HOW TO DEVELOP A SUCCESSFUL ADVERTISING PLAN

James W. Taylor

NTC Business Books
a division of *NTC Publishing Group* • Lincolnwood, Illinois USA

About the Author

James Taylor has spent his entire career in marketing and advertising. A former director of new product development and a marketing manager for Hunt-Wesson Foods, Inc., he has also held senior marketing assignments at Gillette and Arco. His consulting clients include Sea Land Service, Inc., Seattle; KF Fackhandel, Stockholm; Chiat/Day Advertising, Los Angeles; SmithKline Beecham Consumer Brands, Tokyo; and Moray Industries, Auckland, New Zealand.

A distinguished educator, James Taylor is currently Professor of Marketing in the School of Business Administration & Economics, California State University, Fullerton. He has received two appointments as a Senior Fulbright Scholar, and he has held visiting professorships at leading universities in Australia, New Zealand, Portugal, and Spain.

Professor Taylor is the author of more than forty articles and books on advertising, marketing strategy, business planning, and new product development. His work has been published in Spanish, Portuguese, Japanese, Finnish, Norwegian, and Swedish.

Library of Congress Cataloging-in-Publication Data

Taylor, James Walter, 1933–
    How to develop a successful advertising plan / James W. Taylor.—
2nd ed.
     p.   cm.
    Rev. ed. of: How to write a successful advertising plan. c1989.
    Includes index.

    1. Advertising—Handbooks, manuals, etc.   2. Marketing—Handbooks, manuals, etc.   I. Taylor, James Walter, 1933– How to write a successful advertising plan.   II. Title.
HF5823T23 1993
659.1′02′02—dc20

                                             92-30476
                                                CIP

Published by NTC Business Books, a division of NTC Publishing Group
4255 West Touhy Avenue
Lincolnwood (Chicago), Illinois 60646-1975, U.S.A.
3 4 5 6 7 8 9 BC 9 8 7 6 5 4 3 2 1

CONTENTS

Appendix A WHAT AN ADVERTISING PLAN MIGHT LOOK LIKE 231

Appendix B SELECTING AN ADVERTISING AGENCY 235

PREFACE

More than 100 years ago, John Wanamaker, the "inventor" of the department store, is alleged to have said, "Half of the money I spend on advertising is wasted. I just don't know which half." Today, we spend over $100 billion on advertising and John Wanamaker's insight is as valid now as it was then. That means that we *waste* about $50 billion on useless advertising in the United States. An outrageous condition!

We will probably never be able to eliminate all of the waste from advertising, but we can certainly do better than 50 percent, and that is what this book is all about. The more you can plan and control your advertising expenditures, the more you can eliminate waste. Each wasted dollar you recover is another dollar you can spend to compete.

This gives you a double advantage over your competitors. Every dollar you do spend works harder for you *and* you have more effective dollars to spend.

Anyone who has ever had to compete with Procter & Gamble Company will understand the idea immediately. Because Procter & Gamble buys so much media and does it so efficiently, they have a huge advantage over their competitors before the race even starts.

Ed Ojdana, whom you will meet in Chapter Nine, estimates that in 1980 in San Francisco, for example, Olympia Brewing Company was paying $138 per Gross Rating Point (GRP) while trying to compete with Budweiser which paid at $79 per GRP in the market. As you can see, that is a huge disadvantage. The way to offset that kind of competitive advantage in financial clout is to make your dollars work harder and work smarter.

But media is only half of the story. The other half is in what you say to your prospective customers. That involves developing a creative strategy that incorporates how you are going to differentiate your product or service from competition; identifying your most important customer benefit and explaining why this benefit is possible; and describing what you know about who your customers are and how they live.

You will find many, many examples in this book of how to develop an advertising strategy that links your creative strategy and your media plan with your overall marketing plan. This is the best way I know to reduce the waste in your advertising budget. The marketing plan must drive the advertising. Never should it be the other way around.

Many good friends from all around the world made the contributions to this book. Some of them are listed here in alphabetical order: Ann Bailey, Comcast Cablevision, Fullerton, CA; J. A. "Tony B" Buttacavoli, Fullerton Dodge, Fullerton, CA; Bill Cross, Crossolutions Pty. Ltd., Crows Nest, Australia; DeDe Dalton, Dion Hughes, Mary Maroun, and Robert Pellizzi, Chiat/Day/Mojo Advertising, New York, NY; Karly Becker and Suzanne Douglas, Supermarket Communication Systems, Norwalk, CT; Dennis Duffy, Frequency Marketing, Milford, OH; Richard J. Findlay and Keisuke Morimoto, SmithKline Beecham Consumer Products, Tokyo, Japan; Richard Fogg, Land O' Lakes, Arden Hills, MN; Charles Fredericks, DoyleGrafMabley Advertising, New York, NY; Steve Goldman, Carol Madonna, and Richard O'Neil, Chiat/Day/Mojo Advertising, Los Angeles, CA; Setsuko Henne, a terrific freelance translator, Placentia, CA; Takafumi Hotta, Dentsu Advertising, Tokyo, Japan; Chuck Jocoby, Silo, Philadelphia, PA; Robert Jones, California State University, Fullerton, CA; Alan Maclean, Rankin Direct, Mosman, Australia; John Mason, Autoglass, Richmond, Surrey, United Kingdom; Monty McKinney, Kresser Craig D.I.K., Los Angeles, CA; Nick Nickel, Fassett-Nickel Toyota, Cheyenne, WY; John North, Porsche Cars North America, Reno, NV; Edward Ojdana, The Windsor Park Group, Los Angeles, CA; Michelle Rose, Carl Karcher Enterprises, Fremont, CA; Vickie Stafford and Monte Zator, Saatchi & Saatchi DFS Pacific, Torrance, CA; Joanne Taylor, a terrific freelance proofreader, Laguna Beach, CA; and Charlie Walker, C. A. Walker & Associates, Los Angeles, CA.

But the one person who has made the biggest contribution to this book is Jay Chiat. Jay is the most urbane and witty person I know. Over the last 25 years, he has also demonstrated to me that truly creative advertising can sell incredible amounts of goods and services. He has also demonstrated, on occasion, that undisciplined creativity is a disaster. Jay would have you believe that the only thing he is interested in is great advertising. Don't be fooled by that. He has one of the best marketing minds you will ever encounter, and that is where truly great advertising begins.

Thank you one and all! I truly appreciate your generous and cheerfully given help with this book!

CHAPTER 1

The Advertising Business Is in Turmoil

The 1980s have seen more turmoil and turbulence in the advertising business than any time in the last 100 years. There is no reason to expect this to slow down anytime in the 1990s because the underlying factors driving these changes show no signs of mitigating.

The fundamental event that is driving change in the advertising business is that advertisers are diverting their marketing dollars away from advertising and into sales and trade promotions. While it is always difficult to be precise about gross numbers, reasonable estimates are that advertisers spent about 60–65 percent of their promotional dollars on advertising and 35–40 percent on promotions at the end of the 1970s. Now that the way marketing people allocate their funds has become so important, we have much better estimates. The most recent estimates come from Donnelly Marketing, Stamford, Connecticut, which reports that in 1991, advertising accounted for 25.1 percent, trade promotion for 49.5 percent, and consumer promotion for about 25.4 percent.

It is the thesis of this book that many advertisers are pursuing a rational strategy of shifting dollars from marketing tools that *do not* produce sales and profits to marketing tools that *do*. But this raises a very important question. There is an enormous amount of evidence that advertising can make huge contributions to sales and profits in specific situations. So why the contradiction?

The answer is that many advertisers waste large amounts of their advertising budgets without getting results while a few advertisers minimize their wasted dollars and get important results almost every time. The purpose of this book is to make sure that you are in the minority of advertisers who waste very little of their advertising budgets and get big results almost every time.

The sources of waste will be examined throughout this book.

A Quick Look at the Players

There are three main players in the advertising business and a host of supporting players. One of the main players is the advertiser—the company or the person who pays for the advertising messages and for the audiences exposed to these messages. Another main player is the media. The media include newspapers, TV stations, magazines, radio stations, outdoor signs, etc., that develop an audience to sell to the advertisers so they can deliver their advertising messages. The third main player is all of the advertising agencies who help advertisers prepare their advertising messages and who help them select target audiences to see and hear those messages.

The supporting players are a wide variety of companies and people that actually prepare the advertising, deliver the advertising to the media, measure the size of the various audiences, and measure whether the advertising was delivered. Typesetters, photographers, TV commercial directors, photoengravers, and printers are some of the people who produce the advertising messages. Air freighter companies, such as Emory and Airborne, deliver the physical advertising messages to the media. Organizations like the Audit Bureau of Circulation verify the claims of audience sizes and characteristics for magazines and newspapers. Companies like the Advertising Checking Bureau verify that the media actually delivered the contracted advertising messages.

The purpose of the advertising business is to deliver advertising messages to prospective and current customers of the advertisers and to do that job at a per customer cost that is less than it would cost to send actual salespeople to deliver sales messages. You can envision the advertising business like this:

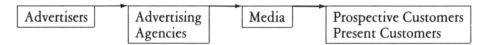

| Advertisers | → | Advertising Agencies | → | Media | → | Prospective Customers Present Customers |

Advertisers

All types of companies, organizations, groups, and individuals are advertisers. Some advertisers are companies with products you know very well. Procter & Gamble Company (which spends more money on advertising than any other company in the world) advertises Tide detergent, Folgers coffee, and Charmin toilet tissue directly to consumers. Procter & Gamble also advertises to retailers—the supermarket people who actually sell their products to the final users—to inform them about trade deals, price promotions, and product improvements. When advertisers direct their messages towards retailers or wholesalers, the advertising usually is called *trade advertising*.

Some advertisers do not sell products at all; they sell services. Humana, Inc., sells the services of its hospitals; Citicorp, Inc., sells its banking services; Connecticut General sells its life insurance services; Jacoby & Meyers sells its legal services; and Dean Witter/Reynolds sells its financial advisory services.

Other advertisers don't advertise to consumers at all; they advertise to other businesses. For example, when the Carlisle Corporation wants to deliver advertising messages about the company's finely drawn, plated, and stranded wire conductors to aircraft manufacturers and aerospace firms, it uses *business-to-business advertising*.

The businesses that spend more money on advertising than any other group of businesses do not manufacture products at all, they run retail stores. The second biggest advertising budget is the dollars spent by Sears, Roebuck & Co. Some advertisers are huge chains selling food products like

Safeway or Kroger. Others are large drugstore chains like Hook Drugs, and some sell clothing, as does the successful Limited, Inc. Other retailers, however, are quite small. Today's *Pennysaver* newspaper carried advertising messages from Accord's Food Market, Shampoo: Hair Designs for Men & Women, Drapery World, and Crown Valley Texaco (among dozens of other small retailers).

Governments also advertise. The U.S. Army has been directing highly successful advertising messages toward young men and women, urging them to ''Be All That You Can Be,'' since the advent of the all-voluntary army at the end of the 1970s. The American Heart Association is an example of a non-profit organization that advertises to raise donations to support its research program. Southern Methodist University is an example of a different kind of nonprofit organization using advertising messages to induce contributions from its alumni.

Finally, individuals advertise. In the *Los Angeles Times* classified section, Franklin J. Slater, Atty., is offering to defend you against a drunk driving charge for a flat $399; somebody is offering a $500 reward for a male West Highland Terrier Scottie that was lost in Orange, California; a doctor's office is trying to hire a licensed massage therapist; and Warren Biggs is offering to sell a fully loaded 1980 Cadillac Seville for $6,995.

All of these companies, organizations, groups, and individuals face the same advertising problem: how to say the right thing in their advertising message(s), how to select the correct advertising medium (media), and how to accomplish the whole thing for the lowest cost. The purpose of this book is to help all of those people answer their questions in the best possible way.

Advertising Agencies

Many advertisers use the services of independent businesses called *advertising agencies* to develop their advertising messages, select the best media, and complete the numerous specialized tasks that are required to ensure that the right advertising messages are delivered to the right audiences at the right time.

There are three major functional areas in most advertising agencies and a number of supporting activities. One major functional area includes the account management people. Their responsibility is to understand the business problems and opportunities of the advertiser who has hired the agency and to translate those problems and opportunities into tasks for the agency to accomplish.

Another major function is the creative area. Here the creative directors, writers, artists, TV producers and others produce the real product of value from the advertising agency, the message to be communicated to prospective customers. The overwhelming reason to hire an advertising agency is to get these people working to build your business.

The third major area is media. The people who work in this area select the best media to deliver your message, negotiate the best prices, schedule the advertising, and make sure that it appears when and where it should.

Additional support comes from traffic departments that make sure things move on schedule, production departments that make sure things get made on schedule, and financial departments that make sure that the money flows in and out of the agency on schedule.

Some advertising agencies also have a research department to help the account people, the creative people, and the media people understand the many questions that arise about who the customers are and why they buy the client's products.

In short, an advertising agency is a collection of people with special talents, skills, and experiences that helps an advertiser deal with many of the problems that arise in developing advertising that gets results and doesn't waste money. An advertising agency is a service business, pure and simple, except for one thing: Advertising is also part show business. More on that in a moment.

An Important Digression—How Advertising Agencies Grow

Every service business has just two ways to grow. One way is through existing clients who grow and spend more money. The other is through *new* business. The factors that drive new business vary from industry to industry. In the advertising agency business, awards and prizes drive new business. That is an extremely important fact for you to understand.

This is the way one of advertising's top executives makes the point. In the September 30, 1991 issue of *Advertising Age*, Philip Dusenberry, Chairman–CEO of the New York office and vice chairman of BBDO Worldwide—one of the world's biggest advertising agencies—said "And make no mistake about it, winning awards *does* matter to us. It sends a signal to our people, to the industry, and throughout the client community. Many big agencies claim that they want to be top creative shops. But most of the time, the words are not matched by action. Awards say you're not just talking, you're doing."

If you think this is an isolated opinion, consider what Jim Jordan, Chairman of Jordan, McGrath, Case & Taylor told the members of the Association of National Advertisers at their 82nd annual meeting in Phoenix on October 27, 1991. "The truth is that more copywriters and art directors and agencies create advertising for their reels than they do for their clients. . . . Agency managements are often no better than their creative departments in keeping their priorities straight. Agency principals perceive that their agencies will get more business if their work is perceived as "chic" or "on the cutting edge" than they will if the ads merely sell a lot of stuff. The point is that you cannot count on your agency to keep its priorities straight; you may have to remind them."

Advertising agencies want to create advertising that wins awards and prizes and gets favorable notice from other advertising people. Part of it is ego, but most of it is hard-headed business sense. When advertising agencies make presentations for new business (the main way that advertising agencies grow and become more profitable), awards like Clios and Belding Cups have demonstrated that they are powerful selling tools, even among the most dispassionate of business people. The problem is that there is no serious evidence that award-winning advertising is advertising that increases sales.

There are, however, anecdotes of award-winning advertising increasing sales. Life cereal's "Mikey Likes It" TV commercial won awards and sold a lot of ready-to-eat cereal. Apple's 1984 TV commercial was shown only once (during the 1984 Super Bowl telecast) and it sold millions of dollars worth of Macintosh computers. The problem is that advertisers can't run their businesses on occasional anecdotes—they must be productive day in and day out, year-round, year after year.

So, the first piece of serious advice for advertisers is this: If you have clearly stated your marketing and advertising objectives to your advertising agency, and the proposed advertising that they are showing you doesn't clearly meet those objectives, DO NOT, under any circumstances, approve the advertising. Such circumstances will probably include direct challenges to your courage and judgment. When you hear, "This is not the kind of stuff that every client in this industry would have the guts to run, but it'll knock the socks off the customers!!" *DO NOT GIVE IN!* Yes, there is a one-in-a-thousand chance that you will actually turn down a "knock their socks off, award-winning campaign," but at the same time you will avoid the risk of wasting your advertising budget.

Remember two things at times like these: One, almost all advertising agencies hate the advertising that Procter & Gamble does, but nobody comes close to having their day in, day out effective advertising. Two, remember that when your internist sends you to consult with a specialist after your annual physical check-up, no matter what she advises, it is still your life you are dealing with, not your doctor's!

The following is a true, but sad story of a little advertiser that got caught up in the glamor of the advertising business and learned to regret abdicating final decision making to its advertising agency. Or, as Jim Jordan might have put it, they failed to keep their priorities straight.

A Strategy Goes Wrong

In 1971, the Los Angeles based Gilbert H. Brockmeyer Ice Cream Company introduced the first all natural ice cream into supermarkets in southern California. The ice cream came in four flavors. It used no artificial preservatives, no artificial colors, and no artificial flavors. It was a health food product ("only natural ingredients") that tasted good and found its way into mass distribution channels. It was moderately successful in sales volume.

Gilbert H. Brockmeyer's Natural Ice Cream accomplished good distribution. Every major food store chain in southern California, and many independents, carried the product. The single exception was Safeway Stores. In southern California, this was not a serious problem because Safeway had a small share of the market. However, it was a very serious problem when Brockmeyer's tried to expand distribution outside of southern California. Safeway had a commanding share of market in virtually every other major market in the West and Midwest. As a result, Gilbert H. Brockmeyer's Natural Ice Cream faced serious limitations in its ability to expand geographically because it failed to gain distribution in any Safeway stores.

In the southern California market (about 5 percent of the total U.S. food business), the brand faced a second problem. The primary advertising medium from the brand's inception had been the Sunday supplement of the *Los Angeles Times, Home Magazine.* When a four-color, full-page ad for the product ran, sales increased by 100 percent the following week, and by 50 percent the second following week (see Exhibit 1.1). By the third following week, sales returned to normal.

Consumer surveys showed that the brand had about a 33 percent awareness level. Coincidentally, the Sunday *Los Angeles Times* reached about 33 percent of all Los Angeles metropolitan households. At the same time, taste tests demonstrated that once consumers became aware of the product, there was a strong possibility that they would become regular customers.

EXHIBIT 1.1

This is an example of an advertising slick. Manufacturers supply slicks and other advertising materials to retailers and wholesalers to assist in advertising the manufacturer's products and/or services.

Through the 1970s, Gilbert H. Brockmeyer's Natural Ice Cream faced serious limitations on its ability to grow within its existing market area because it seemed impossible to increase awareness of the brand, on an affordable basis, in its prime market.

At the end of the 1970s, the brand was doing well, but was stymied in geographical expansion because of its failure to gain distribution in Safeway stores. It was also blocked in building volume because it failed to gain awareness and readership outside of the *Los Angeles Times* Sunday supplement.

In 1979, the food broker who represented Brockmeyer's in San Diego scored a breakthrough by getting the local Safeway district manager to authorize a summer test of the product in San Diego Safeway stores. As part of the deal, the ice cream company agreed to promote the brand heavily in San Diego. Since the deal was made early in June, the long lead time involved in the four-color print advertising process precluded the usual advertising support that the company had been using. The advertising agency suggested using radio because of the short turnaround time. Three commercials were produced using Gilbert H. Brockmeyer's wife, Alma, as the spokesperson (the talent). Alma Brockmeyer had been a housewife all of her life. The actual commercials were crafted carefully word by word, at the production house of Chuck Blore & Don Richman, Inc.

At the end of the summer, there was some fairly strong evidence that

EXHIBIT 1.2

SIXTY SECOND RADIO COMMERCIALS (AS RECORDED)

ALMA

My name is Alma Brockmeyer. We thought it would be so nice if my husband, Gilbert H. Brockmeyer, went on the radio to tell you how delicious his natural ice cream is, but he thinks his voice sounds funny, so here I am. If you've never tried Brockmeyer's Natural Ice Cream, you have no idea how good ice cream can taste. It's natural as can be, with absolutely nothing artificial. All eight flavors are made from the very best that money and my husband's stubbornness can buy. The plumpest raspberries, the choicest bananas, the finest vanilla beans, carob, peanuts, pecans, and walnuts. You'll find Gilbert H. Brockmeyer's Natural Ice Cream in your supermarket, and if it were up to me, I'd tell you to try some right away. Wait a minute, it is up to me to tell you. Gilbert certainly won't. (Chuckles)

ALICE

(SFX—birds twittering) This is a very irritated Mother Nature speaking, and if you ice cream eaters out there don't pay very close attention, I'm going to drop a three ton hailstone on Pasadena. Look, there's a big difference between my genuine vanilla beans and artificial vanilla flavor, vanalin, they call it. Might as well call it Mary Lou for all it tastes like real vanilla. Now stop eating that stuff. Drop down to your supermarket freezer case and get Gilbert H. Brockmeyer's Natural Ice Cream. In the brown carton. Brock uses lots of my very best vanilla beans, fresh milk, and cream, real eggs and honey. No chemicals, no additives, not one thing you can't pronounce. That is why it tastes so delicious. When you finish the vanilla, get started on the rest of Brockmeyer's eight natural flavors and if I ever catch you eating make believe ice cream again, you can try explaining a purple pine tree to the neighbors.

(Male Voice Over) Delicious Gilbert H. Brockmeyer's Natural Ice Cream, from Mother Nature with love.

sales in the total San Diego market had increased by 185 percent! Encouraged by these results, the company management planned to conduct a test of radio advertising in the much larger, much more expensive Los Angeles metropolitan area in the spring of 1980. Since there are 80 radio stations in the Los Angeles metro area, the advertising agency argued that a sizable budget would be required. The company agreed and the entire 1980 advertising budget was put behind the test. To repeat this advertising spending level on an annual, national basis would have required approximately $10 million.

The next recommendation that the advertising agency made involved the advertising itself. They argued that Alma Brockmeyer's lack of professional experience was too limiting from a creative standpoint, that she should be replaced with a professional actress, and that the commercials be rewritten. The company management agreed. Actress Alice Ghostley was hired and three new commercials were produced. The script for one of the commercials is shown in Exhibit 1.2.

Even without hearing the actual voices, just reading the scripts makes it clear that a major change in the content of the advertising message was made.

The test was conducted and no measurable results were obtained. Awareness among ice cream buyers was unchanged and there was no increase in sales. When the peak summer selling season arrived, the company had no funds to advertise the brand and sales began to weaken. Then distribution began to erode and out-of-stock situations began to increase. By 1981, sales continued to trend down and advertising budgets were decreased. A downward spiral began and, two years later, Brockmeyer's was out of business.

Moral: Don't ever change more than one variable in an advertising test and don't ever let your advertising agency talk you into doing something against your better judgment.

More about Advertising Agencies

Advertising agencies come in all sizes and range from the world's largest—Saatchi & Saatchi, Inc., with thousands of employees around the world—to one-person agencies in your town. With a few exceptions, advertising agencies are organized to perform three basic functions. One function is to make contact with the advertiser (called the *client* by most advertising agencies). This involves acquiring a thorough understanding of the client's products, services, marketing plans, and advertising objectives. The people who perform this function are called account executives.

Another function is to create advertising. This is where the creative people in the advertising agency develop solutions to fit the client's advertising objectives. The creative people are also responsible for getting the advertising produced after their ideas have been approved by the client. It is common to find a writer and an art director assigned to work as a creative team on a client's advertising.

The third function is to select appropriate media. The advertising agency is responsible for recommending media and, when plans are approved, drawing up contracts with specific newspapers, magazines, and TV stations.

HOW AGENCIES GET PAID

It is important to understand how money circulates in the advertising business because it is different from every other major business except for travel agents. In the advertising business, the agencies historically have been paid for their work by the media, not by the advertisers.

It all started in Philadelphia in the 1840s when a man named Volney Palmer contracted with the major newspapers of the day to sell advertising space. Palmer contracted for large amounts of space and was able to secure a large discount from the newspapers as a result. As he resold the newspaper space, he found that he had to help his customers with the writing and layout of their advertisements. Palmer used his services in writing and art as inducements to sell advertising space.

That arrangement exists today, although it is changing for reasons we will review later. Here is the way the system works: Suppose an advertiser wants to show a TV commercial about his product in Albany, Georgia. The client describes what he wants to say to the account executive, who in turn relays the need to the creative team, who propose how the commercial might look and sound using a storyboard. The client approves the storyboard and the creative team hires a separate production company to plan, cast, shoot, and edit the actual commercial. Upon completion, the production company sends an invoice for its services to the advertising agency. Since the production company was selected on the basis of their bid to do the work, the agency and the client both know what to expect.

The agency then bills the client for the services of the production house. This invoice may, or may not, include a prearranged percentage mark-up. The advertising agency then contracts with Gray Communications Systems, Inc., for air time on their TV station, WALB-TV, in Albany, Georgia, and sends them a copy of the commercial to air at the agreed upon time(s).

When the commercial has been shown, Gray Communications sends the advertising agency an invoice that looks like this:

Cost of air time	$10,000
Less commission (15%)	−1,500
	$ 8,500
Less 2% discount for payment within ten days	− 170
	$ 8,330

The agency pays Gray Communications $8,330 and the advertising agency sends the client an invoice that looks like this:

Cost of air time	$10,000
Less 2% discount for payment within ten days	− 170
	$ 9,830

The client pays the advertising agency $9,830—exactly what it would have paid Gray Communications if they had contracted directly with Gray. The advertising agency keeps the $1,500 commission as compensation for their services.

While this system of payment has obvious advantages for advertisers, it also has some disadvantages. The two major alternatives are a negotiated commission and a fee system. In a negotiated commission system, the advertiser and the advertising agency agree on a commission percentage smaller than 15 percent, and the advertising agency rebates the difference back to the advertiser.

In a fee system, the advertiser describes the work to be done by the advertising agency and the agency breaks it down to the number of hours required and applies each individual's ''billing rate'' to that amount of time. Out-of-pocket expenses are estimated, hourly charges and expenses are totalled, and an amount is added to cover general overhead and profit.

The fee can cover a specific project or a period of time. The agency submits regular invoices for fractions of the fee on a monthly basis. The agency records the amount of commissions it has received from the media during this period. If the amount is greater than the fee, the agency rebates the excess amount to the advertiser. If the amount is less than the fee, the advertiser is invoiced for the difference.

A 1992 survey by the Association of National Advertisers indicates that the following proportions of its members use the various compensation systems:

Standard 15% Advertising Agency Commission 33%

Negotiated Commission Less than 15% 26%

Fee System (plus all other methods) 32%

Given the way money moves around in the advertising business, it is not surprising that the individual media take great interest in the financial health of advertising agencies before they extend credit to them. In the past, various media have tried to "reach around" an advertising agency by collecting directly from an advertiser, but with no luck.

Variations on Paying Your Advertising Agency

This subject is important enough to warrant further exploration. Let's begin with the commission system, which looks like a "free lunch" for advertisers.

Yes, it appears that the people at the advertising agency are working for you for free if you are paying on the commission system. This is because you pay the same size media bills whether or not your agency bought the advertising (unless you operate an in-house advertising agency). But, in doing so, you should realize that you have constructed a situation where the advertising agency's best interests and your best interests may not coincide. For example, when advertising agencies are paid solely on commission, it is in their best interests to recommend expensive media because 15 percent of a big number is more profitable than 15 percent of a small number. The most expensive media, however, may not be the most effective or efficient media for your business. Also, when advertising agencies are paid solely on commission, it is in their best interests to recommend advertising that they can produce at a minimum cost, and this also may not be in your best interests. Advertising agency managements often protest loudly when these points are raised. They say agencies could not stay in business if their clients' sales did not increase. That response misses the point, which is that the commission system creates a situation where the *possibility* of a conflict of interest exists, and as such, can reduce the mutual trust that is vital to a relationship so demanding of mutual trust. You want a working relationship with your advertising agency that is beyond reproach, and under no circumstances gives any hint of the possibility of a conflict of interests.

A Point of Fact: Television is an expensive medium with low average production costs when a commercial is shown repeatedly; thus, it meets both of the points made above. In 1990, TV work accounted for 58 percent of the revenues of the largest advertising agencies in the United States, but in 1990 TV advertising only accounted for 21 percent of all advertising expenditures. Although this is not a completely valid comparison, it still comes uncomfortably close to making the point.

The objective of this discussion is to make it abundantly clear that you want to have a payment arrangement with your advertising agency that puts your best interests exactly in line with the agency's best interests. The fee-based arrangements discussed above are all steps in that direction.

The ideal payment arrangement is one where your advertising agency is paid based on results. Admittedly, that is difficult in many instances. In direct mail businesses, payment for results is quite simple, but in, say, consumer products sold through supermarkets, so many additional factors affect sales that it is difficult to isolate advertising's contribution. However, just because it is difficult doesn't mean you shouldn't try, or that you shouldn't accept some partial results-based method. Procter & Gamble has been experimenting with results-based compensation methods for over 35 years and they haven't got it right yet. And they haven't given up trying either.

One Thing Not to Do

In the past several years, a number of companies have announced that they have devised agency compensation fee systems based on scores that the agency's advertising gets in various testing methods. In 1990, Carnation and Campbell Soup decided to base payments on test scores. This is a mistake you should avoid at all costs!

If you pay for test scores, that is what your agency will produce—high test scores—because the people who work for your advertising agency are very bright. That is why you hired them in the first place. The painful reality is that there is no evidence that test scores, any kind of test scores, are reliable predictors of sales. The reality is that you may be paying to produce advertising that has absolutely no impact on sales and is just one more way to *waste* your advertising dollars.

There is another hidden price that you will pay. Once upon a time, this author worked for Benton & Bowles on the Tide account, a heavy TV advertiser at the time. During one of Procter & Gamble's experiments with results-based compensation, Benton & Bowles was required to pay all of the production costs on Tide commercials that scored below 20 on the day after a recall test. The agency regularly produced Tide commercials that scored 40, 50, 60, and higher. One time, however, one of the account group suggested another approach to selling Tide, and a different commercial was produced. The new commercial scored only 11, and Benton & Bowles had to pay for production costs out of their own pocket. Thereafter, no new ideas were ever suggested or developed for Tide (a very serious, hidden penalty of the pay for scores system).

Some of "Life's Little Lessons" from a Real Professional

Montgomery N. McKinney is an extraordinary adman who comes from a family of admen. Monty's career in advertising covers over half a century, and includes assignments such as chairman of the board of Doyle Dane Bernbach West, Chiat/Day Advertising; DDB Needham West; and now Kresser, Craig/D.I.K. Not only is Monty one of the most experienced advertising people you could ever meet, he is also one of the nicest. In 1987, the management of DDB Needham West asked Monty to share some of his experiences in advertising with the younger people in the agency. Monty chose to do that by writing a series of stories, ''Life's Little Lessons.'' In his typically gracious way, he has agreed to share some of his stories with you.

The first two are stories about client/agency relationships. The first is Number One in the series and it is about what is probably the most famous bad client/agency relationship of all time: Ernest Gallo and whoever happened to be at his agency at the moment. It is a stark testimonial about how to be absolutely certain you will *not* get your agency's best work.

The second story, ''Virtuosity Rewarded,'' demonstrates how to guarantee that you *will* get your agency's best work, again and again. You will find it extremely instructive to compare the two situations carefully.

VARIATIONS ON THE BASIC ADVERTISING AGENCY

Some agencies attempt only one or two of the functions provided by a ''full service'' advertising agency. For example, some agencies have concentrated just on buying media. They claim that they get better value for their clients because of their specialized knowledge and volume buying practices. These agencies call themselves *media buying services.*

Some agencies attempt to provide only the creative function. These agencies usually are called ''creative boutiques,'' and their popularity probably peaked in the late 1960s. There was a slightly mean-spirited joke in the advertising business (but with a grain of truth) that a creative boutique was an artist and a copywriter sitting around waiting to get a client so they could become a full-service advertising agency.

A few advertisers have decided that they should do the advertising agency's job themselves; these are called *in-house agencies.* An advertiser starts an in-house agency to gain greater control over the people working on the account or to pocket the profits that would have gone to an independent advertising agency that serviced the account.

Even among full-service advertising agencies, there are wide variations. Some agencies specialize in consumer packaged goods accounts, some in industrial products, some in high tech accounts, some in medical products, direct marketing, recruiting, or even fundraising.

In addition, advertising agencies have distinct personalities that reflect the ways in which they attempt to differentiate themselves from other advertising agencies. For instance, some advertising agencies stress their business acumen and present conservative, controlled, stable, old wealth images. Others stress the creative product they turn out so they present modern, unconventional, hip, even avant garde images.

All of this is very important for an advertiser to understand because working with an advertising agency is like getting married. If it is going to work for you, you need to know your partner and select the right one. It is so important that Appendix B is devoted to how to select a new advertising agency or retain the one you already have.

Other Ways to Get the Job Done

Advertising agencies are not the only method that advertisers use to get their advertising messages planned and executed. For instance, most retailers do not use advertising agencies (at least for the bulk of their advertising budgets). They say that retailing is simply too fast paced to afford the luxury of

Stand by Your Convictions

In a famous *NEW YORKER* cartoon from another era, an American Indian in full regalia is shown squatting beside his smoke-signal fire. He is looking across miles and miles of desert to where the mammoth mushroom cloud of an atom-bomb test has formed. Below this dramatic illustration is the simple caption:

"Boy, I wish I'd said that!"

When Jeri Moore and Marianne Ellis suggested that I do a series of mini-essays on what I had seen and learned in my fairly lengthy career in this wild and wonderful business, that cartoon popped into my head immediately. I'll tell you why in a minute.

Meanwhile, let me just say that I agreed to do the series (this is actually the first unit of it) when they soft-soaped me into believing it would be interesting, educational, inspirational, or even all three at once. So here goes.

The thing that put the cartoon in my head was a situation in which *I said what I wanted to say but did not ever deliver it to the target.*

Let me tell you about it. Could be a lesson for you as it was for me.

When I joined DDB, Los Angeles in 1957, it was as account supervisor on Gallo Wines (I didn't learn until too late that my predecessor left because of a nervous breakdown, presumably hastened by Ernest Gallo. Ernest, in addition to being one of America's greatest marketers, was also famous both for the number of heart attacks he caused and for his generosity in caring for the victims).

Ernest was tough, opinionated, and arbitrary. Even more important, he made it impossible to do truly great DDB creative work. Impossible, also, to make a fair profit.

It took only a few weeks on the account for me to realize that the basic situation was unhealthy and wrong. So (even though I was new both to the account and the agency) I elected to put together a recommendation that DDB resign the business. I directed a long memo to Bill Bernbach, Ned Doyle, and Ted Factor (then head of DDB/LA). It was obvious that there was a personal risk involved because I was still relatively unknown and definitely unproved at DDB, but I felt the analysis and evaluation were right and that I had to call the shot.

In the broadest sense I was right. Even though DDB elected not to act on it at the time, the top guys agreed with the conclusions and granted me a couple of merit points for the stand I had taken.

Thereafter, on my own, I carried a copy of the recommendation in my briefcase to every major Gallo meeting. Ernest Gallo was dictatorial, mercurial, impetuous, and unpredictable, and my thought was that at some point I would feel a table-thumping crisis arising; would whip out my comprehensive recommendation before his fist hit the desk, and I would shout, "Wait a goddamned minute, Ernest, you can't fire us, here's our resignation."

It never happened, and we kept the business for what was then the longevity record for any Gallo agency. Finally, we got fired.

A moral? (Many of these mini-essays will contain a moral whether emphasized or not).

For me the moral was: Think things through; say what you believe; stand up for your convictions—even if there is personal risk. You may not always be right. Your recommendations may not always be followed. But you and your opinions will earn respect.

Who could ask for anything more?

Monty McKinney
Chairman, DDB/West

LIFE'S LITTLE LESSONS

Virtuosity Rewarded

The old saying, "Virtue is its own reward," never really appealed to me. In my opinion, virtue is not that easy to attain (or maintain) and it therefore deserves a reward far greater than just more of itself. A golden halo, for instance, in some afterlife—or even a here-and-now big pot of genuine gold.

All of which is preamble to an advertising episode where the possibility of unique reward existed.

Early in my years as Chairman of Chiat/Day, I was called on to develop a contract for a big new client, Yamaha Motors, USA. Yamaha stipulated that they wanted a method of compensation *not* based on the usual media commission system which both they and we normally used.

Among ourselves there was disagreement as to their objective in this request. Some of us feared that Yamaha simply wanted to cut the cost of advertising by reducing agency income and profit. Yamaha was lagging far behind Honda in the motorcycle battle, and the company could hardly be blamed for seeking ways to minimize the big advantage Honda had in marketing and advertising muscle.

Chiat/Day, however, with confidence in the selling strength of its creative advertising, was not the least bit interested in cutting price.

So we designed a proposal based on time spent on the Yamaha account by everyone at every level—with basic hourly salaries of each multiplied to cover full related costs including agency overhead, fringe benefits, vacations, bonuses, and *AGENCY PROFIT AT OUR TARGETED LEVELS.*

While developing this plan with the client, I became convinced that their goal was not to cut into agency receipts, but to eliminate any temptation at the agency to recommend heavy network TV budgets. (Many clients believe that network TV requires less work in all agency departments and is therefore more profitable to the agency.)

I believed that that concern was a reflection on their previous agency rather than on Chiat/Day and we ignored the thought and formulated the method briefly outlined above. All went well, and we were in an important meeting just prior to signing the agreement when I introduced a concern which had troubled me for some time.

"You guys," I said, "come out well in this plan as I see it. You get our best work and effort in every area for a fair cost, and you expect to gain substantially from increased sales and profits. That's fine with us.

"Operating on standard media commission compensation methods, we, too, would have expected to benefit from the growth of your business and budgets, and we would deserve to. Under this plan we would, of course, increase income through some additional work loads but not in amounts really commensurate with our contribution. I miss that incentive and regret its absence."

The Yamaha people (Merle Karst, VP and Sales Manager and John Rinek, Advertising Manager) understood and asked time to consider it. At the next meeting, they said they would like to incorporate into the contract the concept that if Yamaha was pleased with the results of the agency/client association, they could at their option award a cash bonus as an extra fee paid to the agency.

I agreed that it was a gracious gesture, and we added the idea to the actual contract as signed—and forgot it.

an advertising agency, and they do the work themselves. Many media recognize this, and offer a special price schedule called "retail rates" that are lower than the "national rates" they charge everyone else.

At present, the advertising agency business is reducing its employment base. As a result, there are a lot of talented creative people working on their

Chiat/Day's work for Yamaha was spectacular in every way, including sales results. With considerable daring, Yamaha authorized the first big multi-paged insertion in a major publication (*Playboy*) and ran a 24-page insert in the February issue. (Research had shown that the purchase consideration period for motorcycles was 90–120 days and that peak sales occurred in late Spring). So historically, most motorcycle campaigns had begun in April. The Yamaha campaign stole the market; the creative was brilliant; the insert had great value as a dealer catalog; and everything worked superbly.

Most importantly, Yamaha's share-of-market soared—with Honda's share declining almost equally.

Interestingly enough, in the following year, the competition moved its campaign starts up earlier and went to multi-page insertions as well.

Toward the end of Chiat/Day's first year with Yamaha, I received a letter from Mr. Ueshima, President of Yamaha Motor Corp., USA asking for a meeting with him, his associate, Mr. Kimura, Jay Chiat, and me. We worried about wehether this meeting agenda would be to discuss a revision of the compensation agreement—or what. We seldom saw these top Japanese executives alone, although they lived here, and we really did not know what to expect.

Mr. Ueshima and Mr. Kimura met us quite coolly in a Biltmore Hotel suite separate from our second-floor offices in that hotel.

After the usual formal bowing and greeting, Mr. Ueshima handed me an envelope. Opening it with some trepidation, I was startled to find in it both a letter—and a check for $50,000.

I was overwhelmed. Even today the recollection of that afternoon brings a tear to my eye.

I read the letter aloud—as well as I could—and handed the check to Jay.

The next quarter hour was a little difficult. We said everything there was to say. And then said it over again, thanking them profusely in every other sentence.

There seemed to be no way to end the session graciously.

So finally I said, "We are most grateful—but I'm not surprised to see the way the meeting has ended. I have the *letter*—and Mr. Chiat has the *check*."

The meeting broke up—in both meanings.

The bonus, incidentally, was repeated in years two and three, and I believe was later increased.

The review of this delightful incident would not be complete without mentioning the memo Jay sent immediately to the entire C/D staff. After enthusiastically announcing the generous Yamaha bonus to Chiat/Day and his pleasure at all it meant, Jay concluded the memo with a short sentence which said, in effect, that everyone at C/D (not just those who worked on Yamaha) contributed—and that *everyone* would find his or her share of the bonus in next week's paycheck.

Virtuosity rewarded? You bet!
Unique? You bet!

Monty McKinney
Chairman, DDB/Needham West
March 13, 1987

own. Any small- to medium-sized advertiser would benefit from hiring these people. While there may be a few problems, there are also some great advantages. For instance, you can probably get more value for your money because you won't have to subsidize an advertising agency's new business acquisition activities, absorb a full-service agency's overhead, or generate a profit for an outside agency. These things are true of an in-house agency as well, but in-house agency personnel tend to become the advertiser's employees and are with the advertiser for very long periods.

While continuity of employment brings some advantages, it also has one serious drawback. The force that drives good advertising is *new ideas;* overtime, it gets harder for the same group of people to come up with new ideas about the same subject. This problem can be avoided by working with a group of outside, independent creative, media, and research people.

If you elect to work with a group of freelancers, you will have to be prepared to spend a good deal more time directing and coordinating their work than if you were doing the same work with a full-service advertising agency.

And Finally

You should subscribe to *Advertising Age.* This is one of the best business-to-business magazines published anywhere and you should make it a regular part of your reading. You can subscribe by writing to:

Advertising Age
Circulation Department
965 E. Jefferson
Detroit, Michigan 48207

Advertising media are so numerous and varied and so important to successful advertising that all of Chapter 7 and 8 are devoted to the media. Customers are also important enough to warrant a chapter to themselves. An extensive discussion of the importance of customers is found in Chapter 4.

CHAPTER 2

Marketing Planning—
How to Get Started

Advertising is a tool that well-managed businesses use to accomplish specific objectives. The first serious sign that an organization is wasting its advertising dollars occurs when they approach buying advertising as if they were buying yard goods, i.e., "We want to buy some advertising."

Well-run businesses prepare carefully detailed plans describing the tasks they wish to accomplish (including explanations of why those tasks are most important) before they commit the company's always scarce resources—time and money. A successful business practices at least three major types of planning: production, financial, and marketing.

It is easy to see the need for *production planning* and no business can survive long without it, irrespective of whether the company produces goods or services. Production planning anticipates the requirements for labor, raw materials, and the processes for producing finished products or services.

Financial planning anticipates future flows of revenues into the firm and future flows of expenses out of the firm. It identifies periods when revenues may fall short of requirements to cover expenses and allows management to make advance provisions to cover the anticipated short falls. Financial planning is about cash flow. Noted management consultant, Peter Drucker, has observed, "Companies can exist for quite a long time without profits, but they cannot exist at all without cash flow." It is a point that sometimes escapes entrepreneurs in start-up businesses. Experienced businesspeople always understand the importance of cash flow and the need for financial planning.

Production planning and financial planning are internally oriented, i.e., they focus on the internal affairs of the company. Although such plans do consider a few factors that are external to the firm (expected sales, raw material prices, interest rates, etc.), they deal *primarily* with factors that are internal to the firm. They use the firm's resources—time and money—in an efficient and effective way, but in doing so, they assume the external environment as given, or fixed.

Marketing Planning

Marketing planning is externally oriented planning. It examines the environment outside of the firm and looks for opportunities for the firm to expand and grow. It involves careful examination of the outside world. It looks at markets, their sizes, and their growth rates. It observes competitors and their products, prices, and distribution. Marketing planning involves careful examination of the economic socio/demographic, political, technological, and ecological environments. It attempts to organize the firm's scarce resources—time and money—to create the maximum impact on the firm's external environment.

Marketing planning can be viewed as the process of selecting, assembling, and communicating those short-term activities that the firm wishes to engage in to accomplish its relatively long-term objectives. Marketing plans are prepared to assist in decisions concerning:

- Products and/or services
- Prices
- Distribution
- Sales force activities
- Advertising
- Sales promotion

Marketing planning involves management in four general tasks. The first task is developing a comprehensive understanding of the markets where your products or services compete, the position of your products in those markets, and the positions occupied by the products of your major competitors. It requires a clear understanding of the crucial factors that lead to success in your industry. It also involves examining related markets to identify additional opportunities.

Every market or industry competes within environments that are external to the market. Five of those external environments are important in marketing planning: the technological, political, economical, ecological, and socio/demographic environments. Each market must be scrutinized for threats and opportunities.

The second task involves identifying those activities that the company can undertake that hold the greatest prospects for profitability. There is never enough time to undertake all of these activities, so some sort of evaluation system is required to specify which of these activities will be supported by the company. This always involves trade-offs between potential activities. Consider this objective: increasing sales of an existing product line. Company resources could be devoted to any of the following activities, but not to all of them:

- Product quality improvement
- Increased advertising
- Price reduction

- Sales force training
- Guarantee program
- Geographic expansion
- Additional sizes, flavors, and colors
- New distribution channels
- Sales promotion (consumer and/or trade)

Each of these activities has a different cost, a different pay-out potential, and a different risk factor, and they can't all be done at once. Which activities to support and which to forego are the kinds of decisions specified in marketing planning.

The third task involves specifying exactly how the activities selected in the second task will be executed. It is not enough to simply decide to "improve product quality." What product quality is and how it is measured must be determined. Budgets and timetables must be set. Personnel responsibilities must be assigned. The reasons for improving product quality must be stated clearly.

It is not satisfactory simply to increase advertising expenditures. Specific communication tasks must be specified. Target audiences identified. Messages must be agreed upon. A creative strategy must be developed. Media must be evaluated and selected. Timetables and budgets must be determined. Responsibilities must be assigned. In short, an advertising plan must be developed that flows directly out of the marketing plans for the organization.

Developing those advertising plans is the task that this book is designed to assist you in doing.

The fourth task in marketing planning involves review and evaluation of the progress on each of the planned activities. The great British statesman, Benjamin Disraeli, once observed, "What we anticipate seldom occurs, what we least expect generally happens." Some of the planned activities will encounter unexpected obstacles. Others will simply fail to produce the expected results. Still others will surpass all expectations and become rousing successes.

Regular review and evaluation of planned marketing activities will spot the problem programs early enough to allow modifications or abandonment, at the least costs. It will also highlight winners so that they may be expanded, or speeded up, or whatever appropriate actions will maximize the payout from such projects.

DEVELOPING THE MARKET REVIEW

It was noted earlier that the first task in marketing planning involved a comprehensive understanding of your markets, your products, and your competitors. It is necessary to specify clearly the history of how your markets developed, what your market position is and how it got that way, and the market positions of each of your major competitors.

Developing this understanding requires a database—a set of incontrovertable facts—about each of your markets. Marketing plans simply cannot be built on "I think," or "We have always believed. . . ." Marketing plans must be based on facts. A financial planner who reported, "Oh, I guess that we have a few hundred thousand dollars in the bank," would be sent back to rework his assignment. In the same manner, marketing planning cannot be based on "Oh, I guess the total market is probably around a couple hundred thousand units."

The first time you attempt marketing planning, your database will almost certainly be incomplete. That's fine, because as Disraeli pointed out, "To be conscious that you are ignorant of the facts is a great step to knowledge." Now you will know which decisions are based on facts and which decisions are based on suppositions and, as a result, are riskier and must be monitored more closely.

In any event, the planning process is cyclical and repetitive. Part of your plan should be to obtain better data for next year, and the year after.

What Goes into a Database

The exact data that will be most useful in marketing planning vary from industry to industry, and, sometimes, from company to company. Here are some suggestions:

A MARKETING DATABASE*

Note: Don't just collect totals. Get data for geographical areas such as regions, states, metropolitan areas, and counties. Totals will hide important geographical variations in performance and potential. Every product or service has geographic variations.

I. **The Market**
   A. How big is it? Number of units sold, dollar volume.
   B. Trends: Is it growing? Declining? Generally, you will want to collect data for the most recent five years to determine trends.
   C. Total sales (units, dollars per household, per plant, and per customer).
   D. Sales by season, by month.
   E. Sales by geographic area per household, per plant, and per customer. Create a Market Development Index following the instructions on page 22.
   F. How do customers use these products? Are there other products or services that will accomplish the purpose?
   G. Number of wholesalers, distributors? Total volume of sales? Average volume? Key wholesalers, distributors?
   H. Number of retail outlets (at least in major markets) that carry these products, by type of store (drug stores, food stores, mass merchandisers, beauty shops).
   I. Total volume of sales at retail. Average sales per outlet. Per key account.
   J. Changes in distribution patterns?

---

*Database marketing is different. It is discussed in Chapter 8.

(continued)

II. The Competition

List your major competitors, usually three or four. Collect these data about your company and your competitors.

A. Sales volume in units and dollars.

B. Trends: growing, declining, seasonal variations.

C. Market shares: growing, declining, steady.

D. Number of distributors and wholesalers.

E. Number of retail outlets stocking the products.

F. Key accounts.

G. Plant locations, warehouse or distribution center locations. Use a map. Use varying circle sizes to indicate relative capacity for location markers.

H. Individual products: sizes, flavors, and colors.

I. Prices for individual products, manufacturer's prices, wholesaler's prices, retail prices, and sale prices.

J. Distribution by type of outlet.

K. Market shares.

L. Advertising expenditures: total, by media and by geographic area.

M. Examples of current advertising. Identify the primary appeal.

N. Sales promotion expenditures. Examples. Identify the apparent objective.

O. Packaging, examples, or pictures. Labels, ingredient statements, sales literature, etc.

P. How distributed. Sales practices, and terms and conditions of sale.

Q. Number of salespeople and sales territories.

R. Sales training and sales incentive programs.

S. Relative product quality. Complaints.

III. Target Market

A. How are customers identified? Demographics? Location? Product usage? Standard Industrial Classification (SIC) codes?

B. Average amounts spent on product category.

C. Amount of product usage accounted for by heavy, medium, and light users.

D. Ways products are used. Proportion of volume accounted for by each use.

E. Trends in product usage.

Where to Find Data

The data that you need for your database will come from a number of different sources, but they all will fall into one of four classifications:

- Your company records
- Governments
- Trade associations
- Private research firms and other businesses

The data you must start with are called ''secondary'' data because they were collected by someone else for a purpose different from your own. You will discover that there is an enormous amount of secondary data available and most of them will be valuable.

Secondary data have two large advantages and one disadvantage. The advantages are that they already exist and can provide you with history and that they are inexpensive (in fact, a lot of them will be free). The disadvantage is that they frequently do not fit the exact specifications that you need for your own products and markets. For this reason, it is very important for you to understand exactly what definitions and data collection procedures were used in collecting the secondary data you want to use.

Searching for secondary data is a skill that can be developed. Begin by making the acquaintance of the business librarian at your closest large public or university library. Be sure to explain as clearly as possible what it is that you are trying to do and get the librarian to help you. Don't give up easily. There is an amazing amount of serendipity when it comes to searching for secondary data.

HOW TO CREATE
A MARKET DEVELOPMENT INDEX

A market development index is a simple, but very useful tool to deal with demand and sales for products and services that are never distributed evenly on a geographic basis. Some markets are always more attractive than others, both absolutely and relatively. The market development index is frequently used in conjunction with a sales performance index to identify strong and weak markets.

Suppose you manufacture a line of specialty furniture in a plant in Pennsylvania and have distribution in the Northeastern quadrant of the United States. *Sales & Marketing Management* magazine publishes each year a ''Survey of Buying Power'' (Bill Communications, Inc., 633 Third Avenue, New York, N.Y. 10017). In it you will find a wealth of data on U.S. markets. Two items are of interest here: ''Furniture, Home Furnishings, and Appliance Store Sales'' and ''Total Households.'' These data are reported on national, state, county, and SMSA (Standard Metropolitan Statistical Area) levels.

Here are the data from a recent Survey of Buying Power and a first level index.

(continued)

Furniture, Home Furnishings, and Appliance Store Sales

State	($000)	Index
Maine	$ 204,287	15
Vermont	120,317	9
New Hampshire	313,341	23
Massachusetts	1,703,351	124
Connecticut	1,020,327	74
New York	5,792,094	422
Pennsylvania	2,977,545	217
New Jersey	2,755,263	201
Delaware	205,864	15
Maryland	1,517,404	111
West Virginia	367,144	27
Virginia	1,837,304	134
District of Columbia	191,028	14
Rhode Island	215,527	16

Construct this index by dividing total sales by 14 (the number of states) to get average sales per state. Then divide the actual sales in each state by the average sales to create a market development index in its simplest form.

For many industrial products and services, this index is sufficient, but it is often useful to go further. Now divide the Furniture, Home Furnishings, and Appliance Store Sales in each state by the number of households in that state, and use those results to create an additional index. (Industrial product marketers can substitute some other measurement, such as number of plants or number of employees.)

State	Households (000)	Per Household Sales	Index
Maine	431.2	$473	58
Vermont	198.2	607	74
New Hampshire	368.2	851	104
Massachusetts	2,168.1	785	96
Connecticut	1,154.9	883	108
New York	6,676.9	867	106
Pennsylvania	4,492.6	662	81
New Jersey	2,763.5	997	122
Delaware	221.4	929	113
Maryland	1,592.5	952	116
West Virginia	730.7	502	61
Virginia	2,026.3	906	110
District of Columbia	253.7	752	92
Rhode Island	353.0	610	74

(continued)

Now suppose that your eight and a half million dollar sales are divided by state as shown below and you use these data to create a sales per household index.

State	Your Sales ($000)	Per Household Sales	Index
Maine	$ 57	$ .132	37
Vermont	83	.469	130
New Hampshire	161	.437	121
Massachusetts	463	.213	59
Connecticut	341	.295	82
New York	600	.089	25
Pennsylvania	2,309	.513	143
New Jersey	400	.144	40
Delaware	210	.948	263
Maryland	1,130	.709	197
West Virginia	70	.095	26
Virginia	1,812	.894	248
District of Columbia	609	2.400	667
Rhode Island	202	.572	159

Now combine all three indices of Market Development.

State	Absolute Dollar Potential	Relative Dollar Potential	Your Dollar Penetration
Maine	15	58	37
Vermont	9	74	130
New Hampshire	23	104	121
Massachusetts	124	96	59
Connecticut	74	108	82
New York	422	106	25
Pennsylvania	217	81	143
New Jersey	201	122	40
Delaware	15	113	263
Maryland	111	116	197
West Virginia	27	61	26
Virginia	134	110	248
District of Columbia	14	92	667
Rhode Island	16	74	159

Just a few observations to illustrate the power of Market Development Indices:

Maryland and Virginia are large absolute markets with high relative potential where our sales are very good. Find out exactly what we do well in those markets so we can use the findings in other markets.

New York and New Jersey are large absolute markets with high relative potential and we do poorly in those markets. Develop major programs for improvement in those markets.

What to Do Next

Use Planning Pages 2.1 through 2.4 to organize the data you have gathered about total industry sales, your own sales, and your competitors' sales. Calculate market shares and identify trends. Write down your observations about what you think is happening to the total market and to each of the competitors in the market. Check your conclusions with other knowledgeable people in your organization.

PLANNING PAGE 2.1

PRODUCT A

Data source:

_____

Data limitations:

_____

Measurement units used:

_____

Year

	19___	19___	19___	19___	19___	% change, 1st year to last year
Total industry sales	___ 100%	___ 100%	___ 100%	___ 100%	___ 100%	___%
Our sales	___	___	___	___	___	___%
Our market share	___%	___%	___%	___%	___%	_____ Percentage of change
Competitor no. 1 Sales	___	___	___	___	___	___%
Market share	___%	___%	___%	___%	___%	_____ Percentage of change
Competitor no. 2 Sales	___	___	___	___	___	___%
Market share	___%	___%	___%	___%	___%	_____ Percentage of change
Competitor no. 3 Sales	___	___	___	___	___	___%
Market share	___%	___%	___%	___%	___%	_____ Percentage of change
Competitor no. 4 Sales	___	___	___	___	___	___%
Market share	___%	___%	___%	___%	___%	_____ Percentage of change
All remaining competitors Sales	___	___	___	___	___	___%
Market share	___%	___%	___%	___%	___%	_____ Percentage of change

PLANNING PAGE 2.2

PRODUCT B

Data source:

_____

Data limitations:

_____

Measurement units used:

_____

	Year					% change, 1st year to last year
	19___	19___	19___	19___	19___	
Total industry sales	_____ 100%	_____ 100%	_____ 100%	_____ 100%	_____ 100%	___%
Our sales	_____	_____	_____	_____	_____	___%
Our market share	___%	___%	___%	___%	___%	_____ Percentage of change
Competitor no. 1 Sales	_____	_____	_____	_____	_____	___%
Market share	___%	___%	___%	___%	___%	_____ Percentage of change
Competitor no. 2 Sales	_____	_____	_____	_____	_____	___%
Market share	___%	___%	___%	___%	___%	_____ Percentage of change
Competitor no. 3 Sales	_____	_____	_____	_____	_____	___%
Market share	___%	___%	___%	___%	___%	_____ Percentage of change
Competitor no. 4 Sales	_____	_____	_____	_____	_____	___%
Market share	___%	___%	___%	___%	___%	_____ Percentage of change
All remaining competitors Sales	_____	_____	_____	_____	_____	___%
Market share	___%	___%	___%	___%	___%	_____ Percentage of change

PLANNING PAGE 2.3

PRODUCT C

Data source:

_____

Data limitations:

_____

Measurement units used:

_____

	Year					% change, 1st year to last year
	19___	19___	19___	19___	19___	
Total industry sales	_____	_____	_____	_____	_____	___%
	100%	100%	100%	100%	100%	
Our sales	_____	_____	_____	_____	_____	___%
Our market share	___%	___%	___%	___%	___%	_____ Percentage of change
Competitor no. 1						
Sales	_____	_____	_____	_____	_____	___%
Market share	___%	___%	___%	___%	___%	_____ Percentage of change
Competitor no. 2						
Sales	_____	_____	_____	_____	_____	___%
Market share	___%	___%	___%	___%	___%	_____ Percentage of change
Competitor no. 3						
Sales	_____	_____	_____	_____	_____	___%
Market share	___%	___%	___%	___%	___%	_____ Percentage of change
Competitor no. 4						
Sales	_____	_____	_____	_____	_____	___%
Market share	___%	___%	___%	___%	___%	_____ Percentage of change
All remaining competitors						
Sales	_____	_____	_____	_____	_____	___%
Market share	___%	___%	___%	___%	___%	_____ Percentage of change

PLANNING PAGE 2.4

PRODUCT D

Data source:

_____

Data limitations:

_____

Measurement units used:

_____

	Year					% change, 1st year to last year
	19___	19___	19___	19___	19___	
Total industry sales	_____	_____	_____	_____	_____	___%
	100%	100%	100%	100%	100%	
Our sales	_____	_____	_____	_____	_____	___%
Our market share	___%	___%	___%	___%	___%	_____ Percentage of change
Competitor no. 1						
Sales	_____	_____	_____	_____	_____	___%
Market share	___%	___%	___%	___%	___%	_____ Percentage of change
Competitor no. 2						
Sales	_____	_____	_____	_____	_____	___%
Market share	___%	___%	___%	___%	___%	_____ Percentage of change
Competitor no. 3						
Sales	_____	_____	_____	_____	_____	___%
Market share	___%	___%	___%	___%	___%	_____ Percentage of change
Competitor no. 4						
Sales	_____	_____	_____	_____	_____	___%
Market share	___%	___%	___%	___%	___%	_____ Percentage of change
All remaining competitors						
Sales	_____	_____	_____	_____	_____	___%
Market share	___%	___%	___%	___%	___%	_____ Percentage of change

Environmental Analysis

Now that you have developed an understanding of the trends in the sales, market shares, and growth rates in each of your markets, the next job is to scan the external environment to spot developments that may disrupt the historic relationships. The overwhelming evidence is that events that seriously disrupt markets and customers almost always come from *outside* of the industry.

For example, the Japanese engineers that developed light emitting diodes (LED) were trying to make scientific measuring instruments easier to read in daylight. They weren't out to destroy the Swiss watch industry. But that is what they virtually accomplished. Three-quarters of the world's watches used to be made in Switzerland, now it's less than one-third. Except for a government-forced merger between the two leading Swiss watch companies in 1983, there might not be any Swiss watch industry at all.

An important point. Your job in scanning the environment is not to anticipate developments before they occur. Nobody can do that. Your job is to set up an early warning system that systematically searches for existing events that could become disruptive. Seiko did not become the world's leading watch company overnight; it took years. The Swiss could have seen them coming if only they had looked.

Planning Pages 2.5 through 2.9 are designed to help you with environmental scanning.

PLANNING PAGE 2.5

THE ECONOMIC ENVIRONMENT

There are three primary ways in which a changing economic environment can affect your forecasts. First, changes in the overall economic activity in the U.S. (and, maybe, internationally) may have an effect on the total demand for your industry's goods and/or services. Second, changes in the costs of materials and labor may force price changes that affect the competitors in your markets unequally, and thus alter previous competitive relationships. Large price changes may alter the total demand for the industry's output. Third, the cost of money may change and affect your ability to fund your marketing plans.

The purpose here is not to produce razor sharp pictures of the future but to make your assumptions about future events razor sharp so that you can compare your assumptions with the future as it unfolds and make the needed corrections at the right time.

What are the key economic indicators that relate to demand for your industry?

For each of these KEY economic indicators, write down your best estimate for each of the next three years.

	Indicator 1	Indicator 2	Indicator 3
Year 1			
Year 2			
Year 3			

Estimate price changes, up and down, (as a %) for each of the following:

	Year 1	Year 2	Year 3
Materials			
Labor			
Your prices			
Industry leader's prices			

Estimate the level of short-term and long-term interest rates and the Prime rate at the close of your fiscal year.

	Year 1	Year 2	Year 3
Short-term rates			
Long-term rates			
Prime rate			

PLANNING PAGE 2.6

THE SOCIO/DEMOGRAPHIC ENVIRONMENT

Changes in the nature of your customer base (or your customer's customer base if you sell to other businesses) are always fundamental, slow moving, and inexorable. For example, the total U.S. market is getting older. You can see it in the statistics and on the streets. Each of those prospective customers is alive today. There are no abrupt changes in this environment, yet this is often the most difficult to interpret. Try your hand at the four questions below:

1. What fundamental *demographic* changes are taking place that could affect the demand for your products or services (directly or indirectly)?

   _____

   _____

   _____

2. How will this change(s) alter the demand?

   _____

   _____

3. What fundamental changes in social values, or lifestyles, are under way that could affect the demand for your products or services? (Examples: The majority of married women now have jobs outside of the home. The predominant form of family is now a two-person household. Women are now having fewer children and having them much later in life.)

   _____

   _____

   _____

4. How will this change(s) alter the demand?

   _____

   _____

PLANNING PAGE 2.7

THE POLITICAL ENVIRONMENT

The political environment usually produces the most abrupt changes. A legislature passes a new law and, overnight, the rules change. While the details of the changes in the political environment can be abrupt, the general nature of the trends is usually evident well in advance of the actual laws themselves, so you do have some ability to obtain advance warning.

There are two major ways in which changes in the political environment can affect your business: regulation and attitudes toward corporate profits. The questions below are intended to help you organize your assumptions about the political environment. Remember that politics take place at local levels as well as state and national levels.

1. What, if any, are the trends that regulate the way your products or services are made, distributed, or sold?

_____

_____

_____

2. What, if any, are the trends that regulate the competing companies in your industry?

_____

_____

_____

3. What is the government's current attitude toward profitability in your industry?

_____

_____

4. How is that attitude likely to change?

_____

_____

5. What is the government's current attitude toward investment in your industry?

_____

_____

PLANNING PAGE 2.8

THE TECHNOLOGICAL ENVIRONMENT

The technological environment is the hardest to scan because it is so difficult to know what you are looking for. Technology changes usually come from some industry other than your own. The problem then, is *where* to scan.

There are two major ways that technological change can affect your markets. One way is when a change occurs in the production process that fundamentally alters the cost structure of the competitors. For example, fiberglass ski manufacturers abruptly replaced metal ski manufacturers.

The second way occurs when a new technology produces the customer benefit you have been supplying in a less costly fashion or at some new higher quality levels. This kind of technological displacement has taken place in the record industry as compact disks have replaced vinyl phonograph records.

Give some thought to the questions below:

1. What single technological development could cause a major reduction in your production costs? Distribution and selling costs?

_____

_____

2. What would be your response if that development happened?

_____

_____

3. What sort of technological development could provide your present customers with a much better (not incremental) level of satisfaction, or the same level of satisfaction at a greatly reduced cost?

_____

_____

4. What would be your response if that development happened?

_____

_____

PLANNING PAGE 2.9

THE ECOLOGICAL ENVIRONMENT

The ecological environment is the newest and the least understood business environment. Developments in the ecological environment can occur far "upstream" from you and affect the availability and prices of raw materials. Or, they can occur "downstream" at the point of the final consumer, or anywhere in between.

Ecological concerns have affected coal mining in the United States and Germany. Concern over food additives is growing all around the world. The lack of safe disposal of atomic wastes, more than anything else, has brought nuclear power development to a standstill in many parts of the world. Acid rain over the Eastern part of the United States and Canada, and over Norway and Sweden, may be damaging lakes, forests, crops, fish, animals, and buildings. Hydrocarbons from aerosal spray cans, refrigeration units, and burning hydrocarbon fuels may be changing the temperature of the earth by strengthening the "greenhouse" effect with far-reaching implications for food production. The destruction of the rain forest in the Amazon Basin is worrying scientists about the availability of oxygen throughout the world.

The questions here will help you start thinking about the ecological environment.

1. What production processes or procedures do you use that could be criticized as harmful to the environment?

   _____

   _____

2. What production processes or procedures do your suppliers use that could be criticized as harmful to the environment?

   _____

   _____

3. How is your packaging handled after it is removed by the customer? Is there a potential waste disposal problem here?

   _____

   _____

4. What would you do if your responses to any of these questions indicated that ecological problems exist?

   _____

   _____

Forecasting

The lesson that most astute businesspeople have learned in the past decade or so is that it is impossible to predict the future with any great degree of accuracy. But you still have to forecast because all of your plans support that forecast. The message is that it is not very useful to spend a lot of time and effort developing sophisticated forecasting methods because they aren't likely to be any better than simple methods, which are faster and cheaper.

Start by simply extending the trends from the past that you have documented in Planning Page 2.1 into the future for each of the next three years. The first future year, called *out-year,* is the one for which you will prepare plans in detail, with lesser detail for the second and third "out" years. Then go back to Planning Pages 2.5 through 2.9 to see if there are any developments that may upset those historical patterns. If so, adjust the forecasts to reflect the impact those developments may have on demand for the total industry and on the individual competitors.

Doing this accomplishes three things. First, it provides you with a reasonable forecast of sales volumes for the next few years so you can begin to plan the programs to make your forecasts become a reality. Second, it calls your attention to just how fragile those forecasts are. This is a great way to avoid believing that sales forecasts are "set in concrete." Third, it focuses your attention on possible developments in a way that will cause you to keep a close watch on the progress that those developments make. In short, you reduce the likelihood that changes sneak up on you.

CHAPTER 3

Marketing Planning— Understanding Your Strengths, Weaknesses, and Competitors

Now you have a good understanding of how your industry has developed and your current position within it. You also have sales estimates and forecasts for the near term that are based on recent trends in your markets and are consistent with trends developing in the environments in which you operate. The normal reaction at this point would be to begin to develop the specific programs that would make those sales estimates come true. But don't do that just yet. There are three more concepts that must be mastered if your plans are going to work the way you want them to work: understanding your strengths, weaknesses, and competitors.

Understanding Your Strengths and Weaknesses

The first two concepts you should understand are the strengths and weaknesses of your company. Far too many companies act as if they have only strengths, no weaknesses. This is foolish. As an individual, you know that you have areas where your performance is good, because of natural abilities, practice, affinity, etc. Those are the areas where you seek out assignments because you know you will most likely do well. You also know there are some things that you don't do so well, and those are the assignments you try to avoid.

In the same way, organizations come to be good at some things and not so good at others. Corporate cultures that are created, by design, accident, or both can attract certain kinds of talents, skills, and experience. It is not possible for anyone or any organization, however, to be outstanding in everything.

The point is that if your marketing plans are to succeed, they must be built on your strengths, not on your weaknesses. It is amazing the number of companies that do not understand this simple fact of life. Texas Instruments, Inc. is a good example. Here is an organization that is superb at inventing and engineering. Ever since Texas Instruments' engineers figured out how to use transistors in the 1950s, there has been a stream of state-of-the-art inventions flowing from their labs—the first integrated circuit in 1958, the first microprocessor in 1971, and so on. They are, however, bad at marketing. They tried to market hand-held calculators and lost money. They tried to market digital watches and lost money. They tried to market home computers and lost an enormous amount of money ($330 million). Anybody can make a mistake once, but three mistakes in a row?

You may want to dismiss Texas Instruments as an isolated example of a group of engineers and scientists who were simply out of touch with the marketplace, but that would be a mistake. The world's largest retailer, Sears, Roebuck & Company, is certainly in touch with the marketplace, but they too, failed to understand their own strengths and weaknesses, on a grand scale.

As you know, Sears is a very large organization. Their current sales are about $40 billion. They operate over 800 stores in the United States. Sears's great strength has always been their superb control systems. Electronic cash registers link virtually every department of every store directly to its Chicago headquarters where merchandising decisions are made. In this way, Sears can make volume purchases at the best possible prices.

In the late 1970s, Sears's growth began to slow as the population growth of the United States also declined. This decline, however, did not affect the number two retailer in the United States, K mart, which runs a very different kind of department store. K mart is a promotional store. Buyers buy for just a few local stores, and if the merchandise sells, they quickly order more. If it doesn't sell, they quickly mark it down, recover all the cash that they can get, and invest it in other newer merchandise. Make a decision—quick—see the results—quick—make another decision—quick.

For some reason, Sears's management decided that it should become a promotional store. Tens of thousands of Sears employees who were trained *not* to make sudden decisions were now expected to do so and take on responsibilities unlike anything they had ever done before. Sears cut prices and advertised aggressively. Both activities were controlled from headquarters.

But in the stores, the special merchandise that was promoted and had been bought centrally piled up while store employees just looked at it and waited for someone to tell them what to do. After turning in one of the first money-losing quarters in the company's history, management abandoned their attempt to become a promotional retailer.

Sears's great strength, then and now, is in its control and communication system. Its great weakness is the lack of entrepreneurial spirit among its employees. In spite of this, Sears's management put in place a program built not on the company's strengths, but on its weaknesses. If Sears can make that kind of mistake, most other companies can also make it. That is why it is important to assess your strengths and weaknesses honestly. Successful plans must be built on your strengths.

Understanding Your Competitors

The third concept you should understand in considerable depth is your major competitors. The reason is simple: You can only execute those plans that your competitors *allow* you to execute. The following example illustrates this important concept.

Procter & Gamble, Kraft, Hunt-Wesson Foods, and several other companies manufacture and sell shortening to the food service market. McDonald's uses it to fry their french fries, Kentucky Fried Chicken fries its chickens in it, and the bakery in your neighborhood uses it to make cakes. There is little difference between these products; all are made by refining raw soybean and other oils. It is very easy for customers to shift from one brand to another.

The products are bulky, heavy, and of relatively low value so most of the business is done through local market distributors. Price is very important as a competitive tool. Procter & Gamble, the price leader, changes prices with a view toward replacement costs of the raw soybean oil and uses soybean futures as an indicator.

Hunt-Wesson Foods assigned a new vice president to their food service division with instructions to improve the margins generated by the division. Accordingly, he began to make a number of changes in the way the company did business, and in doing so, offended many people in the industry. Eventually, he raised his prices unilaterally because soybean futures had risen sharply and Procter & Gamble had not raised their prices. He fully expected that all of the competition would raise their prices as well (they were also under profit pressure).

Not one single competitor followed the price increase. Distributors stopped buying Hunt-Wesson shortening—not just slowed down—stopped. The division normally received $5–$6 million in orders every month and suddenly it received none. After three weeks of no orders, the vice president lowered his prices again. Two days later, Procter & Gamble *raised* its prices and all of the competitors followed suit. The "new guy on the block" had been taught a lesson. And that lesson is that you can't execute a strategy unless your competitors will permit you to do it.

Analyzing Your Strengths and Weaknesses

To analyze your strengths and weaknesses, start by developing a list of business factors that contribute to success in your industry. The list should be comprehensive and act as a profile of your business. The objective is to get a number of people in your company to rate it on each of the items.

Planning Page 3.1 gives you a place to begin. It lists a number of items that are important, organized by functional areas of business. First, go through the items shown and cross out those that aren't really important in your business. Second, go through again and add items that are important in your business. Talk over this working list with managers in other areas of your business (finance, production, and purchasing). Explain what you are trying to do and get them to help you. You are quite likely to learn a lot more about your company.

Whenever there is a question about whether or not to include an item, go ahead and include it. It is better to have too many items than to have too few.

When your list seems complete, you will need to get a number of people in your organization to rate your company on all of the items about which they have reasonable knowledge. Instruct them to leave items blank unless they are reasonably confident about their knowledge of the competition. After all, what you are trying to do is understand your real competitive position in the market.

In addition to your item list, you will need a written set of criteria that each individual can use to evaluate each item. Many systems work well. Letters like A, B, C, D, and F, or words like "excellent," and "very good," or number systems like 100%, and 90% all work well. The important part is the written descriptions of what the criteria define.

As you write the descriptions, remember that you want to keep the distinctions between the levels of ratings as sharply defined as possible. Here are some examples to help you get started:

1. A Rating: Best there is. Nobody is better. Unquestioned leader. Best in the market. Stronger than any competitor. Clearly the best in the business.

2. B Rating: Good as any competitor. Equal to the best. Leading edge of technology. Very good.

3. C Rating: About average for our industry. Adequate for now. OK, not a big problem now. Better than some, not as good as others.

4. D Rating: Most of our competitors are better. Division managers have a lot of trouble with this. Competitors use it against us. Not good.

5. F Rating: A very serious problem. Competition beats our brains out. Must be corrected now. We're seriously behind here. Needs immediate attention.

As you think about how you want to go about administering the strengths-weaknesses analysis, there are two tendencies that you should be aware of as you draw up your plans. First, upper-level managers will want to concern themselves with broad issues and ignore the operating details. Lower-level managers do just the opposite; they will tend to focus on operating details and ignore broader issues. Also, upper-level managers tend to give optimistic evaluations and look at things with rose-colored glasses; lower-level managers tend to give more pessimistic evaluations.

Second, be aware of the tendency of managers to substitute their own criteria when rating items. Further, those criteria tend to be different for weaknesses than for strengths. In areas of strength, there is a tendency to use historical criteria ("We're a lot better than we used to be"). But for weaknesses, there is a tendency to use normative criteria ("We could be better in that area"). Both of these criteria are wrong. You must make your raters understand that the competition sets the criteria. Nobody makes any money competing with the past or with some abstract norms. Profits come from beating today's competitors. That's the message to communicate.

PLANNING PAGE 3.1

STRENGTHS AND WEAKNESSES ANALYSIS

Definition of A ratings: _____

_____

Definition of B ratings: _____

_____

Definition of C ratings: _____

_____

Definition of D ratings: _____

_____

Definition of F ratings: _____

_____

Item	Rating				
Marketing Area	**A**	**B**	**C**	**D**	**F**
Market share	___	___	___	___	___
Product quality	___	___	___	___	___
Distribution extent	___	___	___	___	___
Distribution quality	___	___	___	___	___
Size of sales force	___	___	___	___	___
Sales training	___	___	___	___	___
Selling expense	___	___	___	___	___
Prices	___	___	___	___	___
Customer base	___	___	___	___	___
Advertising budgets	___	___	___	___	___
Advertising creative	___	___	___	___	___
Market research	___	___	___	___	___
Warehousing	___	___	___	___	___
Inventory levels	___	___	___	___	___
Prompt delivery	___	___	___	___	___
Distribution expense	___	___	___	___	___

(continued)

PLANNING PAGE 3.1 (continued)

STRENGTHS AND WEAKNESSES ANALYSIS

	A	B	C	D	F
Customer service	___	___	___	___	___
Customer satisfaction	___	___	___	___	___
Product line completeness	___	___	___	___	___
_____	___	___	___	___	___
_____	___	___	___	___	___
_____	___	___	___	___	___
_____	___	___	___	___	___
_____	___	___	___	___	___

Production Area

	A	B	C	D	F
Plant capacity	___	___	___	___	___
Plant location(s)	___	___	___	___	___
Expand capacity ability	___	___	___	___	___
Age of plants	___	___	___	___	___
Age of equipment	___	___	___	___	___
Equipment versatility	___	___	___	___	___
Labor availability	___	___	___	___	___
Labor force quality	___	___	___	___	___
Raw material availability	___	___	___	___	___
Manufacturing costs	___	___	___	___	___
Labor costs	___	___	___	___	___
Quality controls	___	___	___	___	___
Inventory controls	___	___	___	___	___
Union relations	___	___	___	___	___
_____	___	___	___	___	___
_____	___	___	___	___	___
_____	___	___	___	___	___
_____	___	___	___	___	___
_____	___	___	___	___	___

PLANNING PAGE 3.1 (continued)

STRENGTHS AND WEAKNESSES ANALYSIS

Financial Area	A	B	C	D	F
Cash flow	___	___	___	___	___
Profitability	___	___	___	___	___
Dividend record	___	___	___	___	___
Credit rating	___	___	___	___	___
Available capital	___	___	___	___	___
Plan to actual performance	___	___	___	___	___
Bad debt record	___	___	___	___	___
Inventory turnover	___	___	___	___	___
Currency of receivables	___	___	___	___	___
Total assets	___	___	___	___	___
Current liabilities	___	___	___	___	___
Long-term debt	___	___	___	___	___
Shareholder equity	___	___	___	___	___
Equity/debt ratio	___	___	___	___	___
Share book value	___	___	___	___	___
Share P/E ratio	___	___	___	___	___
Sales per employee	___	___	___	___	___
Ownership	___	___	___	___	___
_____	___	___	___	___	___
_____	___	___	___	___	___
_____	___	___	___	___	___
_____	___	___	___	___	___
_____	___	___	___	___	___

(continued)

PLANNING PAGE 3.1 (continued)

STRENGTHS AND WEAKNESSES ANALYSIS

Administrative Area	A	B	C	D	F
Clerical skills	——	——	——	——	——
Office facilities	——	——	——	——	——
Office procedures	——	——	——	——	——
Administrative costs	——	——	——	——	——
Customer service	——	——	——	——	——
Administrative skills	——	——	——	——	——
Training costs	——	——	——	——	——
Office equipment	——	——	——	——	——
Office automation	——	——	——	——	——
Data processing ability	——	——	——	——	——
_____	——	——	——	——	——
_____	——	——	——	——	——
_____	——	——	——	——	——
_____	——	——	——	——	——
_____	——	——	——	——	——

Management Area					
CEO experience	——	——	——	——	——
Top executive experience	——	——	——	——	——
Middle management experience	——	——	——	——	——
Middle management depth	——	——	——	——	——
Management turnover	——	——	——	——	——
Salary levels	——	——	——	——	——
Communications	——	——	——	——	——
Information access	——	——	——	——	——
Decision-making ability	——	——	——	——	——
Well-defined responsibilities	——	——	——	——	——

PLANNING PAGE 3.1 (continued)

STRENGTHS AND WEAKNESSES ANALYSIS

	A	B	C	D	F
Quick reaction time	___	___	___	___	___
Management group cohesiveness	___	___	___	___	___
Incentive plans	___	___	___	___	___
Management expense	___	___	___	___	___
Planning ability	___	___	___	___	___
Operations systems	___	___	___	___	___
Board of directors	___	___	___	___	___
_____	___	___	___	___	___
_____	___	___	___	___	___
_____	___	___	___	___	___
_____	___	___	___	___	___
_____	___	___	___	___	___

Technology Area	A	B	C	D	F
Age of product technology	___	___	___	___	___
Age of process technology	___	___	___	___	___
Engineering capability	___	___	___	___	___
Product patents	___	___	___	___	___
Process patents	___	___	___	___	___
R & D depth	___	___	___	___	___
R & D management	___	___	___	___	___
R & D budgets	___	___	___	___	___
R & D track record	___	___	___	___	___
_____	___	___	___	___	___
_____	___	___	___	___	___
_____	___	___	___	___	___
_____	___	___	___	___	___
_____	___	___	___	___	___

Other Areas

_____	___	___	___	___	___
_____	___	___	___	___	___
_____	___	___	___	___	___
_____	___	___	___	___	___

In your cover memo, be certain that the raters know that their ratings will be confidential. Then arrange a blind return system that allows for identifying individuals who have not responded within the deadline and require prompting.

When all of the Planning Pages are returned, prepare a summary of the ratings, item by item. Show the number of As, Bs, etc. in a distribution for each item. Then take a blank Planning Page to summarize those distributions. Use the modal score to record on the Planning Page (the mode is the score received most often). Give all of the participants a copy of the summary and schedule a meeting a week to ten days later to review and analyze the results.

What to Do at the Review Meeting

The first thing that you want to accomplish at the review meeting is to gain agreement that the results are an accurate assessment of the company. There may be disagreements. Listen carefully to the reasons for them. They may indicate other management problems that need attention.

The next thing to do is to examine the D and F items, if there are any. They represent real competitive vulnerabilities and require immediate attention. Clear assignments and responsibilities must be attached to these items, and make sure that everyone understands the timetable for actions dealing with D and/or F items.

Now it is time to tackle the A items. Use a big art pad, or a chalkboard, to list them. Try to find clusters that seem to make sense together, for example, customer satisfaction, product quality, extensive distribution, delivery, and customer service. These clusters are your strengths and they are the basis for building your marketing plans.

Next, look at the B items that fit logically into the strength clusters. Estimate what is required to upgrade each item to an A rating. For every item that can be upgraded, make a clear assignment with a timetable.

Now take those A and potential A clusters and give them short, descriptive names. This exercise will give you a sharper understanding of the nature of your strengths and will make future communications and the development of your marketing plans much easier.

Finally, turn your attention to the C items. Look for places that could be upgraded with a minimum of effort and money. You simply can't do everything at once; however, there may be some opportunities to strengthen the whole company with a modest investment.

Analyzing Your Competitors

A thorough understanding of your competition is an absolute requirement for developing successful marketing strategy and plans. It is very clear that Steve Jobs did not understand his main competitor when he decided *not* to make Apple computers IBM compatible. He didn't understand the commitment of IBM's customer base, he didn't understand the strength of its sales and service force, and he didn't understand the importance of IBM to software developers. Well, Steve Jobs is no longer at Apple Computer, Inc. and his successor, John Sculley, is backpedalling as fast as he can to make

Apple as IBM compatible as possible. Understanding your competitors is very important.

What you want is a way to organize the wealth of publicly available information about your competitors. You should find some way to organize the data so that you can develop the best answers to the following six general questions.

1. What are the major strengths and weaknesses of each major competitor? Only the three or four biggest competitors are of interest to you. These companies are the ones whose actions can have a significant effect on the market. Your plans will have a much greater chance of being executed if you attack your competitors' weaknesses, not their strengths.

2. How do your competitors actually manage their businesses? Managers almost always assume that the competition manages the same way they do. Wrong. Just as companies develop different patterns of strengths and weaknesses, so do they develop different management styles. The popular press refers do it as the "corporate culture." Whatever you choose to call it, it is instrumental in what actions a company will and will not take in the marketplace.

3. What are the priorities of your competitors? What do they spend money on first? What things do they insist on having? What do they like to brag about? What do the sales people stress to the customers?

4. Are your competitors satisfied with their position in the market? Are they going to spend large amounts to grow in this market? Or will they assign those resources to growth in other areas?

5. If a competitor is not satisfied with its present position, what change in behavior seems to be most likely? How fast could such a change be implemented? What would be the early warning signs? What would be the effect on you? On other major competitors? Would they retaliate? How?

6. What specific actions could you take that would be the most threatening to each competitor? What reaction would that action most likely evoke?

The President of Levi Strauss International, Thomas Tusher, described competitive analysis to the 1983 ESOMAR Conference on Strategic Planning this way:

> All too often we tend to define our markets and objectives in isolation from the marketplace actions of our competitors. The best laid strategic plans and marketing executions often go astray from failure to analyze our competitors, *their* strategies, and *their* likely response to our *own* strategies and actions.
>
> Thus we need to define who our competitors and potential competitors are, to put ourselves in *their* heads to define their objectives and priorities, and what their strengths and weaknesses are compared to ours. We need to understand their market resources and strengths, their points of weakness and vulnerability, and their *management* resources, capabilities and tendencies. We need to define *their* key strategies, how they are likely to change in the future, and *their* probable response to specific actions or executions on our part.

AN EXAMPLE OF A FRAMEWORK FOR
COMPETITOR ANALYSIS

   I. Current strategy and long-term goals
      A. Strategic position
         1. Historical development
         2. Corporate culture
      B. Strategic performance
         1. Financial
         2. Operational
         3. Source of competitive advantage
      C. Organizational strengths and weaknesses
      D. Functional strengths and weaknesses
      E. Management characteristics
  II. Future strategy and long-term goals
      A. Most probable strategic changes
      B. Strategic threat to us from this competitor
      C. Strategic opportunity for us presented by this
         competitor

In addition to gathering publicly available information about your competitors, here are some other things that you should be doing.

• Do some reverse engineering. Tear down your competitors' products. Evaluate their costs, manufacturing methods, etc. Evaluate their product quality from a customer's standpoint.

• Use Planning Page 3.1 as a way to summarize what you and the other managers know about each of your major competitors.

• Develop "Competitive Activity Reports" for the field sales force to use in communicating with headquarters. Be very specific about what you expect the sales people to do for you (or they won't do anything) and make certain that they understand that the reports are read and acted upon (or they won't do anything).

• Use one of your own company's management employment application forms and fill it out for the CEOs of your competitors. Write a subjective profile. How does he or she make decisions? Is he or she a risk taker or a risk avoider? The chief executive officer of each of your major competitors is of particular interest because this is the one person who sets the tone for the whole organization. Most importantly, this person makes the final strategic decisions for the company.

• Find a way to get your top managers to spend time calling on your key customers and potential key customers on a regular basis. Get written reports of customers' reaction to competitors' behavior.

• Prepare an investment history. When does each competitor spend capital funds, where are they spent, and for what? Prepare a spending history of each competitor's advertising budgets. How much do they spend? Does it vary from year to year? If so, why? How do they spend it market by market? Which media do they spend it in? Does that change? Over time? By geography?

- Analyze your competitors' advertising, sales promotion, and sales literature to identify what they think is important to customers and what they think are their strong points.

- Use a map to locate all of your competitors' plants. Use a different color to identify each competitor. Vary the size of the circle to represent plant capacity.

- Use another map to locate all of your competitors' distribution points or warehouses. Use a different color to identify each competitor. Vary the size of the circle to represent inventory levels.

Planning at Procter & Gamble

There can be little question that one of the premier consumer products companies in the world is Procter & Gamble, Inc. Its managers are meticulous at planning and are determined about carrying through on execution. The company has distilled its approach to business into ten major business principles (Exhibit 3.1). Each of these principles should be considered as you bring your marketing plans together.

Building on Your Strengths—An Example from Australia

The new car market in Australia is a fiercely competitive one. There are five domestic manufacturers and a legion of importers, ranging from Alfa Romeo to Volvo, competing for a market of approximately 400,000 units. By way of comparison, Honda sold 544,000 units in the United States in 1986.

Exhibit 3.2 shows recent trends in market share among the major competitors in the Australian market. As you can see, Ford and Toyota have the best growth records. Toyota has built its growth record on its major strength—an outstanding, aggressive dealer network.

Toyota Australia capitalizes on its dealer network by organizing tightly focused, intensely promoted sales events several times a year. Exhibit 3.3 demonstrates dramatically how these sales events generated sales in a single year, as an example. To achieve such results in this competitive market, three groups have to plan meticulously and execute with precision. They are the Toyota factory representatives, the Toyota dealers, and their advertising agency, SSB Weston Advertising. This is the way they work it.

Australia is divided into television marketing regions. Television is important in marketing there because of the great distances involved. In each television marketing area, the Toyota dealers contribute an agreed-upon amount (usually A$25 to A$50) per unit into a "spending pool," the Toyota Dealers Advertising Fund (TDAF). Toyota also contributes to the TDAF and the total amount is used to fund the advertising and sales promotion activities that are at the center of the sales events.

Bill Cross, general manager at SSB Weston, says the purpose of the TDAF sales event is to "generate incremental store traffic in the dealers' showrooms by adding a sale tonality to the TV communications and to the point of sale, as well as press/radio efforts." To ensure that the various sales events stay tightly focused, SSB Weston follows a set of guidelines devel-

---

EXHIBIT 3.1

PROCTER & GAMBLE'S STATEMENT OF MARKETING PHILOSOPHY

Business Principles

1. *Plan all action in advance*—Always forecast business in relation to expenditure, always check that the business is reacting according to forecast, and always be ready to adjust plans as necessary.

2. *Base all action on facts*—One fact is worth many judgments. Strive always to find the factual truth on a subject before acting. This applies to all fields of the business: product, packaging, advertising, promotions, and expenditures.

3. *Always know the objective of your actions*—Know what advertising, individual promotions, and sales plans are intended to do and judge their success by whether they achieve objectives.

4. *Sell a better product*—Even if it costs more; it is not necessary to compete on price, we compete on product quality and marketing skill.

5. *Make a reasonable profit*—Profit related to field in which operating.

6. *Spend advertising and promotion money to build business*—If necessary, forego profit temporarily to build business, but only if adequate profit is assured when business is built.

7. *Spend big money only against proved techniques*—Never spend big monies (and hence potential profit) on large scale unless efficacy has been tested in small scale first.

8. *Spend some money to test possible improvements*—Unless new plans and techniques are tested now, future broad-scale progress is impossible.

9. *Wherever possible, limit our activities to those in which we are specialists*—We are product performance specialists and marketing specialists. We try to stick to these activities and do as little else as possible. (Let the firms who specialize in other activities perform them for us.)

10. *Generate competition between our own brands*—Only in this way can we properly meet competition from other brands of other companies.

---

oped by Toyota's U.S. advertising agency, DFS Dorland, Inc. The guidelines and their application to the first Sales Event of the calendar year 1987 follow:

EXHIBIT 3.2

THE AUSTRALIAN AUTOMOBILE MARKET (MARKET SHARES—1982 TO 1986)

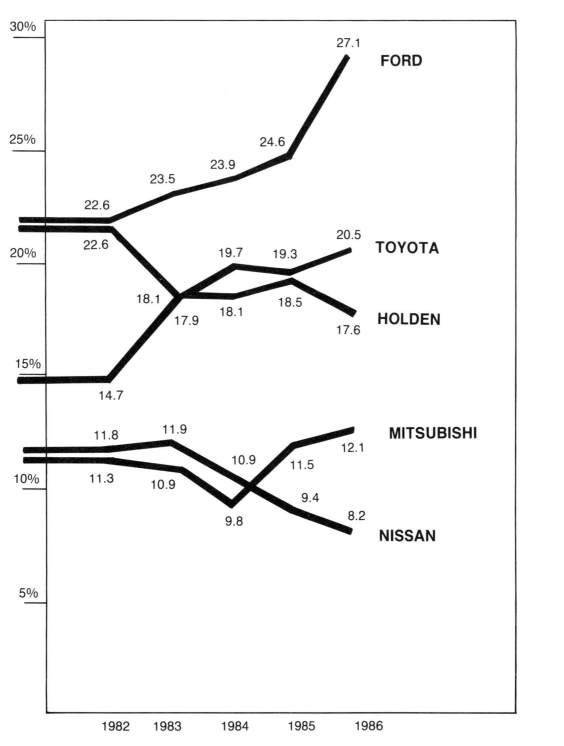

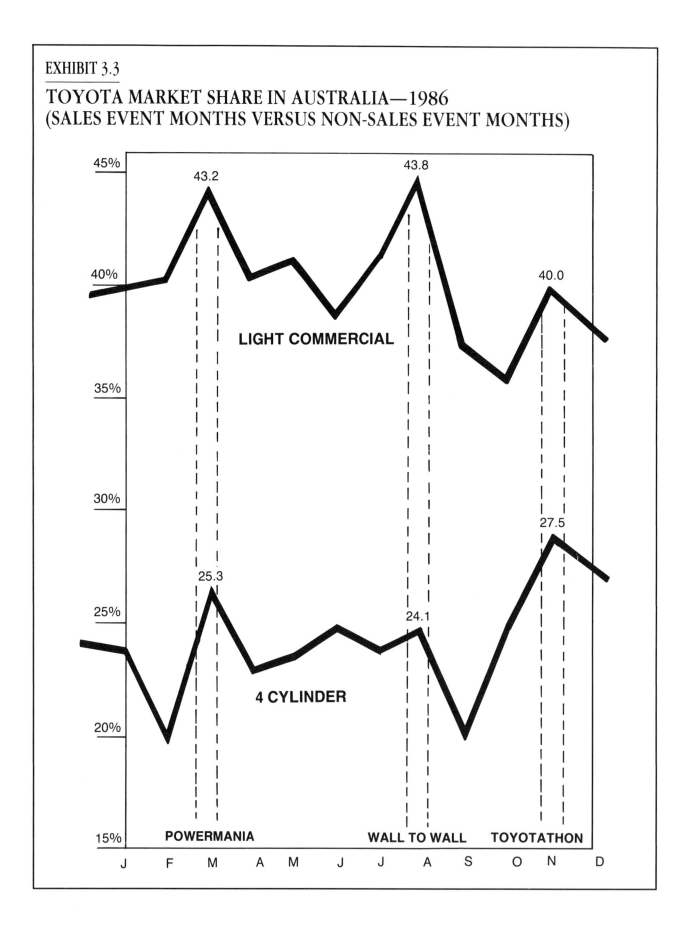

EXHIBIT 3.3

TOYOTA MARKET SHARE IN AUSTRALIA—1986
(SALES EVENT MONTHS VERSUS NON-SALES EVENT MONTHS)

THE SUCCESSFUL EVENT FORMULA

INGREDIENTS	FIRST SALES EVENT—1987
1. Call to action	OUT OF CHAIR Want to get excited. Toyota's March Excitement Sale is on! But Hurry Toyota's Excitement Sale ends March 31st.
2. Limited time	CAN'T WAIT March Excitement Sale from now to end of March. 5,000 Vehicles by the end of March. End March 31st.
3. Implied offer	SOMETHING IN IT FOR ME Giving away Millions of Dollars. Price Leaders. Trade-ins are up, up, up.
4. Sales goal	DEALER WILL TRY HARDER Move 5,000 Units by the end of March.
5. Reason to deal	IT'S GENUINE To move 5,000 Units by the end of March.

PACKAGING

1. Surprise openings	GAIN ATTENTION Want to get Excited? Attention getting set.
2. Humor	REASON TO ATTEND In Customer Reactions.
3. Lots happening	WHAT AM I MISSING? Lots of People in Background. Quick Cuts.
4. In showroom	BUILD *TOYOTA TERRIFIC/P.O.S. IDENTIFICATION* Studio/Showroom
5. Large selection	I'LL GET WHAT I WANT Corolla Corona Cressida Hilux Tarago Landcruiser Wagon

This first sales event of 1987 is titled EXCITEMENT DEALS. The centerpiece is a 30-second TV commercial. Exhibit 3.4 is the first storyboard for the EXCITEMENT DEALS 1987 commercial and Exhibit 3.5 is the script for the storyboard.

After review and discussion by all three parties, the commercial was revised (Exhibit 3.6). It was revised slightly one more time to make sure all parties, including the legal department, were in complete agreement. Exhibit 3.7 is the script of the final version of the commercial that went on the air in Australia on March 12, 1987. Although it is not indicated in the script, the final version uses the Pointer Sisters singing their song ''I'm So Excited'' as background music. Exhibit 3.8 shows how this theme was translated into radio commercials for individual dealers. Examples of ad slicks that were provided to individual dealers to use in their newspaper advertising are shown in Exhibit 3.9.

Toyota's goal is to be the number one selling automobile in Australia by 1990. If they continue to build on their strengths, they just might accomplish that goal.

EXHIBIT 3.4

FIRST DRAFT STORYBOARD
(EXCITEMENT DEALS—1987)

EXHIBIT 3.5

TV COMMERCIAL SCRIPT—EXCITEMENT DEALS
(FIRST DRAFT)

CLIENT:	TOYOTA
PRODUCT:	EXCITEMENT DEALS
KEY NO:	
DATE:	FEBRUARY 17th, 1987
DURATION:	30 SECONDS

VIDEO	AUDIO
Open on Presenter in front of Toyota excitement centre display.	PRESENTER: Want to get excited? Your excitement centre is right here!
Young blonde woman with her new Corolla can hardly contain her excitement. Super the price.	WOMAN: The deal on my Corolla . . . wow!
	MUSIC: I'm so excited.
Presenter then pans across Toyota range with windscreen banners. SUPER: New Factory Incentives. Family man with Tarago R.V. at picnic scene. He & wife hug excitedly. SUPER: Super value new Tarago R.V.	PRESENTER: Factory incentives mean Toyota Dealers around Australia have over 1 million dollars to give away this week. *The* most exciting deals ever on all Toyotas . . . including the all new Tarago R.V.
	MAN: Incredible deal!
	MUSIC: I'm so excited.
Worker feeling really flash with his new Hilux. SUPER: The price.	PRESENTER: Toyota Dealers have got the money so trade-ins are up, up, up.
Worker does excited dance.	MAN: New Hilux and I got more for my oldie than I paid.
Presenter amongst cars & excitement centre display. SUPER: Offer ends April 30.	MUSIC: I'm so excited.
	PRESENTER: Come into your Toyota Dealer and get new car excitement you can now afford.
Split screen of 3 above excited customers doing Toyota jump.	TAG: Oh What a Feeling Toyota.

EXHIBIT 3.6

TV COMMERCIAL SCRIPT—EXCITEMENT DEALS (SECOND DRAFT)

CLIENT:	TOYOTA DEALERS (TDAF)
PRODUCT:	MARCH EVENT—EXCITEMENT DEALS
KEY NO:	STT698
DATE:	20th FEBRUARY, 1987
DURATION:	30 SECONDS

VIDEO	AUDIO
	Clarion Call.
Open close on Presenter & quick pull back to reveal him in front of the Excitement Centre display and range of vehicles.	PRESENTER: Want to get excited? Your excitement centre is right here! MUSIC UNDER: I'm so excited etc. . . .
Vivacious young woman with her new Corolla can hardly contain her excitement as she smiles and gestures.	WOMAN: The deal on my Corolla . . . great!
SUPER: Excitement Price $10,990 Corolla	MUSIC: I'm so excited etc. . . .
Series of shots of the Toyota range with customers inspecting, deciding to buy and showing excitement at the prospect of owning one etc. Tarago RV and Corona are prominent with windscreen banners —All New! Super Value Tarago RV —Exciting Corona Run-Out Deals	PRESENTER: From now 'till the end of March Toyota Dealers around Australia will be giving away millions of dollars for the most exciting deals ever on any new Toyota you want. All models and colours.
SUPER: Factory Incentives	MUSIC: I'm so excited etc. . . .
Cut to a feature vehicle and the owner showing genuine excitement at the deal he got (e.g., Corona Wagon or Hilux 1.6L)	PRESENTER: Toyota Dealers are go, go, go to move stock by the end of March, so . . . trade-ins are up, up, up! MAN: I got more for my trade than I paid!
Brief cuts to series of excited customers	MUSIC: I'm so excited etc. . . .
Cut to Presenter amongst Excitement Centre display and range of Toyota vehicles.	PRESENTER: This *is* new car excitement you can afford. But hurry! . . . these deals last 'till the end of March only!
SUPER: Ends March 31st (Ends This Week)	
Cut to split screen as Corolla and the feature vehicle buyers do the jump.	TAG: Oh What A Feeling. Toyota!
SUPER: Toyota	

EXHIBIT 3.7

TV COMMERCIAL SCRIPT—EXCITEMENT DEALS (THIRD DRAFT)

CLIENT:	TOYOTA DEALERS (TDAF)
PRODUCT:	MARCH EVENT—EXCITEMENT DEALS
KEY NO:	STT698
DATE:	FEBRUARY 24th, 1987
DURATION:	30 SECONDS

VIDEO	AUDIO
	Clarion Call
Open close on Presenter & quickly pull back to reveal him in front of the excitement sale display and range of vehicles.	PRESENTER: Want to get excited? Toyota's March Excitement Sale is *on now*!!
Vivacious young woman with her new Corolla can hardly contain her excitement as she smiles and gestures.	MUSIC UNDER WOMAN: (100%) The deal on my Corolla . . . great!
SUPER: Excitement price Corolla hatch from $10,990.	MUSIC: I'm so excited.
Series of shots of the Toyota range with customers inspecting, deciding to buy and showing excitement at the prospect of owning one etc. Tarago RV and Corona are prominent with windscreen banners. —All New! Super value Tarago RV —Ripper runout Corona deals	PRESENTER: From now till the end of March Toyota Dealers are giving away millions of dollars to make the most exciting deals *ever* on any new Toyota you want. MUSIC: I'm so excited.
SUPER: Factory incentives on now!	PRESENTER: Toyota Dealers are go, go, go to sell 10,000 vehicles by the end of March . . . so . . . trade-ins are up, up, up.
Cut to feature vehicle and the owner showing genuine excitement at the deal he got (e.g., Hilux 1.6L)	MAN: I got more for my trade than I paid.
Brief cuts to series of excited customers.	MUSIC: I'm so excited.
Cut to Presenter amongst excitement centre display and range of Toyota vehicles. SUPER: Ends March 31st (Ends This Week).	PRESENTER: But hurry Toyota's Excitement Sale ends March 31st.
Cut to split screen as Corolla and the feature vehicle buyers do the jump. SUPER: Toyota	TAG: Oh What a Feeling, Toyota.

EXHIBIT 3.8

SAMPLE RADIO COMMERCIAL SCRIPT—EXCITEMENT DEALS

*Broadcast tapes of these radio commercials are available on request
to Craig McNeilly, SSB Weston (02) 358 5366*

SAMPLE RADIO SCRIPT USING POINTER SISTERS MUSIC TRACK & PRESENTER INTRODUCTION FROM T.V. COMMERCIAL

Clarion Call

Music Under

Presenter: Want to get excited? Toyota's Excitement Sale is on *now*! New car excitement you *can* afford!

Chorus: I'm So Excited

Announcer insert example: Right now at John Smith Toyota, Smithtown, you'll get *the* most exciting deal in town on any new Toyota—Corollas, Coronas, Hi Lux. All models, all colours—we'll do the deal to excite you!

Chorus: I'm So Excited

John Smith Toyota are go, go, go, to move stock by the end of March so trade-ins are up, up, up. Could even get more for your trade than you paid!!

Chorus: I'm So Excited

But hurry! The Excitement Sale ends March 31st.

Tag: Oh What a Feeling, Toyota.

EXHIBIT 3.9

AD SLICKS FOR USE BY TOYOTA DEALERS IN THEIR OWN ADVERTISING (EXCITEMENT DEALS—1987)

These reproductions have been produced in such a manner that all you need do is cut out the print required and stick it on to your layouts or finished art. Your printers or publications will then produce your blocks for printing. If required, more of these sheets are available on request.

TOYOTA Excitement Sale IS ON NOW!

WITH MILLIONS OF DOLLARS TO GIVE AWAY.

Yes, from now until the end of March Toyota Dealers are giving away millions of dollars to make the most exciting deals on every new Toyota in the range.

Toyota Dealers are all go to sell 10,000 vehicles by the end of March so trade-ins are way up. See your Toyota Dealer now for exciting deals and mammoth trade-ins.

But hurry – sale ends March 31st. The excitement goes on and on.

TOYOTA
Oh what a feeling!

BUT HURRY – SALE ENDS MARCH 31ST

EXHIBIT 3.9 (continued)

AD SLICKS FOR USE BY TOYOTA DEALERS IN THEIR OWN ADVERTISING (EXCITEMENT DEALS—1987)

These reproductions have been produced in such a manner that all you need do is cut out the print required and stick it on to your layouts or finished art. Your printers or publications will then produce your blocks for printing. If required, more of these sheets are available on request.

MORE BUILDING ON YOUR STRENGTHS— AN EXAMPLE FROM WYOMING

This story is intended to make three points very firmly.

1. It is still the best idea to build on your strengths.

2. Good ideas can come from *anywhere*.

3. Good ideas are fragile and require careful handling.

As the example from Australia demonstrated, the job for advertising is to get prospective customers into the Toyota dealer's showroom where the actual sale takes place. This is just as true in Cheyenne, Wyoming as it is in Sydney, Australia.

In Cheyenne, there is a Toyota dealership owned and managed by Nick Nickel. Fassett-Nickel Toyota has been a leading Toyota dealer for 12 years. Nick Nickel also owns and operates a Ford dealership, and has gained some interesting insights into what happens when a prospective customer arrives at the showroom.

Nickel is a serious professional and, as do all serious professionals, he thinks a lot about what he does and how to do it better. One of the things he *knows* is that the Toyotas he sells retain more of their value when it comes time to trade them in than do most other cars. He knows that new car buyers should be informed of this when they make their decision to purchase a new car.

But he also knows that when people come to shop for a new car, it is a very exciting time for them. The shiny paint, the new fabrics, and the new sensations all tend to focus the prospective customer on immediate considerations. When people are in the process of buying a new car, trade-in time is a million years and a million miles away.

So Nickel asked himself how he could bring the important information about trade-in value "forward" in the decision-making process. After considerable thought, he came up with a plan. Nickel says, "First, we work out the details of the potential sale, i.e., body style, color, accessories, etc. Then the financing on that specific car is worked out. Sale price, less trade-in, plus tax, license, financing charges, etc. and a monthly payment for some time period is calculated. Say $300 per month for 36 months is the result as an example." Then Nickel turns to the prospective customers (and he has trained all of his salespeople to do exactly the same thing) and says, "Look, that Chevrolet Caprice you told me you were also considering buying had a payment of $300 for 36 months, but that is not actually quite right. Let me show you something."

Nickel then takes out his Kelly Blue Book and shows the prospective customer that in 36 months the Toyota is probably going to be worth $5,000 and the other car will be worth only $2,000. The missing $3,000 would require the prospective customer to pay an additional $83.33 for each of those 36 months to account for the missing $3,000.

The monthly payments for automobiles that are similar in appearance are quite different. $300 versus $383.33 is enough difference to bring the importance of trade-in value all the way forward into the immediate purchase decision. As a result, Fassett-Nickel Toyota's sales increased over 20 percent the first year Nickel used this method. *That is building on your strength.*

In 1989, at a meeting of the Greater Denver Toyota Dealer's Association, Nickel happened to mention what he was doing to Monte Zator, vice president and manager of the Retail Division, Saatchi & Saatchi DFS Pacific, the association's advertising agency, and asked whether he thought the agency might be able to do anything with the idea. Zator has *never* believed in the NIH (Not Invented Here) syndrome because he *knows* good ideas can come from *anywhere*.

Zator took the idea back to the creative group at the agency's headquarters in Torrance, California and asked them to give it their best. And their best turned out some pretty terrific advertising. Exhibit 3.10 shows the storyboard from one of five TV commercials that were developed around Nick Nickel's idea. Exhibit 3.11 shows how the idea worked in print.

Sales went up over 10 percent and within months, Toyota Dealer Associations all across the United States were using Nickel's idea for their own advertising. (If you don't think that was an impressive increase in sales, go back and look at total sales in the United States for that year!)

So far, our story has demonstrated that building on your strengths is a good idea and that good ideas can come from anywhere. Now we come to the "Ideas are fragile things" part of the story.

At the 1990 annual advertising planning meeting of the Greater Denver Area Toyota Dealers, there was a lot of congratulating each other going on, but there was also a little grumbling. The creative people at the agency were complaining that the format was too restrictive and that they couldn't be creative enough. (Does this sound familiar to you? If not, go back to Chapter 1, and review the story of the Gilbert H. Brockmeyer Ice Cream Company. The point is that it happens all of the time and you must constantly be on guard against letting it happen to you.) By the time the advertising committee had satisfied everyone's point of view for the 1991 campaign, a terrific advertising idea looked a lot like Humpty Dumpty (after the fall), but the agency thought it was creative.

By 1992, the Greater Denver Toyota Dealer's Association recognized that they had made a mistake and asked Saatchi & Saatchi to think about "how to fix Humpty Dumpty." The agency came up with a pretty terrific idea to revive the original hard-working advertising. They shot film of the new 1992 models, edited the original commercials, and inserted the new products. Exhibit 3.13 shows the storyboard from one of the 1992 commercials; the advertising is once again bringing customers back into the Toyota dealers' showrooms.

Remember these three lessons: Build on your strengths; good ideas can come from anywhere; and good ideas can be fragile. They will all save you money, make money for you, and give you hard-working advertising. (Don't buy into the notion that advertising that works for you isn't creative.)

EXHIBIT 3.10

SAATCHI & SAATCHI DFS
RETAIL DIVISION, SOUTHERN CALIFORNIA

TELEVISION COPY

File Name: T2-005	**Campaign/Project:** COST OF OWNERSHIP	**AS PRODUCED**	
Client: DENVER TDA			Page 1 of 3
Job No.: T2-005	**Tide:** ''4 × 4 SMARTS/92''	**Code No.:**	TSTR 0410
Acct. Exec.: C. BONILLO	**Product:** 4 × 4	**Length:**	:30
Rev. No.:		**Writer/tr/wp:**	DS/jb/mm

1. VID   BRUCE ELLIS ON CAMERA.
    AUD   *BRUCE:* I've driven Toyotas a half a million
          times.

2. VID   BEAUTY SHOT OF 4 × 4.
    SUPER: *A VALUE STORY FROM YOUR*
    TOYOTA DEALER
    AUD   In 1982 I bought a Toyota 4 × 4 . . .

3. VID   BRUCE ON CAMERA.
    SUPER: *BRUCE ELLIS TOYOTA OWNER*
    AUD   *and 8 years later I got over $3,100 dollars*
         back for it.

4. VID   SUPER: *AS LITTLE AS $100 A MONTH TO*
    OWN
    DISCLAIMER: BASED ON RESALE.
    AUD

5. VID   BRUCE ON CAMERA
    AUD   That means I owned that truck for about
         $100 dollars a month.

EXHIBIT 3.10 (continued)

SAATCHI & SAATCHI DFS
RETAIL DIVISION, SOUTHERN CALIFORNIA

TELEVISION COPY

File Name:	T2-005	**Campaign/Project:**	COST OF OWNERSHIP	**AS PRODUCED**
Client:	DENVER TDA			Page 2 of 3
Job No.:	T2-005	**Tide:**	"4 × 4 SMARTS/92"	**Code No.:** TSTR 0410
Acct. Exec.:	C. BONILLO	**Product:**	4 × 4	**Length:** :30
Rev. No.:				**Writer/tr/wp:** DS/jb/mm

6. VID BRUCE ON CAMERA.
   AUD I use my truck in field work as an
   archeologist.

7. VID BEAUTY SHOT OF 4 × 4.
   SUPER: *QUALITY THAT LASTS*
   AUD 155,000 miles and all I replaced was an
   alternator.

8. VID BEAUTY SHOT OF 4 × 4.
   AUD I just bought a new 4 × 4 Toyota pickup.

9. VID SUPER: *YOU'LL LOVE IT.*
   AUD It's easy to see why . . .

10. VID BRUCE ON CAMERA.
    AUD I love my new Toyota!

(continued)

EXHIBIT 3.10 (continued)

SAATCHI & SAATCHI DFS
RETAIL DIVISION, SOUTHERN CALIFORNIA

TELEVISION COPY

File Name: T2-005	**Campaign/Project:** COST OF OWNERSHIP	**AS PRODUCED**
Client: DENVER TDA		Page 3 of 3
Job No.: T2-005	**Tide:** "4 × 4 SMARTS/92"	**Code No.:** TSTR 0410
Acct. Exec.: C. BONILLO	**Product:** 4 × 4	**Length:** :30
Rev. No.:		**Writer/tr/wp:** DS/jb/mm

11. VID   SUPER: *SEE YOUR TOYOTA DEALER TODAY*
            "I LOVE WHAT YOU DO FOR ME."
            TOYOTA
      AUD   *ANNCR:* Toyota quality pays for itself. That's why it pays to see your Toyota Dealer now.

EXHIBIT 3.11

CHAPTER 4

Finding Your Customers

As stated in Chapter 1, the whole purpose of the advertising business is to be able to deliver a message to current or prospective customers at a cost lower than any other form of delivery. But to do that job efficiently and effectively, it is necessary to know who your customers are. There are two main reasons.

One reason is that each of the many media delivers a different kind of audience (people with different characteristics). Therefore, if you are going to select audiences that have the best value in terms of delivering current and/or prospective customers, you will have to have a very good idea of the characteristics of your customers.

A second reason for needing to know your customers is that you will have to fashion an advertising message toward them. If you are to make that message interesting to your customers, so they will stop and pay attention to it, you have to know a lot about who they are, how and where they live, and how and why they use your product or service. Too many advertising messages contain material that is interesting to the advertiser but not to the customer. That kind of advertising may give the advertiser a warm feeling, but the money spent is wasted if nobody else pays attention to it.

You must remember that the average American, on an average day, is exposed to a thousand advertising messages. Obviously, nobody pays attention to all of those messages. We all use *selective perception* to sort out those few messages that are of interest to us. If you expect your advertising message to stand out in that overwhelming barrage of messages, it had better make a very specific promise to a very specific individual.

Market Segmentation

Understanding who your customers are starts with the idea of market segmentation, or target marketing. The idea is that somewhere between the total market and each individual, there are groupings of people who share common characteristics and have a similar need for your product or service. The total market is always the wrong market. There is no producer of goods and/or services that can satisfy *every* prospective and present customer. At the other end of the spectrum, there are very few producers that can afford to make custom products for one customer at a time.

Somewhere in between the total market and each individual, there is a group of customers that represent your "market segment." To be useful, a market segment must meet the three following requirements.

EXHIBIT 4.1

MARKET SEGMENTATION

CONSUMER PRODUCTS

Marketing Conditions

Distribution channels
Amount of competitiveness
Advertising effectiveness
Service importance
Information needs

Buyer Behavior

Amount of product consumed
Previous use of product
Product loyalty
Purchase motives
Product satisfaction
Price levels

Demographics

Age
Sex
Marital status
Family composition
Occupation of head of household
Education of head of household
Household income
Number of employed adults
Home ownership

Psychological Characteristics

Intelligence
Personality
Hobbies
Lifestyles
Values

Geographic

Location
City size
Population density
Climate

INDUSTRIAL PRODUCTS

Organizational Characteristics

Industry (by SIC or STIC codes)
Location
Size of plants
Production configuration
Technology level
Profitability
Buying procedures

Purchase/Use Characteristics

Application
Importance of the purchase
Volume purchased
Purchase frequency
Number of individuals influencing the
    purchase
Criteria for decisions

Needs/Preferences for Product Characteristics

Performance requirements
Assistance from suppliers
Brand preferences
Desire features
Quality level
Service requirements

1. It must be measurable in some specific operational manner. For example, a market segment defined as "couples between 25 and 49 years of age who want to vacation in Hawaii in May, 1989" is probably an important group of customers for the Hawaiian Tourist Bureau. But since there is no practical way to measure such a segment, it is of little practical value.

2. It must be reachable with advertising in some affordable way. For example, winter tourists are an important source of income for both the merchants and the city of Laguna Beach, California. But since winter tourists come from all over the United States and Canada, there is no affordable way to advertise to them.

3. It must be large enough to service economically. It has already been noted that the ultimate segment—an individual—is too expensive to service for almost all producers. However, exactly how big a market segment has to be to be profitable varies widely across industries. Exhibit 4.1 shows some common ways to segment markets.

AN EXAMPLE OF SEGMENTING A MARKET

American Express is a diversified financial services company offering insurance, stock brokerage, investment management, and various financial instruments as well as their familiar travellers checks and charge cards. American Express uses age and income to create market segments. This is how they do it:

MARKET SEGMENTS FOR FINANCIAL SERVICES

Segment Name	Definition
Up and comers	Up to 50 years old with annual incomes over $40,000
Affluent established	50 years old to retired with annual incomes over $40,000
Affluent retired	Retired with annual income over $40,000
Successful beginners	Up to age 35 with annual incomes between $15,000 and $40,000
Mainstream family	Age 36 to 50 years old with annual incomes between $15,000 and $40,000
Conservative core	50 years old to retired with annual income of $15,000 to $40,000
Young survivors	Under 35 years old with annual incomes less than $15,000
Older survivors	35 years old to retired with annual incomes less than $15,000
Retired survivors	Retired with annual incomes less than $10,000

The U.S. Census of Population provides a wealth of detail on population in terms of age and income. American Express can calculate market potentials, market shares, and geographic location with considerable accuracy. It can also compare media in terms of the number of, say, families with a head under 50 years of age and an annual income of over $40,000, against per household delivery costs. Just a moment's thought makes it very clear that each of these segments will have different needs and interests, and for those with large enough profit potential, American Express will have to create different advertising messages.

LEVI STRAUSS

While simple age and income provide good segments for American Express, Levi Strauss finds it valuable to add attitudinal, lifestyle dimensions to their segments. Levi's basic customer is male, between 18 and 49 years old, with modest incomes and above. However, Levi finds that within that broad segment of the market for clothing, there are some very different segments. They divide the market into five submarkets, which they describe as follows:

1. Utilitarian Jeans Customer (about 26 percent of the total). This is the Levi blue jeans loyalist. He wears jeans for work and for play. He doesn't care much about style.

2. Trendy/Casual Customer (about 19 percent of the total). This customer is very interested in high fashion because he likes to be noticed. He is usually younger.

3. Price Shopper (about 12 percent of the total). This is an older customer whose main concern is price. He shops department store sales and discount stores.

4. Mainstream Traditionalist (about 22 percent of the total). This man is also older. He has quite conservative tastes in clothing. He likes to shop with his wife and likes to shop in department stores. He favors polyester fabrics.

5. Classic/Independent (about 21 percent of the total). This late twenties/early thirties man is a real "clothes horse." Clothes are very important to him and he spends more on clothes than any of the other segments. He likes to shop alone. He likes to patronize specialty stores and he prefers traditional styles.

Here you can see that market segmentation affects media, advertising message, distribution, and product styling decisions.

PORSCHE CARS NORTH AMERICA

Steve Goldman, senior vice president at Chiat/Day/Mojo Advertising, Los Angeles makes a very important point. He points out that it is extremely important to know exactly who your prospective customers are when you are working with a small advertising budget because you can't afford to waste a single dollar in such situations. (Not that you can afford to waste money with larger budgets; it's just in that case you have a little more "cushion.")

Here is an example of the kind of results you can get from a small budget that is targeted at exactly the right audience with exactly the right message. Chiat/Day received an assignment from their client, Porsche Cars

North America, Inc., Reno, Nevada, to introduce the Porsche 924S model into the U.S. market during the summer of 1986. The marketing situation surrounding the assignment went like this:

Porsche manufactures a line of expensive, high-performance sports cars in Germany. The 1987 suggested retail prices were:

928S	$58,900
911 Turbo	58,750
911 Cabriolet	44,500
911 Targa	40,500
911	38,500
944 Turbo	33,250
944S	28,250
944	25,500
924S	19,900

In recent years, the growing demand for two-seat sports cars has been one of the bright spots in U.S. automobile sales. However, most of that growth has been in the $13,000 to $19,000 price range. Mazda's RX7 and the Nissan ZX series are good examples. Thus, a substantial price gap existed between Porsche's lowest priced model and the top price of the (mostly) Japanese sports cars. Porsche intended the 924S to reduce that gap and to get the Japanese sports car buyers to consider buying a Porsche.

The 924S has the same drive train, brakes, running gear, and electrical system as the 944. John North, president of Porsche Cars North America, summarized the new model by saying, ''In effect, the 924S provides Porsche fans with a car similar in performance to the 944, but with sleeker styling.'' In addition, the 924S had been sold in Europe since 1976 and was a thoroughly tested product.

Some Real Problems

The advertising plan had to recognize and deal with the following problems.

• Budgets—Car makers with entries in the lower price range sell a lot of units and can afford to spend a lot on advertising. The 1986 RX7 budget of $16.2 million and the 300ZX budget of $21.8 million vastly overshadowed Porsche's budget.

• Attitudes—Prospective customers correctly perceived that the Japanese sports cars and the Porsches were in different classes.

There were only a limited number of 924Ss available, so it was important that 924S sales were not simply substitutes for 944 sales, that is, the 924S shouldn't cannibalize the 944s. It was also important that the price of the 924S not ''cheapen'' the image of the 944. Porsche has never been a price brand and there was no desire to change that fact.

Prospective Customers

Buyers of upper-end Japanese sports cars and European sporty sedans were 25 to 40 years of age, had incomes of $45,000 or more, and were 30 percent female. It was believed that some portion of this market segment wanted to own a "Porsche badge" and would be willing to "stretch" a little to achieve that ownership. They are automobile enthusiasts.

The Advertising Strategy

To reach the prospective customers with exactly the right message, two-page, four-color ads appeared in *Car and Driver, Road and Track, Motor Trend,* and *Automobile* magazines during July and August, 1986.

The real customers of Porsche Cars North America are its dealers. A complete dealer advertising program was developed to support the national campaign at the local level. Plans were prepared for 29 major markets (geographic segmentation). A TV commercial was produced and ran in June, 1986 in the major markets. It allowed a five-second, individual dealer "tag" at the end to make the commercial really local. Exhibit 4.2 shows the story-board of that TV commercial.

How Did It Work?

It worked like gangbusters! Here are some of the key measurements.

• Floor Traffic—Increased almost 100 percent in the major markets. The proportion of showroom customers seriously considering a 924S *before* the campaign ran was 12 percent. After the advertising ran, the proportion increased to 37 percent, a 300 percent increase.

• First-Time Shoppers and Buyers—Dealers recorded a 30 percent increase in first-time shoppers and an increase of 15 percent in first-time buyers. In other words, the campaign generated new customers for the Porsche dealers.

• Advertising Awareness—Awareness of any Porsche TV advertising among shoppers increased from 23 percent before the campaign to 54 percent at the end. Awareness of the specific 924S commercial increased from 2 percent before to 31 percent at the end of the program.
• Sales—Porsche had the biggest sales month in the history of the company. The previous monthly high was back in 1974. Specifically, Porsche sold 3,100 cars in June, 1986, a 30 percent increase in sales over June, 1985. Sales increased for all models, so there was no cannibalism created by the 924S. In addition, this sales momentum carried over into July and August, typically soft sales months for Porsche.

GLENFIDDICH SCOTCH WHISKEY

For decades, American taste in liquor has been changing. First came a shift in taste from what the industry calls "brown goods" (straight whiskeys, blended whiskeys, Canadian whiskeys, and Scotch whiskeys) to "white goods" (vodka, gin, and rum). More recently, this has been followed by a shift from hard liquor to beer and wine, as well as a shift from alcoholic beverages altogether. Among all of these shifting tastes and preferences, Scotch whiskey has taken a severe beating. Sales have fallen by almost one-third since the mid–1980s. As you can imagine, this is a tough market to operate in at a profit.

There are a few bright spots in this vortex, however, and single malt Scotch whiskey is one of them. This high-quality, high-priced product's sales continued to grow all through the 1980s. But by 1990, the U.S. recession, the weakened U.S. dollar vis-a-vis the British pound, and the 1991

EXHIBIT 4.2

:25/:05 Now in America

V/O: The most popular Porsche in Europe . . . is this one.

The Porsche 924S. For the past year or so, Europeans have been happily putting it through its paces.

On everything from the twistiest mountain roads . . . to the German autobahns, where the speed limit is whatever they want it to be.

But now the real fun begins.

Because now . . .

. . . the 924S . . .

. . . is available . . .

. . . in America.

(:05 Dealer Tag)

federal excise tax on luxury goods all combined to bring an abrupt end to the growth of single malt scotch whiskeys.

Some Real Problems

There are two major brands of single malt whiskey, The Glenlivet (a Jos. Seagram, Inc. brand) and Glenfiddich (a William Grant & Sons, Inc. brand). Michael Lufthglass, senior vice president and director of marketing, William Grant & Sons, Inc., had some sizeable problems to deal with to keep his brand from developing into an endgame strategy.

The Glenlivet has at least 50 percent greater distribution than Glenfiddich, and Seagram's large and effective sales force was threatening Glenfiddich's existing distribution. To make matters worse, there were rumors that Seagram was going to selectively cut wholesale prices as much as 30 percent in selected Glenfiddich markets—reductions that Glenfiddich simply could not meet. As the end of 1990 approached, senior management at William Grant began to think that flat sales in 1991 would be a remarkable feat.

Prospective Customers

The customers for premium Scotch whiskey are easy to define demographically: males, aged 25 to 49, with household incomes of $40,000 or more. In addition, they are people who are constantly searching for "premium" products, new experiences. They love challenges and new experiences.

An important characteristic of these customers is that they have specific criteria for judging the quality of Scotch whiskey. They believe they can accurately evaluate the "smoothness" of Scotch whiskey, and that smoothness is a surrogate for quality.

The Advertising Strategy

The advertising objectives here were twofold and straightforward—head off the expected decline in the sales of Glenfiddich. To do that, the advertising had to increase awareness of Glenfiddich among premium Scotch drinkers and, more importantly, increase trial purchases of Glenfiddich. This is because management believed that when premium Scotch drinkers tried Glenfiddich, they would become loyal customers.

But if halting the sales slide was a short-term objective, there was also a long-term objective. Almost half of Glenfiddich's regular buyers were 45 or older, and the long-term health of the brand depended on bringing younger customers into the Glenfiddich franchise.

The good news: the media needed to reach the prospective customers were easy to identify. More good news: the basic selling message that needed to be communicated was clear and specific.

The not so good news: the budget was very limited and there was no reason for increasing it.

With all of this in mind, the Glenfiddich acount group at Chiat/Day/ Mojo in New York (Elena Salij, senior account planner and Blake Olson, vice president and account supervisor) set to work with the creative group to create a print advertising campaign that would accomplish those objectives.

Robert Pellizzi, associate media director, says there were three key media strategies that contributed to the success of the 1991 Glenfiddich campaign:

1. Magazines that reached upscale, educated, and sophisticated men were selected:
US News, Fortune, Esquire, GQ, M, The Atlantic, and the *New York Times Magazine,* plus upscale regional magazines in the key Glenfiddich markets of New York, Los Angeles, San Francisco, Chicago, Houston, and Dallas.

2. Magazine space contracts were vigorously negotiated to help offset the limited media budget:
A 25–30 percent increase in the "value" of the purchased media was accomplished without an increase in the budget.

3. Part of the vigorously negotiated contracts included high visibility positions in the magazines. This increased awareness dramatically.
Back covers
Inside covers
Table of contents
Inside back covers

Exhibit 4.3 shows the Glenfiddich advertising media plan for 1991.

Exhibit 4.4 shows three of the print ads that were created for the Glenfiddich 1991 campaign. Chiat/Day/Mojo senior copywriter Dion Hughes is a great admirer of this creative work even though he did not work directly on the project. He says, "The visual element of these ads is extremely important. The creative team chose to stay away from traditional Scotch imagery, i.e., rolling heathers; dark, cozy drawing rooms. This gave them the freedom to create more eye-catching images: A man playing golf on a billiard table, a roadster being driven inside a large mansion. The shots still "feel" like Scotch because they are warm and aspirational. But the unusual subject matter, and the surreal, quirky humor in the photographs, and the copy makes Glenfiddich more accessible to younger drinkers."

Results

All things considered, "amazing" may be an inadequate term to describe the Glenfiddich campaign results. Here are the highlights:

Measurement	1990 (%)	1991 (%)	% Change
Unaided awareness (What brands of Scotch can you think of?)	10.2	18.0	+76
Aided awareness (Have you ever heard of any of these brands of Scotch?)	28.5	39.4	+38
Ever tried (Drank in past six months)	19.8	32.0	+62
Share of category	July/August 1990 (%)	July/August 1991 (%)	
Case sales	24.6	30.6	+24
Dollar sales	23.3	29.6	+27

EXHIBIT 4.3

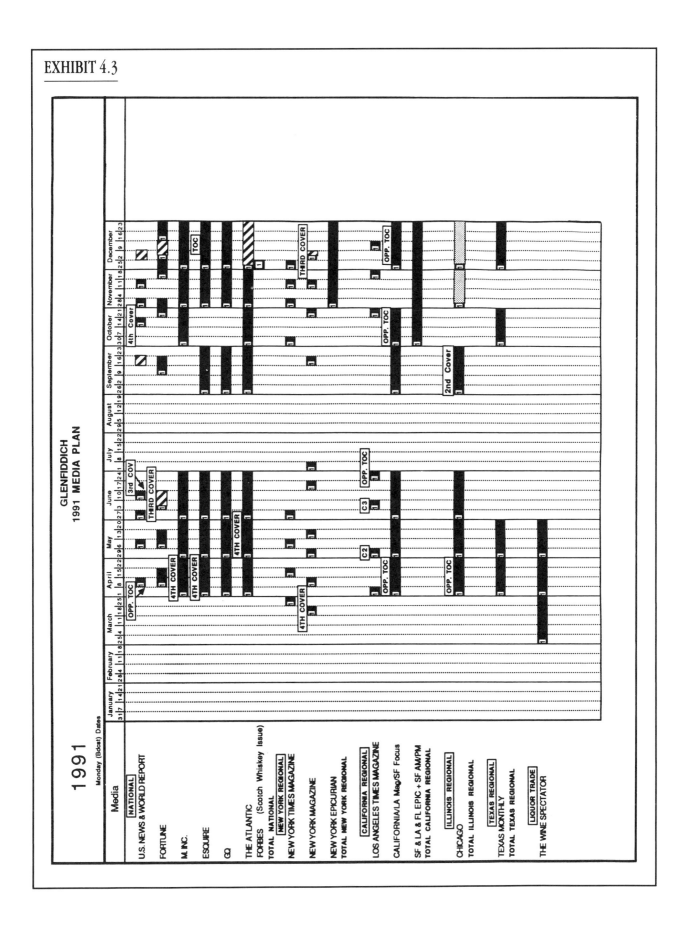

EXHIBIT 4.4

AS SOON AS I LAID EYES on my Uncle's '53 Jaguar, I prayed he'd let me take it for a spin. "Son, I'm afraid these roads aren't smooth enough," he said. "Not even *once* around the Estate?" I queried. He shook his head. "How about the circular drive?" I pleaded. As if to close the subject, he handed me a glass of *Glenfiddich single malt* and declared, "The road would have to be as *smooth as this Scotch* before I'd ever let her roll." As I savored my first sip, I had an inspiration. My Uncle laughed. But the next morning we gave it a whirl.

PURE MALT SCOTCH WITH EXTRAORDINARY CHARACTER.   DISTILLED AND BOTTLED BY THE GRANT FAMILY SINCE 1887.

NOT BLENDED WITH GRAIN WHISKIES.   NOT MATCHED BY ANY BLEND.

TO SEND A GIFT OF GLENFIDDICH ANYWHERE IN THE U.S., CALL 1-800-238-4373.
VOID WHERE PROHIBITED. BOTTLED IN SCOTLAND. 43% ALC/VOL (86 PROOF). © WILLIAM GRANT & SONS INC., NEW YORK, NY 10020.

EXHIBIT 4.4 (continued)

WHAT A MAGNIFICENT DAY FOR SAILING. A constant breeze starboard side. Not another boat in sight. And the most serene water. Such ideal conditions provided us with *the smoothest* course I had ever navigated. It was all the inspiration I needed to rechristen this heavenly vessel. Would it be sacrilege, I wondered, to rename her *"The Glenfiddich"*? No, I corrected myself. It would be my usual tendency toward exaggeration.

PURE MALT SCOTCH WITH EXTRAORDINARY CHARACTER.   DISTILLED AND BOTTLED BY THE GRANT FAMILY SINCE 1887.

NOT BLENDED WITH GRAIN WHISKIES.   NOT MATCHED BY ANY BLEND.

TO SEND A GIFT OF GLENFIDDICH ANYWHERE IN THE U.S., CALL 1-800-238-4373.
VOID WHERE PROHIBITED. BOTTLED IN SCOTLAND. 43% ALC/VOL (86 PROOF). © WILLIAM GRANT & SONS INC., NEW YORK, N.Y. 10020.

(continued)

EXHIBIT 4.4 (continued)

I BEAT HIM at the country club. The grass was *too long*. I beat him at Pebble Beach. The grass was *too short*. I beat him at St. Andrews. There was a ROCK in the way. Finally, I called his bluff. This time, it was the FELT. "*How smooth does it have to be?*" I begged. Smiling, he held forth his glass of *Glenfiddich single malt Scotch*. I sighed. Tennis anyone?

PURE MALT SCOTCH WITH EXTRAORDINARY CHARACTER.

DISTILLED AND BOTTLED BY THE GRANT FAMILY SINCE 1887.

NOT BLENDED WITH GRAIN WHISKIES.

NOT MATCHED BY ANY BLEND.

TO SEND A GIFT OF GLENFIDDICH ANYWHERE IN THE U.S., CALL 1-800-238-4373. VOID WHERE PROHIBITED. BOTTLED IN SCOTLAND. 43% ALC/VOL (86 PROOF). ©WILLIAM GRANT & SONS INC., NEW YORK, NY 10020

All of these increases happened while The Glenlivet's sales were flat and the total category continued its long-term decline.

And finally, Glenfiddich is changing the composition of its loyal customers and is getting ready to face whatever the future brings.

Glenfiddich bought in last six months	1990	1991
Age 21–44	56%	67%
Age 45 and over	44	33

The wildly successful Glenfiddich campaign is an example of carefully crafted advertising directed at clearly identified customers that was achieved on a limited budget. These are the kinds of results you can expect every time *if* you do the job right in the first place.

Note: The prospective customers for Porsche 924S and for Glenfiddich Scotch were very similar; however, it was necessary to use different media to reach these prospects in each case. It will be worth a few minutes of your time to stop now and think about the differences in the marketing problems and why the chosen media were used.

New York Life Insurance Company

Well-managed insurance companies understand that the best prospects for new services are their own satisfied customers. Talk about knowing your own customers? What could be clearer or easier than to know your own customers? Here is a story about one company that forgot, for a little while, the simple truth that your best new customers are your regular customers. (We will discuss this further in the section on frequency marketing.)

New York Life Insurance Company is the fifth largest life insurance company in the United States. New York Life has over $50 billion in assets. This is a substantial base of satisfied customers, indeed.

One of the products offered by the life insurance industry is Long Term Disability (LTD) Insurance. In the case of New York Life, 50 percent of its existing customers were qualified for LTD, but only 3 percent owned such policies. By comparison, Northwestern Mutual, a direct competitor of New York Life, sold over 15 percent of its customers LTD policies. That is more than a 500 percent difference!

Inequities among competitors like this do not occur by accident; there are underlying reasons. In this case, New York Life failed to effectively teach their agents how to sell LTD policies. The market for LTD insurance is white-collar professionals who think they do not need LTD policies. In their view, this kind of insurance is for blue-collar workers who get hurt on the job in industrial accidents. The real need for LTD is to cover *illness,* and that can strike anyone. Because the commission structure for life policies and LTD policies is the same, the agents elected to continue doing what they did best: sell life insurance policies.

Some Real Problems

In real life, there are ''windows of opportunity'' that open and close as life goes on. The management at New York Life was afraid that one such ''window of opportunity'' for LTD was closing on them. They asked Daisy Chan, director of advertising, to organize one last attempt to build a market for LTD among New York Life's customers.

Chan faced two problems. It was necessary to convince prospective customers that they needed LTD policies and, at the same time, convince New York Life agents that LTD was not too difficult, complicated and time consuming to sell. She asked the Chiat/Day/Mojo account team to make a recommendation for the New York Life account, and to do it quickly to beat the closing window.

Jon Shrair, account supervisor, and Rosemarie Ryan, senior account planner, decided that the best move New York Life could make was to select a single market and put up a demonstration project. If the project failed, costs would be minimum. If, however, the project was a success, the results could be widely and quickly merchandised to New York Life agents in other markets across the United States. Daisy Chan accepted their ideas and, together, they selected Charlotte, North Carolina for the demonstration project. Their reasoning was that if they could sell LTD insurance in a tough market like Charlotte, they could sell it anywhere.

Prospective Customers

The advertising had to reach two audiences simultaneously. The prospective policy owners were male, white-collar professionals, between the ages of 25 and 45, and they needed to understand that illness, not an industrial accident, is the biggest threat to family breadwinners.

At the same time, however, the advertising had to be good enough to convince the New York Life agents in Charlotte that LTD was a viable product that could be sold successfully. To make certain that New York Life agents in other markets would accept the results of a successful program, the agents were asked *to set criteria for success in advance of the Charlotte experiment.* The agents said they would judge the proejct a success if LTD applications in Charlotte increased by 50 percent and actual LTD sales increased by 25 percent. Those are tough goals for an advertising program scheduled to run for just three months.

The Advertising Strategy

The Chiat/Day/Mojo creative group developed six print ads filled with facts about the real needs for LTD insurance. Exhibit 4.5 shows four of those ads.

Once again, associate media planner Robert Pellizzi was called on to add value to the campaign through media selection. Here is what he had to say about his selections: "The primary goal in magazine selection was to ensure that we could reach upscale, white-collar professionals in publications that would lend credibility and immediacy to New York Life's message, and do it primarily in news and business environments. Here is what we recommended:"

1. Daily newspapers
The *Charlotte Observer* and the *Wall Street Journal* provide "must read" news affecting the day-to-day business of white-collar professionals.

2. Regional business publications
The *Charlotte Business Journal* and *Business North Carolina* provide executives with a broader perspective than newspapers regarding trends and issues relating to their businesses.

EXHIBIT 4.5

A NEW YORK LIFE STORY

by

LLOYD WILSON

As a life insurance agent, you sometimes hear thoughts clients are unable to voice to their closest friends or family members. According to Lloyd Wilson, it's just the nature of the business. Those who know him would disagree. They'd say it's more the nature of Lloyd Wilson.

"We had a large family corporation here in Birmingham where the patriarch of the family–the big tree–passed away. He was a neighbor of mine, and right after his death something happened that surprised me.

"A while back, he became disabled. Seems his heart didn't work as well as it once did, and his doctors told him he shouldn't work anymore. And so, during that time, we got to know one another, and we ended up becoming pals.

"Here he was, sixty-three or -four years old, and I was thirty-four or -five, and we'd go and do things together. He was a character...a wonderful person. Sometimes, I'd take a day off, and we'd drive out to his ranch–maybe check on the animals–and we'd talk. A lot. We'd discuss business and things that maybe we didn't talk about with other people. We were, I suppose, sounding boards for one another.

"Well, when he died, his two sons who had been running the family business came to me and said, 'Lloyd, this might sound strange, but if anyone knows what dad hoped to have happen now, it's you.

What do you think that he wanted us to do?' I guess it was surprising to me because I wasn't really their father's life insurance agent, yet they were asking me for guidance.

"At that point, we sat down and immediately set up some things that we've been enhancing ever since. His sons have become wonderful clients...and good friends.

"What's interesting is, I can see them taking on the same enthusiasm for life that he had. To me, it's one of the greatest batons he passed on to them."

Lloyd Wilson (center), President of the Agent's Advisory Council, the main link between New York Life and its 10,000 agents. John (left) and Dave Wood (right). Their business friendship with Lloyd has been around for three generations.

The Company You Keep.®

(continued)

EXHIBIT 4.5 (continued)

At one time or another everything in your office has broken down. Why should you be any exception?

"It'll never happen to me." "I don't know anyone who's ever needed it." "I think I'm covered at work."

It's easy to come up with reasons why you shouldn't have long-term disability insurance. It's even easier to come up with reasons why you should.

After all, disability insurance isn't just for people who have lost a limb. The fact is, most cases involve people whose problems are far less tangible.

And yes, it could happen to you. If you're not convinced, just sample some of these recent disability statistics.

One out of five people suffers from a mental/nervous disorder, which is the leading cause of disability.[1] And which, along with heart disease and high blood pressure, is often brought on by common stress.

One out of seven people will be disabled *for more than a year by the time they're 65*.[2]

And to top it off, less than 20% of employees have group long-term disability coverage.[3]

Starting to reconsider your need for long-term disability coverage? If so, simply call New York Life at 1-800-331-7622 for more information. We may not be able to help you when your copier breaks down, but if anything ever happens to you, we'll be there.

NEW YORK LIFE

The Company You Keep.

1. New York Life Claim Reserve File of policies issued since 1983. 2. 1985 Commissioners' Individual Disability Table A (people ages 25-60). 3. HIAA: Source Book of Health Insurance Data (1984-85).

EXHIBIT 4.5 (continued)

What millions of disabled Americans rely on as their sole means of support.

When you become disabled, and you're not insured, life as you know it begins to change.

First you stop going to work. Then you figure out how long you'll be receiving sick pay. And then you start calculating the amount of time your savings will last. And how long it might be before you have to sell off your car. Or for that matter, your home.

When you become disabled, and you *are* insured, life as you know it–at least from a financial standpoint–continues along pretty much as it was before.

Your benefit payments arrive punctually every month. And chances are, you'll still get to drive the same car, and park it in the same driveway, in front of the same home.

At New York Life, we hope you'll never have to deal with a disability. But the fact of the matter is, one out of seven people will be disabled *for more than a year* by the time they're 65.* If you'd like to make sure you're protected, feel free to call us at 1-800-331-7622.

We'll help you choose a long-term disability plan that meets your personal needs. So that no matter what should ever happen, you'll always have a leg to stand on.

NEW YORK LIFE

The Company You Keep.℠

(continued)

EXHIBIT 4.5 (continued)

Get well cards aren't the only things disabled people receive in the mail.

If you become disabled, and lose your source of income, how long would your money last?

Two years? One year? Six months? Six weeks?

Many Americans are just a few paychecks away from financial disaster. And yet the majority of us continue to live on the edge, failing to consider the consequences of becoming disabled.

At New York Life, we're getting more of our customers to think seriously about long-term disability insurance.

After all, according to recent statistics, 1 out of 7 people will be disabled *for more than a year* by the time they're 65.[1] And a large percentage of those will be individuals who suffer from such common problems as hypertension and lower back pain.

To learn more about long-term disability insurance, and how we can custom design a policy for you, contact New York Life at 1-800-531-7622.

We can help you feel a lot more secure about what the future— or your mailman—may bring.

NEW YORK LIFE

The Company You Keep.®

1. 1985 Commissioners' Individual Disability Table A (people ages 29-45).
©1990 New York Life Insurance Company, 51 Madison Avenue, New York, N.Y. 10010. All rights reserved.

3. Newsweekly publications in regional editions
Time, US News, and *Newsweek* reach the educated prospects we were targeting with a leisure time, read more relaxed, and involved environment than the business publications listed above, but these magazines still convey the seriousness and "newsworthiness" of New York Life's message.

Exhibit 4.6 is the New York Life Disability Test Plan media schedule.

Results

The results were spectacular! Although applications and LTD policies written on a national basis were down compared with the same month a year earlier, the Charlotte market showed very large gains compared with last year. Here are the numbers:

LONG-TERM DISABILITY APPLICATIONS
(VERSUS LAST YEAR)

Period	Market	
	Charlotte (%)	National (%)
October, 1990	+ 112	+ 12
November, 1990	+ 100	− 12
December, 1990	+ 65	− 12
January, 1991	+ 20	− 16

LONG-TERM DISABILITY POLICY SALES
(VERSUS LAST YEAR)

October, 1990	+ 43	+ 16
November, 1990	+ 35	− 38
December, 1990	+ 20	− 50
January, 1991	+ 45	− 16

Not only did the experiment out-perform all of the goals that the national agents had set for it, the agents were so impressed that they requested similar programs for other insurance products in their portfolios.

Note: The advertising in the Porsche problem and the New York Life problem had to reach two markets simultaneously to be successful. This is a much more common situation than one might think at first glance. For example, almost all food, health and beauty aids, and over-the-counter drug product advertising is designed to reach the prospective customers and the reatilers who carry the products. The point is that it is important to think carefully about *all* of the people who your advertising will reach.

How to Get to Know Your Customers

Developing a profile of your customers—a description of your market segment—is going to take some work. There is no one way to go about the job, but here are some ideas.

EXHIBIT 4.6

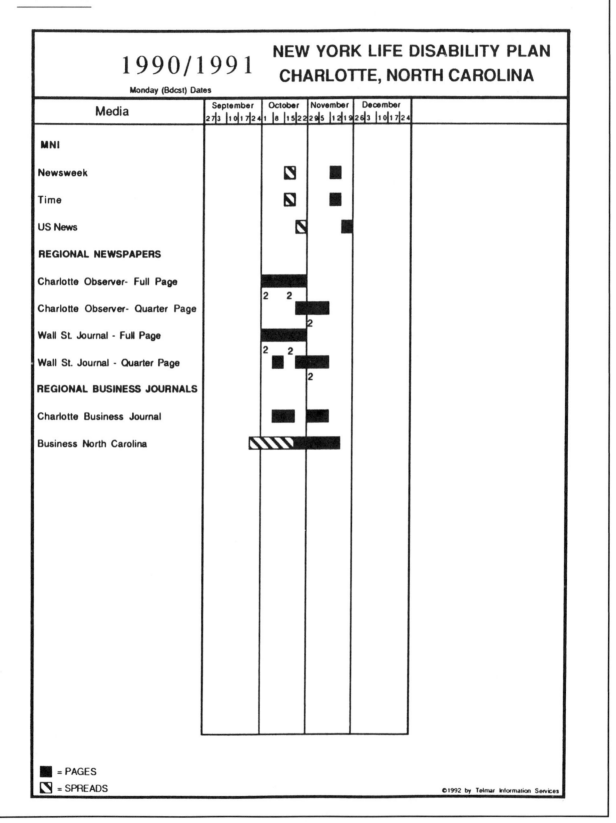

| 1990/1991
Monday (Bdcst) Dates | NEW YORK LIFE DISABILITY PLAN
CHARLOTTE, NORTH CAROLINA |

Contact a trade or industry association that may have conducted research on the nature of the industry's customers. It's a place to start. The same thing holds true for trade magazines that serve your industry. They may have some research as a service to their advertisers.

Retailers can conduct a contest among patrons and get them to fill out ''entry forms'' that ask for additional information about the person.

Manufacturers, who are farther away from the end customers than are retailers, can pack warranty cards into their packages for return by prepaid mail. Try to obtain these.

There is no question, however, that the best way to go about the job is with the help of a professional marketing research firm. Start with your local Yellow Pages, probably under Marketing Research & Analysis. Look for ads that talk about doing survey research. Call up three or four of the firms and explain that you are interested in doing a customer survey. Invite any of the interested firms to your office to learn more about your requirements. Establish in your head a rough budget that you can afford. Costs for marketing research are primarily time costs (plus overhead) and most good researchers will be able to tailor a program to fit your budget. You may have to suffer some limitations in precision and/or comprehensiveness under a limited budget, but it is still a good trade-off.

If you can't find a satisfactory survey firm in your town, call Charles A. Walker, Walker and Associates, Inc., 3800 Barham Blvd., Los Angeles, California (213) 850–6820. Charlie Walker's firm has done hundreds of customer surveys for large and small companies and for large and small budgets.

The Ultimate Level of Sophistication

Up to this point, our discussion of market segmentation has ignored competitors and treated all of the products and/or services offered to the market segment as identical. We also have treated all of the customers within the market segment as identical. But they are not identical. The question then is what separates all of these different customers with different needs, and all of these products or services that provide different benefits and divide market segments into market shares for individual companies?

We can begin to understand the answer to that question by turning to an idea first introduced by Bruce Henderson, founder of the Boston Consulting Group, Inc. He called it the *served market concept*. The served market concept says that market shares are created because customers with varying needs select the product or service that best suits them. In this process, each competitor serves some group of customers in a way that gives that competitor an absolute advantage over all of the other competitors in the market (see Exhibit 4.7).

What is of interest to you is the boundary lines between your served market and your competitor's served market because those are the areas of *zero* competitive advantage for either competitor. Therefore, all competition in a market takes place at the boundaries of served markets. Further, over time, those boundary areas change as competitors introduce new products and services.

In summary, a served market is that combination of customers' needs and product or service benefits provided by a competitor, representing an

EXHIBIT 4.7

THE TOTAL MARKET SEGMENT

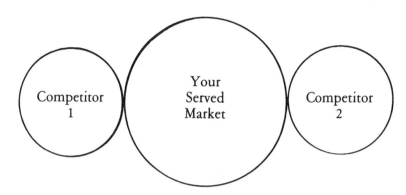

advantage over all other competitors in the market. It is each competitor's position of absolute advantage. All competition takes place along the boundaries of served markets.

Truthfully, there is not much that you can do with the served market concept. For instance, it probably won't help if you buy media. What it will do, however, is force you to think seriously about why your customers are your customers and why the other guy's customers are his (or hers). When you begin to grasp those ideas, you will be in a good position to develop your own "creative strategy," the subject of the next chapter.

What to Do Next?

Planning Pages 4.1 through 4.4 are designed to help you organize what you know (and what you think you know) about your customers and your competitors' customers. First, define your market segments. Even if you don't have hard data yet, write down what you *think*. Try to be specific. Don't say younger, say 18 years old to 30 years old.

When you have defined the market segment, try your hand at specifying your served market and each of your major competitors' served markets. Finally, try to identify what may be the area of zero competitive advantage.

Always Remember That Customers Are Changing and That Your Advertising Must Be Changing

Another one of Monty McKinney's "Life's Little Lessons" (about when customers changed but the advertising didn't or couldn't) appears on page 97.

PLANNING PAGE 4.1

MARKET SEGMENTATION—PRODUCT A

Definition of total market:

_____

_____

Definition of segments you compete in:

_____

_____

_____

_____

Description of your served market:

_____

_____

_____

Description of Competitor 1's served market:

_____

_____

_____

Description of Competitor 2's served market:

_____

_____

_____

PLANNING PAGE 4.2

MARKET SEGMENTATION—PRODUCT B

Definition of total market:

_____

_____

Definition of segments you compete in:

_____

_____

_____

_____

Description of your served market:

_____

_____

_____

Description of Competitor 1's served market:

_____

_____

_____

Description of Competitor 2's served market:

_____

_____

_____

_____

PLANNING PAGE 4.3

MARKET SEGMENTATION—PRODUCT C

Definition of total market:

_____

_____

Definition of segments you compete in:

_____

_____

_____

_____

Description of your served market:

_____

_____

_____

_____

Description of Competitor 1's served market:

_____

_____

_____

Description of Competitor 2's served market:

_____

_____

_____

_____

PLANNING PAGE 4.4

MARKET SEGMENTATION—PRODUCT D

Definition of total market:

_____

_____

Definition of segments you compete in:

_____

_____

_____

_____

Description of your served market:

_____

_____

_____

Description of Competitor 1's served market:

_____

_____

_____

Description of Competitor 2's served market:

_____

_____

_____

_____

LIFE'S LITTLE LESSONS

Teamwork

For me, the greatest thrills in the agency business have been to be part of a team that literally turned a client's business around—particularly when nothing else changes. Product, market, sales force, budgets—all stay the same, but sales soar and everyone acknowledges that fresh, focused creative advertising alone made the dramatic difference.

Situations in which all other marketing elements do remain constant are rare. So, although advertising successes are not infrequent, pure documentable advertising triumphs don't happen every day.

A very memorable one occurred in the early 60s when Doyle Dane Bernbach was appointed by the Sicks Brewing Company, Seattle, to handle Rainier Beer. The battle in those days was fought principally by strong regional brands, and the Rainier competitors were primarily Olympia from Tumwater, Washington; Blitz Weinhard from Portland; and much less from the nationals such as Schlitz, Budweiser, Pabst, and Miller's, which were there but not strongly.

In planning strategy and campaigns for Rainier, we, in Los Angeles who had gained the account, conferred with our colleagues in New York who were having great success with Utica Club Beer in upstate New York. I remember vividly a debate with Ned Doyle over how we should construct our first-year budget recommendation for Rainier.

Ned, one of the three unique founders of Doyle Dane Bernbach and a superb strategist and marketer, strongly urged that we base our plan on Rainier's usual advertising-to-sales ratios and that we do so on projected sales increases we could almost guarantee with DDB's unique and forceful creative work.

I resisted this approach feeling sure that the recommendation of a budget increase would be regarded suspiciously and as a greedy, money-hungry tactic by a bunch of sharpies from Los Angeles and New York.

After a fair amount of arguing, we went in with a budget equal to that of the year prior to our appointment—although Rainier's sales were down 5% in that prior year. Over a little resistance, the budget was approved.

Our creative team consisted of two young DDB stars from New York—Ron Rosenfeld and Len Sirowitz, now heads of Rosenfeld, Sirowitz, Humphrey & Strauss, New York, and still, I'm sure, creating outstanding campaigns. For Rainier, they developed a campaign centered on a big, tough, completely bald Prussian Brewmaster who, though kind to dogs and children, was a mean, nasty tyrant about every aspect of his beer or the brewing of it. (Actually, the real Rainier brewmaster had a comparable attitude and character and undoubtedly inspired the theme).

They cast the Rainier Brewmaster right off the Broadway stage, shaved his head for every shoot, and created a memorable, believable, impressive character who sold Rainier *by the vatful!*

The campaign took off from the start. Sales shot up and, although the campaign didn't start until late spring, the gain for the year was 7% over the year before—a *net* gain over the trend of 12%. Thereafter, Rainier continued to show annual gains, and we continued to budget on the increases.

This history, to be complete, has to continue to a fairly sad ending—at least for DDB. Taste trends in beer were moving toward the "light" end of the spectrum, and there was considerable worry about whether the tough, stubborn Rainier Brewmaster could effectively promote lightness. Although we contended that he could be firm about light beer, too, and we tried that and other variations, we ultimately had to bid Rainier and the Brewmaster farewell.

Happily, both Rainier and DDB Needham are still doing fine in the beer business.

Monty McKinney
Chairman, DDB/Needham West
November 30, 1987

CHAPTER 5

What to Say to Your Customers—Developing a Creative Strategy

Differentiating Your Product or Service

The search for the best possible sales message starts with the idea of product or service differentiation. It means asking the question, ''In what meaningful way to customers is my product or service different from my competitors?'' Notice that this idea is different from market segmentation discussed in the last chapter. Market segmentation dealt with how customers were different; differentiation deals with how products and services are different from one another.

Also notice the words ''*meaningful to customers.*'' There is simply no point in building a sales message around some feature that has no meaning to customers regardless of how important that feature may be to you. This is a fact that is repeatedly ignored by businesses. Two examples: Since the 1950s, America's taste for liquor has been changing. The shift has been away from brown products (bourbons, blends, and Scotches) to light products (vodka, rum, and gin). Virtually the entire liquor industry (Seagram, Schenley, Barton, National Distillers, and Brown-Forman) decided that customers wanted a light-colored whiskey. Every one of those companies introduced a new, light-colored whiskey in 1971 or 1972.

Do you remember FROST 8/80? It was the first and most flamboyant of the white whiskies, costing Brown-Forman over $6 million before they withdrew the product. Even if you do not remember FROST 8/80 or any of the other dozen white whiskey products that also failed at the same time, you should remember the point of the story. Customers did not care about the color of the products; they cared about the *taste* and white whiskey still tasted like whiskey.

The other example represents the other side of the coin. During the late 1970s and early 1980s, Coca-Cola steadily lost market share to Pepsi-

Cola, which is sweeter and more appealing to younger people. By 1982, top management at Coca-Cola decided to respond by making Coca-Cola sweeter. After three years of product development and testing, management thought they had removed the differential between Coke and Pepsi, and brought New Coke to market with much fanfare and a big budget.

As you probably know, New Coke was a disaster. Every day for over three months, Coke received more than 1,500 telephone complaints and the complaining mail was measured in tons. It was obvious to Coca-Cola that its customers did care about taste. Coca-Cola lost its differentiation when it changed its formula.

CONTAC SOGO

For a successful example of product differentiation, we can look across the Pacific to Japan and study the experience of CONTAC 600, SmithKline Beecham Consumer Brand's time released cold medicine (the same formula CONTAC you buy from your local pharmacist). CONTAC was launched nationally in Japan in 1967 and its differentiation made it an extremely successful business for many years: "You only have to take one in the morning and one in the evening to relieve three specific symptoms: nasal congestion, sneezing, and runny nose." In 1969, another product was introduced. CONTAC Seki, a product specifically formulated to suppress coughing. For the next 14 years, the two products' sales grew at a compounded rate of 17.5 percent.

By the end of the 1970s, however, Japanese competitors matched CONTAC's time release system and developed broadly effective cold remedies (CONTAC 600 is effective against sneezing, nasal congestion, and runny nose, but does not relieve pain) and the new competitors were beginning to make serious inroads into CONTAC's business. Top management responded by spending more money on advertising and providing very wide margins to pharmacists (in Japan, about 40 percent of the medicine bought over-the-counter (OTC) is recommended by the pharmacist), but nothing worked. Between 1982 and 1985, CONTAC lost 25 percent of its market share. By 1985, Keisuke Morimoto, long-time vice president of marketing, SmithKline Beecham Consumer Brands, knew something had to be done immediately, so he authorized a major consumer study. The major findings were startling:

Think CONTAC is:	CONTAC purchasers (%)
For a usual cold	41
For early symptoms of colds	29
For a head cold	21
All other answers	14
	Multiple answers

The study showed that the biggest reason customers purchased CONTAC was for applications for which CONTAC was not designed to work. Not only had CONTAC lost its differentiation, it had also lost a clearly defined position in the minds of its customers.

Up to this point, top management resisted the idea of introducing a broad-acting cold medicine for fear of reducing the sales of CONTAC 600, but with these data in hand, Morimoto convinced top management that there was a greater risk in doing nothing. Accordingly, a crash project began to develop a new multi-symptom cold remedy. As the work progressed, it was decided to include a water soluble vitamin C in the formula because research showed that 70 percent of all Japanese think vitamin C is effective for colds. None of the competitors had vitamin C in their products.

The marketing and advertising task was to walk the narrow path between trading too heavily on CONTAC's reputation while still benefitting from CONTAC's excellent reputation. Much of this task was accomplished in packaging, pricing, and advertising. The new product was named CONTAC Sogokamboyaku (multi-symptom cold medicine in English), or Sogo for short, to assist consumers in differentiating it from CONTAC 600.

Takafumi Hotta, account supervisor, Dentsu, Inc. (Japan's largest advertising agency and CONTAC's first and only advertising agency), had the task of creating television advertising that would clearly differentiate CONTAC Sogo from CONTAC 600. After considering many alternatives, Dentsu decided that a spokesperson was needed to give the CONTAC Sogo commercials continuity. He hired popular movie star, Kaoru Inoue, to fill that role. The photoscript in Exhibit 5.1 is the lead commercial and is called ''Panic.'' In the photoscript, a crowd is demanding CONTAC Sogo, but the pharmacist tells them he is sold out. At the last instant, the viewer sees that the pharmacist has secretly saved one package of CONTAC Sogo to treat his own cold.

The research disclosed that the market for cold remedies was segmented by the form of the medicine, and that many customers would only buy medicine in their preferred form. The preferences were:

Tablets	35%
Capsules	25
Granules	20
Liquid	15
All others	5

Based on these data, it was decided to introduce CONTAC Sogo in capsule form, and then follow with tablets and granules (with herbs because of the Japanese fondness for herbal remedies) over the next three years.

During the introduction of CONTAC Sogo, heavy advertising supported CONTAC 600 to help reduce confusion between the two products. The careful efforts paid off in a big way. Sales were double the forecast, market share had reached a very significant level at the end of the first year, and Japanese pharmacists voted CONTAC Sogo as the best new product of the year.

But there is more. The consumer research discovered that a sizeable group of customers were buying CONTAC 600 in the spring for help with allergies. To address these customers directly, SmithKline Beecham Consumer Products introduced CONTAC Bien for allergies—another successful new product was launched.

Exhibit 5.2 shows the cover of a 1991 SmithKline Beecham Japanese trade brochure that illustrates the various CONTAC products the company sells. As a result of the careful differentiating that has taken place over the past five years, the product line is now:

EXHIBIT 5.1

Contac Sogokamboyaku

PANIC version 15 sec.

Performer (Kaoru Inoue)
'' Contac Sogokamboyaku is
sold-out ! There is none left ! ''

People :
'' It should have anti-pyretic
action ! ''

'' It must also contain Vitamin C ! ''

Narration :
'' Contac Sogokamboyaku ,
with containing vitamin C ,
now on sale ''

Caution

EXHIBIT 5.2

Number in Exhibit 5.2	Product	Use
1	CONTAC 600	Runny nose and sneezing
2	CONTAC Seki	Coughing
3	CONTAC Sogo Capsules	Multi-cold symptoms
4	CONTAC Sogo Capulets	Multi-cold symptoms
5	CONTAC Sogo Granules	Multi-cold symptoms
6	CONTAC Bien	Allergies

Each product is clearly differentiated from each other and from the competition; CONTAC remains one of the few non-Japanese brands that is successfully marketed in Japan.

Now we need to turn product differentiation into successful advertising, and that requires a creative strategy.

Advertising Is Different from Personal Selling

There is a very important difference in what works when you are communicating to your customers through advertising compared with direct sales. When your salesperson makes a presentation to a customer, or a prospective customer, the salesperson has the undivided attention of the customer. This is true whether it takes place in a department store concerning a pair of shoes, or in the Pentagon about a jet-fighter plane. Both parties know they are there to do business. They are there because they both want to be there.

When you communicate through advertising, this scenario almost never exists. You seldom get undivided attention for your advertising message. The fact that your advertising message and your customer come in contact at all almost is accidental (almost, but not quite). As a result, the first thing that your advertising message must do is to get the attention of your intended audience. If it doesn't do that, then it doesn't do anything except waste your money.

The second important difference between a sales call and delivering an advertising message is that the salesperson gets instant feedback from the customer each time a sales point is delivered. If the feedback is positive, the salesperson expands and strengthens that particular sales point. If the feedback is negative, the salesperson abandons that particular point and goes on to another sales argument.

But when you deliver an advertising message, the feedback takes months to reach you, if it ever does. As a result, an advertiser is limited in its ability to adjust sales messages. Therefore, it is critical that you select the *best possible sales message to use in your advertising.* You may not get a second chance.

A Creative Strategy

The tool that helps you select the best possible sales message to use in your advertising is called a *creative strategy.* It links your advertising plans to your marketing plans and ensures that your advertising messages reinforce and support your marketing objectives. It is amazing how often advertising execution gets unhinged from the best laid marketing plans.

CREATIVE STRATEGY IN A NUTSHELL

I. What Is Creative Strategy?

   A. Extension in creative area of marketing strategy . . . a part of total marketing plan.

   B. Long-term document—states net impression of brand we want consumers to have. States *what* we want to say to consumers.

II. What's in It?

   A. Basic benefit or promise we offer to the consumer.

   B. Reason why this benefit is possible.

   C. Personality or character we are trying to build for the brand.

   D. How the product is to be used.

III. Factors Controlling

   A. Product and what it will do.

   B. Competitive situation in the market.

   C. Product and market research results.

   D. Previous experience on this or other brands.

IV. How It Is Used

   A. Guide in the development of advertising.

   B. Benchmark for evaluating advertising.

V. Value

The creative strategy assures that our advertising is a direct outgrowth of the basic marketing strategies of the brand. In addition, as a long-term document, it provides continuity of impression in a brand's advertising that, over a period of time, will help that brand stand for something specific in the minds of consumers. It helps a brand achieve distinction and stature in a competitive market.

VI. Who Develops It?

Since the creative strategy is a logical extension of the marketing objective and strategy of the brand, the marketing group and the agency account team are responsible for the initiation and the development of a new or revised creative strategy.

With that overview in mind, a creative strategy was described in detail as follows:

CREATIVE STRATEGY

The creative strategy statement is an extension and elaboration of a brand's marketing strategy principles into the brand's advertising or creative area. It picks up from a creative standpoint where the marketing strategy leaves off, indicating agreed-upon basic and relatively long-term selling approaches to the consumer. Its basic function is to define clearly:

1. The total net impression that advertising is expected to leave with a specific target group.

2. Other *basic* decisions that will shape and direct the content and form of the advertising copy.

Thus the creative strategy describes how a product is to be distinguished from competitive products, how the product is to be positioned in the minds of the target group, or how it will be given a distinct identity.

It is used as a guide in the development of advertising and as a benchmark of evaluating advertising.

Creative strategy should be thought of as long-term strategy because one of the purposes of this statement is to give continuity to the advertising program over a period of time. Basic creative strategy is ordinarily changed only when there is a fundamental change in the character of the market or product, a major competitive threat, or a demonstrated failure of the existing strategy to achieve specific objectives.

Since the creative strategy is a logical extension of the marketing objective and strategy of the brand, the marketing group and the agency account team are responsible for the initiation and development of a new or revised creative strategy.

WHAT THE CREATIVE STRATEGY INCLUDES

Every creative strategy should include the specific selling idea(s) or the basic concept(s) that the product's advertising is designed to establish with the consumer and, as a result, motivate her to purchase the brand in preference to competition.

The following kinds of ideas will ordinarily appear in a creative strategy (not all of them need appear in any one statement).

1. A concise statement of the principal benefit offered by the product. This idea represents the basic reason consumers are expected to purchase the product in preference to a competitive product. It is important to note that this part of the statement is not an analysis of all possible product benefits, but represents a decision as to which of these benefits are to be emphasized in advertising.

2. A statement of the principal characteristic(s) of the product that makes it possible to claim this benefit—that is, the reason why this benefit exists and has meaning to the target group. (Examples: an ingredient, a process, a quality standard.) Stated another way, these ideas identify points of product distinctiveness or superiority that bear directly on the consumer benefit claimed.

3. A statement of the character or personality that is to be built for the product and that will be reflected in the mood, tone, and overall atmosphere of the advertising (long term). Elements of such a product character might include ideas like feminine, progressive, vital, playful, conservative, wholesome, and luxurious.

4. A statement of what the product is and what the product is used for (if the answers to these questions are not obvious). Examples: Is it a meal or a snack? A food dish or an ingredient? A beverage or a multiple-use product? A basic food or a problem-solving dietetic? In short, answers to the question "Where is this product supposed to fit into the consumer's experience?"

Note: This particular creative strategy document was developed by a company that makes and sells food products to women. You can adapt this document to fit your own situation, however, without any difficulty.

A Creative Strategy Statement

Here are some important points you should not overlook.

The primary purpose of preparing a creative strategy statement for each of your products or services is to clearly *link* the marketing plans you developed in Chapters 2 and 3 with the advertising plans you start to develop now. It is certain that your advertising dollars will end up wasted if your advertising plans lose sight of your marketing objectives.

The creative strategy statement is a long-term strategy document. Another way to waste your advertising dollars is to continually change what you say to your customers about your products or services. Remember how advertising is different from a personal sales call? The instant you make it difficult or confusing for your customers to understand and follow your advertising messages, they will tune you out. A creative strategy document keeps you focused on what you are trying to accomplish over a long period of time. It also keeps continuity in your advertising even though new marketing managers and new account executives may come and go.

It should be changed only when one of two things happen. One, a very fundamental change in the demand for your products or services occurs. (That is why Chapter 2 concentrated on getting a thorough understanding of your markets.) You will be in a better position to distinguish real shifts in demand from seasonal or cyclical ups and downs. The second reason to shift strategy is when the one you have selected is no longer working. No manager has ever batted 1,000 percent. If you have given your strategy a good try and it is not working, don't fret about it. Cut your losses and try a new strategy.

A creative strategy statement forces you to think seriously about the position you want your products or services to occupy in your customers' minds. Remember the exercises about your served market? Well, the creative strategy is a formal expression of what you desire to communicate about your products to your served market. It helps to ensure that your fundamental position in the market is the one communicated in your advertising.

A creative strategy statement is an important communication tool between you and your advertising agency people. It sets out clearly to your account people (they may have had a hand in developing it) what your advertising objectives are. In turn, it helps the account service people explain those objectives to the creative and media people at the agency. And, after everyone else has left, it gives your creative group at the agency a guideline for evaluating the rough ideas they invent. It protects you from being a "yard goods" buyer of advertising.

And *very* importantly, it gives you a way to talk to your advertising agency people about the creative ideas and programs they propose. It gives you a clear way to say, "Look, here is what we all agreed we were trying to say. I don't think this says that," or, "I don't see how this says _____. Maybe you can show me what I'm missing." The *worst* thing you can say to your advertising agency's people is, "I don't like it. I just don't like it, that's all." That is instantly demoralizing. "That was our best stuff! What the heck do they want anyway?" When a conversation like that one starts up on the way back to the agency after a presentation, you are in big trouble because you will no longer be getting the best minds in the agency thinking about how to solve your advertising problems.

Every creative strategy statement contains a principal benefit. This is your statement of how you differ from your competitors. It is not a list of all the ways you are different; it is a decision about which of those differences is most important to your customers.

A "reason why" is important in your creative strategy because it makes your claimed benefit legitimate and believable. Sometimes, there is no identifiable "reason why" and there is nothing you can do except make a "naked" claim. Since this is a much weaker position, you should be thinking about how you can build a "reason why."

The statement of character or personality usually turns out to be a list of adjectives that provide a feeling for how the advertising should look and feel. This is helpful as you move from one medium to another, and from year to year.

The optional part of the creative strategy statement is number 4, what the product or service is, or how it is used. This takes some careful thought and marketing research. For existing products, the question is whether you want to say just when the product should be used, or whether you want the customers to use it any time they can think of a use. Not an automatic decision. The most difficulty usually comes with new products and services—those that don't have an existing track record or position in the customer's experience.

Knudsen, Inc. was a large Los Angeles-based food products company that once was in the *Fortune* 500. Knudsen introduced a single-serving refrigerated combination of cream cheese, flavoring, and topping called "Knudsen's Cheesecake Dessert." But their advertising never bothered to tell the customer how to use the product. The original introduction was a complete disaster. At one point, sales were so bad that the company was taking back more out-of-date products than it was shipping new stock. They ran a $1 coupon (for a product that retailed for 30¢, but that is another story) in the *Los Angeles Times* (with a million plus circulation), and got just five coupons redeemed.

Six months after the product was introduced (in western U.S.), Knudsen management retained a marketing consultant in an attempt to breathe life into the product. After some modest research with homemakers, the consultant pointed out that the product could occupy any of these positions:

- mid-morning pick-up for a busy homemaker

- dessert to pack into blue-collar husband's lunch pail

- special dessert to pack into children's lunch sacks

- high-calorie single-item lunch for Mom

- treat for kids when they come home from school

- mid-afternoon reward for Mom for surviving the day so far

- individual dessert for various members of the family on those nights when everyone eats on a different schedule

The same research told management that its prospective customers said this, "If the company doesn't know what it is for, why should I bother?" And, of course they didn't.

AN EXAMPLE

The creative strategy statement for the natural ice cream described in Chapter 1 looked like this:

Principal benefit: Tastes good.

Reason why: Made with only natural ingredients. No artificial flavors. No artificial preservatives. No artificial colors.

Personality: Honest, old-fashioned, earth tones, soft, rich feeling, sweet, full-flavored, soft, homey, friendly.

When to use: Not needed.

AN EXERCISE

Make a rough recording form for yourself that looks like this:

Advertiser	Principal benefit	Reason why
_____	_____	_____
_____	_____	_____
_____	_____	_____
_____	_____	_____

Make spaces for 20 to 25 advertisements. Make one for TV and one for magazines. Then spend an evening watching your favorite TV programs. When a commercial comes on, fill out your form. Who was the advertiser? What was the single most important benefit about the product or service that the advertiser wanted you to know? Why was that benefit possible? Then take your favorite magazine and do the same exercise.

You will be amazed at the number of advertisers who have no discernable benefit to convince anyone to buy their products or services. It is advertising without a creative strategy. It is bad advertising.

BURGER KING AND HERB

If the above exercise doesn't convince you that an enormous amount of money is being wasted on advertising that has no creative strategy, then perhaps the case of "Herb" will convince you. You probably saw at least some of Burger King's 1986 advertising campaign, primarily on television. The basic premise early in the campaign was that in all of the United States, there was just one person who had not eaten at Burger King, a nerdy guy named Herb. Later in the campaign, the "real" Herb was introduced: a middle-aged, balding man with glasses who wore white socks with his black suit and shoes. Yes, a real nerd! After Herb was introduced on camera, a contest was started. If anyone spotted Herb in a Burger King restaurant, they would win prizes. The results of the campaign were spectacular—sales went *down!* Everything went down: awareness, attitudes, images, and favorable feelings.

What happened? One hundred undergraduates in an advertising course at a large university supplied the answer with 100 percent accuracy. It goes like this: Herb is a nerd. Herb now eats at Burger King. Nerds eat at Burger King. I am not a nerd. I do not eat at Burger King.

How could this have happened to one of America's largest advertisers and the second largest fast-food chain in the country? Well, there are two stories in the trade. In one story, the advertising agency tried to make a big impression on the new president of Burger King and whipped up this new creative campaign, "Herb," just to show their cleverness. The second story is that it was the idea of one of Burger King's strong regional operating vice presidents who forced the agency to present the idea to the new president, who had also held an operating post prior to becoming president. This version has it that the new president had to approve the campaign to support his old ally, the regional vice president.

It doesn't make the slightest bit of difference how "Herb" got approved. The fact of the matter is that "Herb" *never* would have been approved if Burger King had a creative strategy and used it.

What to Do Next?

Planning Pages 5.1 through 5.4 are designed to help you develop creative strategy statements for four of your products or services. If you have more than four, make additional copies.

PLANNING PAGE 5.1

CREATIVE STRATEGY—PRODUCT A

Principal benefit: _____

_____

_____

_____

_____

Reason why: _____

_____

_____

_____

_____

Personality/Character: _____

_____

_____

_____

_____

What it is/How to use it: _____

_____

_____

_____

_____

PLANNING PAGE 5.2

CREATIVE STRATEGY—PRODUCT B

Principal benefit: _____

_____

_____

_____

_____

Reason why: _____

_____

_____

_____

_____

Personality/Character: _____

_____

_____

_____

_____

What it is/How to use it: _____

_____

_____

_____

_____

PLANNING PAGE 5.3

CREATIVE STRATEGY—PRODUCT C

Principal benefit: _____

_____

_____

_____

_____

Reason why: _____

_____

_____

_____

_____

Personality/Character: _____

_____

_____

_____

_____

What it is/How to use it: _____

_____

_____

_____

_____

PLANNING PAGE 5.4

CREATIVE STRATEGY—PRODUCT D

Principal benefit: _____

_____

_____

_____

_____

Reason why: _____

_____

_____

_____

_____

Personality/Character: _____

_____

_____

_____

_____

What it is/How to use it: _____

_____

_____

_____

_____

How to Get the Most out of Your Advertising Agency

This is a good place to discuss the general question of how to get the best work out of your advertising agency. The rules are few and they are simple. Following them is somewhat more difficult, however.

Rule 1. Make sure they are paid fairly. All that an advertising agency has to sell is the time of the people who work there. All that you buy from them is their best ideas. If you have a large account, you may be able to bargain down the agency's compensation. If you do, you'll end up buying discounted time and second-rate ideas.

Rule 2. Make sure that you treat all of the advertising agency people as equal members of your marketing and sales team. There is something about the client/agency relationship that causes some advertisers to act as if it were a master/slave relationship and agency people are relegated to "go-fer" status. This is a sure way to get second-rate ideas for your advertising.

Rule 3. Communicate clearly, openly, and honestly with your advertising agency. If you have a creative strategy for each of your products or services, you have a good start. If you are going to have a productive partnership with your agency, they will need to know you, warts and all. Make sure they know what is going on and they know it promptly. Don't keep secrets from them; secrecy is one of the silliest ideas in the business world. There are no secrets for long.

Rule 4. If you have managed to accomplish the first three rules, then and only then, the final rule is to trust their recommendations. You picked the best advertising agency around and you picked it because they knew their business. Now, when they give you their best work, trust them; don't second guess them.

Monty McKinney has some specific ideas about managing the creative part of the advertising process. In "Life's Little Lessons" called Mass Transit, he makes a point about advertisers trusting their agencies, and in "Today's Little Lesson Is for Top Managers" he calls attention to the need to have trust in your advertising agency.

LIFE'S LITTLE LESSONS

Mass Transit

Back in the early '60s, Doyle Dane Bernbach dramatically increased its creative preeminence with an uninterrupted series of brilliant billboards for Volkswagen. Many are still remembered as true classics in the medium. Simple and strong conceptually and visually, they each slammed home a selling point for VW and helped accelerate VW's historic marketing triumph.

Many of you (however young you may have been at the time) will remember these few examples from that era:

Nobody's perfect—with its red VW tilting on a flat tire toward its owner crouched beside it, surprised.

$1625 each—showing only a plain blue VW beetle but putting full focus on a price so low that buying more than one at a time made sense.

Two can live as cheaply as one—with two VW's in a single garage.

Month after month, outdoor boards like these went up in Los Angeles and elsewhere, and the natives strove to be the first to exclaim over each new one.

My personal favorite—only partly because of its history—was a design which never was posted in this market.

Here's what happened.

The headline was *Mass Transit,* and the illustration was a VW Bus surrounded by a group of 9 nuns in their traditional habits, obviously about to board and take off for a convent or church—or maybe a cathedral.

In appearance, the nuns were an appealing assortment of lovely, dedicated women—tall, short—thin, plump—young, old—they were radiant, beautiful, and beatific. The two-word headline with its three-way pun and four-star charm was the perfect zinger for a brilliant poster.

But the client refused to approve it!

Everyone at DDB was stunned. We had submitted the design to the Catholic Diocese in Los Angeles as a normal precaution, and they found it wholly acceptable. True, when we asked if they could provide 9 nuns for the photograph, they had declined, saying that they would prefer not to do so, but they did approve the ad.

We reviewed all that with the client, but he stubbornly insisted that many good Catholics would be offended, and he simply would not approve the ad.

It should be recorded here that the top VW executive in Los Angeles at that time was a great guy and an excellent businessman. Unfortunately, he was a Scotch Presbyterian—not a Catholic. He was predicting the reactions of a group he neither belonged to nor understood. And he was adamant. He would not O.K. that ad.

He did, however, agree to let us submit the ad to the Catholic Diocese in New York, then headed by the reknowned Cardinal Spellman (not that the Cardinal actually evaluated it, but I'm an eager name dropper).

In New York the official response was as positive as it had been in Los Angeles. No one saw anything questionable or worrisome in the ad, and full permission to use the ad was given.

Further, when the New York committee was asked if they would recruit 9 nuns, they responded with this question: *"Can we keep the bus?"*

We said yes.

So they helped select the sisters, and we gave them the bus.

Although originally created for our client, the Southern California VW Distributor, the poster was offered to and run by distributors elsewhere and ran in many markets. Later, I believe, it was run as a national magazine ad and in newspapers in other markets.

As far as I know, the ad never drew a negative comment anywhere, and it took a well-deserved place in VW's gallery of truly great outdoor posters.

So really, everyone was right: the creative stars, Si Lam and Ed Bigelow; the church authorities in Los Angeles and New York; and even the overly cautious head of VW here. (The never-seen-here VW poster got no resentment, cost no sales, and created no bad PR.)

And the big winners, of course, were VW and the New York Diocese. VW got sales, and the Church got the bus.

Monty McKinney
Chairman, DDB Needham West
January 30, 1987

LIFE'S LITTLE LESSONS

Today's Little Leason Is for Top Management Only.

It covers a kind of stupid, thoughtless mistake from which many of us suffered as AE's or even as supervisors. We then proceeded to forget it—only to make the same kind of mistake ourselves as agency executives and principals.

HEAR MY STORY.

Stopette, an underarm deodorant packaged in a plastic squeeze-spray bottle (predecessor of roll-ons and aerosols), was the largest client at Earle Ludgin & Company, Chicago, where I started in advertising. The brand led the category in dollar volume, even though 50 percent of deodorant sales were still in cream form in jars.

We urged the company to create a cream form so we could offer both types (each with the same established Stopette protection) and thereby double Stopette's business.

Finally, the company did so, and we constructed a plan to introduce the new product on network TV via our very popular program, "What's My Line?"

Having two of the three commercials per program, we confidently recommended allocating all of our spots to the new product for a 4-week introductory period to pound the news into the ears, eyes, and minds of all viewers.

In a major meeting, we presented the whole introductory program including TV, print, and promotion.

Attending the meeting was a major agency executive recently named agency president and not previously involved with the account.

Toward the end of the meeting, he rose and expressed his concern that all commercials for the period were on this new product, forsaking the "foundation of the business during the peak summer season."

From the podium, I tried to cover with this comment, "Thank you for bringing that up. I had forgotten to say that we, too, were worried about that but concluded that the greater risk lay in so diffusing the impact as to weaken the announcement of the new form of Stopette. We feared that viewers, paying only partial attention, would only half register the first announcement. Then, when the second came along and it was for the old type, they would react somewhat in this way, "Well, I thought I heard something different, but I guess not.""

After the meeting, the new president forced a review of our position and a revision of our recommendation—one each on new cream Stopette, the other on the original spray type.

At the end of the second show, research demonstrated that we were not registering the advent of a new item adequately, and we went back to the original plan. Late. Wasteful. Lamentable.

Looking back, I see these lessons, and I hope I learned them:

1. Trust the troops.

2. If you can't trust them, change them.

3. Raise your basic questions before the big meeting—or outside the meeting.

4. If you are a key executive, review points 1, 2 and 3 regularly.

July 15, 1986

CHAPTER 6

Advertising for Retail Stores

There is a great difference between planning and managing the advertising for products or services, and doing the same job for one or more retail stores. The manufacturer takes his products to his customers who can be just about anywhere; if they move, he can even follow them. A retail store, on the other hand, is tied to a piece of geography. While the manufacturer advertises to a "market," the retailer advertises to a "trading area."

A *trading area* is the geographic area immediately surrounding the retail store location. Your trading area, by definition, accounts for 60 to 70 percent of your business. It is the geographic area in which, usually, you hold an advantage over your competitors. It is the source of the bulk of your business.

If the idea of trading areas is new to you, try this exercise. Suppose you have a retail store in downtown St. Louis. Do you believe that a customer in Chicago, 284 miles away, is likely to shop at your store? No, not likely. Well, how about a customer who lives in Springfield, Illinois? That is only about 90 miles away. No, still not likely. Then, how about somebody who lives in East St. Louis? That is just across the river. Now, the answer is maybe, and it depends.

The point is that there is some distance from your store at which point it becomes more convenient not to shop at your store. If you find that point in all directions from your store location, you have outlined your trading area. Note that not all of your customers are going to come from inside of your trading area. In the course of a year, you are likely to get a customer from Nome, Alaska. It turns out she was visiting her sister-in-law who lives just two blocks from your store when she discovered she needed a gadget you sell. You are also going to get a customer from Washington, D.C. His Winnebago motorhome broke down in the same block as your store is located. He came in to buy a gizmo from you to help fix his motorhome so he and his family can get on with their vacation to Yellowstone Park.

The woman from Nome and the man from Washington had never been in St. Louis before and they will never visit again, but for one moment they were your customers. They never were your customers before and they never will be again. There is nothing you can do about that; therefore, you must turn your attention to the place where you can do something to affect customer behavior, and that is your trading area.

Defining Your Trading Area

There are a number of ways to go about collecting the data to define your trading area. If you have a business that produces receipts with customers' names and addresses, that is a fine place to start. Go to a table of random numbers (you can get one at the library, if you don't have one) and pick a sample of 20 to 25 day numbers (1 to 365). Look up those days on a calendar and discard any that are for days when you weren't open for business. Now go to your records for those days that you randomly selected and pull all of the receipts you wrote on those days. Plot the addresses by sticking colored dots on a detailed map of your area. Somewhere around 200 to 300 addresses is a good place to take a first look (assuming they come from all of the sampled days equally).

Try to draw a line around two-thirds of the customer addresses closest to your store. It is as much art as anything. Look for natural or almost constructed boundaries. Freeways, and major highways, and rivers cut off trading areas. The trading area in Exhibit 6.1 is for a jewelry store in Huntington Park, California and was prepared by sampling invoices as described above. Note how a freeway on the right-hand side restricts customer movement. At the top of the exhibit, the adjacent town is 100 percent industrial and nobody lives there, thus no customers.

If you don't have customer records, you will have to do a survey among your customers. Wienerschnitzel, Inc., is a Newport Beach, California headquartered fast food company with franchisee-owned stores in the western United States. Wienerschnitzel management understands how important it is to advertise and merchandise within each store's trading area. Exhibit 6.2 shows the detailed set of instructions that Wienerschnitzel has prepared to help each of its franchise store owners identify their trading areas. You can easily adapt these instructions to fit your situation.

Estimating the Sales Potential in Your Trading Area

You will need to estimate the total potential sales in your trading area so you can compare your sales and determine your market share. The best way to do this is to begin by plotting your customer data on a map that has U.S. census tracts identified on it. Next you should obtain from the U.S. Government Printing Office copies of the most recent U.S. Census of Population reports for your city. You can either write to the Superintendent of Documents, U.S. Government Printing Office, Washington, D.C. 20402, or buy it directly from the closest GPO book store.

A census tract is a small piece of geography with specific boundaries. Originally, the intention was to have each tract represent about 400 households, but over time, that goal became too difficult. In any case, each of the census reports will contain a map showing the boundaries of the census

EXHIBIT 6.1

TRADING AREA

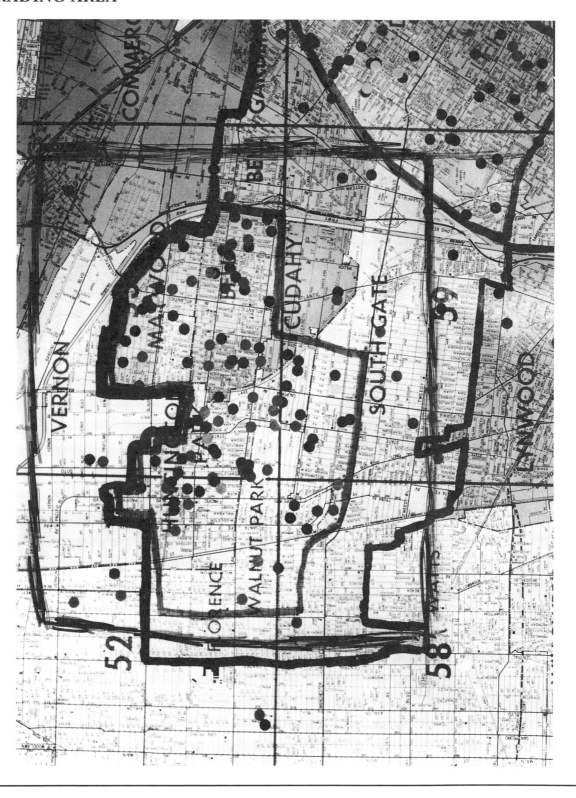

EXHIBIT 6.2

TRADING AREA SURVEY INSTRUCTIONS

INTRODUCTION TO THE TRADING AREA SURVEY

In order to fulfill the purpose of the Trading Area Survey, you must first know the mechanics required to successfully carry it out. A very complete step-by-step explanation follows. To say it's "a little something to do in your spare time" would be an understatement! And it will involve money as well. But the amount of information you will receive is well worth the effort. Used properly, it can make you a specialist in your own trading area.

I. HOW YOU GO ABOUT IT

You've decided to do a Trading Area Survey? Good! Plan on spending about two weeks in gathering information, preparing materials and interviewers, and one week actually doing the survey.

A. GATHERING BACKGROUND INFORMATION
(Sales volume by day, by hour)

TWO WEEKS PRIOR TO INTERVIEWING:

1. Choose four days of the week for the survey.

For example:

We recommend interviewing on Saturday and Sunday and two weekdays which you judge to be most typical of your Monday–Friday business.

2. Divide these four days into meal "periods."

For example:

Lunch	11–2
Afternoons	2–5
Dinner	5–8
Evening	8–11

ONE WEEK PRIOR TO INTERVIEWING:

3. Review your sales volume by hour for each day of the week. Use your hourly reading sheets to determine hourly volume. The purpose of this review is to help you get the most representative profile of your business.

4. Now calculate the number of interviews to be conducted for each meal period in each day. It is recommended that a total of at least 600 interviews be conducted during the four days. Therefore, you will need to complete 150 interviews a day. Lower sales volume restaurants may require an extra day for interviewing in order to meet the minimum number of interviews required.

Taking hourly sales volumes, you can now compute how the interviews are to be divided by periods of the day.

EXHIBIT 6.2 (continued)

For example:

Suppose your hourly sales volumes for one day of the previous week (Thursday) looked like this:

11–2	$	300	=	30%
2–5		200	=	20
5–8		400	=	40
8–11		100	=	10
	$1,000		=	100%

Total Daily Volume:

Let us say that you want to complete a total of 800 interviews (200 per day), then you would allocate the total of 200 interviews as follows:

11–2	.30 × 200	=	60
2–5	.20 × 200	=	40
5–8	.40 × 200	=	80
8–11	.10 × 200	=	20
	Total Interviews:		200

B. MATERIALS YOU WILL NEED
(Map, heavy cardboard, gummed dots, questionnaire, clipboard)

1. Obtain a detailed street map of your area (ideally your store should be located in the center). This map can usually be obtained from a gas station, Chamber of Commerce office, stationery or office supply store.

If the map is too difficult to read, have the map "blown up" (enlarged) in order to facilitate customers locating the areas from which they've come. The map should include an area of at least a $3^1/_2$- to 4-mile radius from the store or a minimum 24-inch by 24-inch map size depending on specific geographic boundaries.

(Street names should be large enough to read and any existing or potential traffic generators—shopping centers, amusement areas, highways, schools, etc., should be on the map.)

2. Have the map mounted on heavy cardboard or artist's pressboard. Four acetate or plastic overlays representing the first day, the next the second day, and so on, should be attached to the top of the mounted map. The top overlay will be used for the first day of interviews and folded over to give you a new acetate for the second day.

To mark where your customer is coming from, you will also need at least 800 small, round adhesive stickers—200 each of four different colors—each color representing a meal period and each dot approximately $^1/_8$ inch in size. (Stickers can also be purchased at a stationery or office supply store.) The colored dots will enable you to quickly see just where your customers are coming from by meal period.

3. A questionnaire will be used to survey the customers. Specific information on this questionnaire follows in the section, "Questions to Be Asked."

The advertising agency with whom you deal in planning your local advertising and promotions can probably handle all of these procedures for you—enlarging the map, mounting it, attaching overlays, providing stickers, and printing the questionnaire—but you should be able to do it yourself with very little effort.

(continued)

EXHIBIT 6.2 (continued)

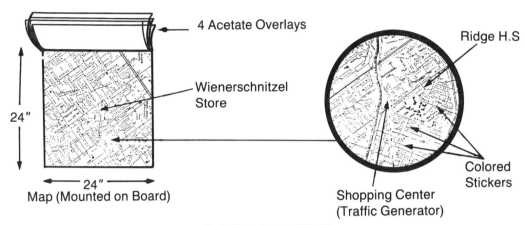

4 Acetate Overlays

Wienerschnitzel Store

24"

24"
Map (Mounted on Board)

Ridge H.S

Colored Stickers

Shopping Center
(Traffic Generator)

C. WHO TO SURVEY
(A representative sample of your customers)

It is important to keep in mind that for the best results you will want to talk to a group proportionate to your daily and hourly customer traffic.

There are two ways of insuring a sample representative of your customers:

1. If you are not sure of the makeup of your customers during specific meal periods, randomly select anyone coming in.

For example:

If you calculated that you want to interview 60 people during Thursday lunch, then speak to *any* 60 customers during that time on that day. If the interviewer approaches a group of people who come together, be sure only one person from the group is interviewed; otherwise, the sample will be inaccurate. Or—

2. If you are confident you know the makeup of your customers during each of the meal periods for each day, you can be more selective in determining whom to sample.

For example:

If you know that your lunch customers on Thursday are comprised of 50 percent adults (age over 27), 40 percent young adults (age 20–27), and 10 percent teens (age under 20), then try to interview the same proportion of customers, i.e., of the 60 customers you calculated to interview, try to interview 30 adults (50 percent), 24 young adults (40 percent), and six teenagers (10 percent). Calculate the number of interviews by age in advance with your hourly and daily schedules, and be sure to give your interviewers a copy of the hourly breakdown so they will know who (by age group) to talk to.

Sounds like a lot for an interviewer to remember? Experience tells us that it is possible to interview customers in exact proportion to the actual age makeup of hourly traffic *if* the estimate of the breakdown is accurate. Remember, use the second method only if you are confident you know your customers by age; otherwise, you are safer with the first method.

D. THE INTERVIEWER

1. Use competent personnel.
It is essential that interviews be conducted by dependable personnel and, if possible, by the same people on all four days. The manager or assistant manager should do at least a few interviews to get a feel for the survey. Team members have also been used to obtain good results. We've found that

EXHIBIT 6.2 (continued)

by using Wienerschnitzel personnel, you not only gather trading area information, but you also generate enthusiasm among your workers and likewise among your customers. Whomever you decide to use, consider them public relations representatives for you and Wienerschnitzel.

Note: For peak periods (where you need more than 30 interviews per hour) you will need additional interviewers and questionnaires. And, one interviewer should be designated as responsible for maintaining meal period survey quotas.

2. Meetings required.
An initial meeting (two weeks before the survey) should be held with all those who may be involved in the survey including: agency personnel, store managers, and team members. At this meeting, the purpose of the survey should be outlined as well as how to actually conduct the interviews.

A second meeting should be held one hour prior to the commencement of the Trading Area Survey with those who will actually administer the interviews. At this meeting, the interviewing technique should be reviewed and last-minute questions answered.

E. INTERVIEWING PROCEDURE

1. The questionnaire should be placed on a clipboard for easy marking.

2. The mounted map should be placed on an easel, chair, or table at the front of the store for Concept 80s and A-frames that do not have drive-thrus. If your store is an A-frame with a drive-thru, the map can be placed either before the speaker box or between the speaker box and the drive-thru window. Use whichever method you feel will work best for your restaurant.

3. Greet the customer you want to interview *before* he or she orders as follows: ''Good morning/afternoon/evening. I'm from Wienerschnitzel and I wonder if I could ask you a few short questions about fast service restaurants. Thank you.''

4. Take your customer over to the map and proceed to ask the survey questions.

F. QUESTIONS TO BE ASKED

1. ''The Three Basic Questions''

QUESTION #1: Would you please show me on this map approximately where you are *now* coming from?

QUESTION #2: Where ''on the map'' (or ''off the map'') are you *now* coming from (city, town, etc.)?

QUESTION #3: Where are you going immediately after you leave Wienerschnitzel?

2. Additional Survey Questions That Can Be Asked—''The Extensive Questionnaire''
Some operators and managers may have questions they would like answered in addition to the ''Three Basic Questions.'' If this is so, and if more *money* and time are available, it would be a good idea to take advantage of this opportunity to talk with your customers.

By extending your survey to more than three questions, your questionnaire writing, interviewing, and tabulating become more complicated and should definitely involve the research know-how of your advertising agency or an outside research firm. (You can still use your crew for interviewing but writing and analysis of the questionnaire would best be done by professionals.)

(continued)

EXHIBIT 6.2 (continued)

Here are some examples of additional questions you might want to include if you decide to broaden your range of information.

Question #4: How often do you visit a fast-service (or Wienerschnitzel) restaurant?

Question #5: Do you have any suggestions for improving the restaurant or its service?

Question #6: Is there anything you don't like about this store?

Question #7: Demographics of your customer such as age, size of family, family income, etc.

Question #8: Did you walk or drive to the store?

Question #9: Where will you eat—in the car, at home, at the store?

G. WHEN TO CONDUCT THE SURVEY

It is recommended the same survey be conducted twice a year (once in the winter and once in the summer) to measure seasonal influences such as summer business/winter business, in-school/out-of-school business, etc. Results of both surveys can be very different. And, remember, when determining how many interviews to conduct during specific meal periods, use sales data that reflect the same type of customers you are to interview (data from a week or two before is best).

---

tracts. The report itself will contain a wealth of data about the families that live inside each of those tracts.

Your task will be to identify all of the census tracts that fall inside of your trading area. You can then summarize all of the data about the households in your trading area by referring to the report book. In particular, you will want to know the total number of households in your trading area.

The next job is to find a way to estimate how much of your merchandise an average household buys in a year. If you know that and multiply it by the number of households in your trading area, you will have a good estimate of the total sales potential. The U.S. government sometimes makes such data available. Industry associations and trade magazines may have what you need as well.

If all else fails, you can use County Business Patterns or the U.S. Census of Retailing to identify sales in a larger area, say the county you are in, and divide by the households in that county. Adjust it to reflect anything you know is different about your trading area's population from the index base.

If you calculate that you have a market share over 50 percent, you will want to spend your major efforts looking for new locations where you can replicate the success you are presently enjoying. Expanding a market share that large isn't usually cost efficient, i.e., you can use the dollars better some other way.

If, however, you have a small market share, you will have the basis for building your business at its existing location. The first tool that you will have is an estimate of the profit that each new customer generates for you. This will give some good guidelines about how much money you can spend to gain new customers.

Identifying Your Competitors

Go back to your trading area map and locate your competitors on the map. Estimate their sales and use customer counts at their stores for time periods that you can compare to your own. Try to draw in their trading areas. Calculate their share of market in your trading area. Identify what you think each competitor's strongest selling points are and what weaknesses seem to exist.

Measuring Your Trading Area Position

There are three things that advertising can do for a retailer. Advertising can make your store and its location known to people in your trading area (i.e., create "awareness"). Awareness is obviously a precondition to sales. The second thing that advertising can do is to motivate people who know about your store to come in for a shopping visit (create trial shopping). And third, advertising can encourage existing customers to come back again (become repeat shoppers).

You should measure just where you stand on each of these three factors with households in your trading area that purchase your merchandise. You can do that with telephone interviews of a sample of households in your trading area. You can begin by selecting a systematic sample of streets in your trading area, including the block numbers that occur inside of the trading area.

Then you should rent (from your local telephone company) a reverse directory, or a criss-cross directory as it is sometimes called. Such a directory lists telephone subscribers by alpha/numeric address instead of alphabetically. For example:

101 Adams Blvd., Mary K. Smith 333-8878
103 Adams Blvd., Harry Briggs 545-9123

Select a systematic sample of telephone numbers from within the streets and blocks that run through your trading area.

Then you will need a questionnaire that covers these points:

1. Have you or anyone in your family shopped at a (your store type) in the past (purchase cycle for your merchandise)?
   If no, thank you and good bye.
   If yes, be sure you are talking to the person that does the _____ shopping.

2. When you think of (your store type), which stores come to mind?
   If your store is mentioned, skip to 4.
   If your store is not mentioned, ask 3.

3. Have you every heard of (your store name)?
   If no, thank you and good bye.
   If yes, ask 4.

4. Have you ever shopped at (your store name)?
   If no, ask 5.
   If yes, ask 6.

5. Why is it that you have never shopped at (your store name)?
   Record complete answer, thank you, and good bye.

6. How many times have you shopped at (your store name)?
   If once, ask 7.
   If more than once, ask 8 and 9.

7. Why is it that you have only shopped once at (your store name)?
   Record complete answer, thank you and good bye.

8. What do you particularly enjoy about shopping at (your store name)?
   Record complete answer.

9. Is there anything that you don't like about shopping at (your store name)?
   If yes, ask ''What would that be?'' Record complete answer, thank you and good bye.
   If no, thank you and good bye.

To do this job, you can either use the marketing research firm you found in Chapter 4, or you can approach the marketing research instructor at your local business school and suggest this as a class project, with the provision that you pay for expenses and make a donation to the school when the project is completed.

WHAT TO DO WITH THE RESULTS

If your awareness level isn't above 60 percent, your advertising will have to create awareness. If it is 60 percent or greater, however, there is not much more that you can do that is cost effective to drive awareness higher.

Among those prospective customers who are aware of your store, at least two-thirds of them should have made at least one shopping trip. If it is not that high, then advertising is needed to generate trial shopping. The answers to questions about why they haven't shopped and why they only shopped once can be helpful in formulating plans at this point.

Finally, at least half of those who have made trial shopping trips should be regular customers. The answers to what they particularly enjoy about shopping, and what, if anything, they don't like will be helpful here.

Defining the Demographics of Your Customers

Different media deliver different kinds of audiences who are most often described in terms of demographic characteristics. Therefore, if you are going to make good media choices, you will have to compare media in terms of their costs for delivering your kinds of customers.

You may be able to find this kind of information from your industry association or from a trade magazine covering your type of store. If you conduct an on-site trading area survey, you may generate your own data as a part of that study. Exhibit 6.3 is the questionnaire that Wienerschnitzel uses in their on-site interviews.

If all else fails, at least make your own estimates. Make up a recording form that has categories for these demographics: sex, age, income, and occupation. Then spend some time observing your customers and filling out the recording form. Keep after it until you are sure you know your customers.

EXHIBIT 6.3

CUSTOMER PROFILE SURVEY EXAMPLE

Day Interviewing		1
Thursday		1
Friday		2
Saturday		3
Sunday		4

Good morning/afternoon/evening. I'm from
Wienerschnitzel and I wonder if I could ask
you a few short questions about our restaurant?
Thank you.

Time Interviewing		2
Red 11-2		1
Yellow 2-5		2
Black 5-8		3
Blue 8-11		4

1. How often do you eat at a Wienerschnitzel
   restaurant?   **3**

Several times a week	1
Once a week	2
Once every couple of weeks	3
Once a month	4
Once every 3 months	5
Less than once every 3 months	6
The first time	7

2. Where are you now coming from?   **2**   **3**
   Is it:

	4-5	6-7
Where you live	1	1
Working in Brookfield shopping area	2	2
Shopping in Brookfield shopping area	3	3
Other shopping area	4	4
School	5	5
Office	6	6
Factory or other place of work	7	7
Just passing by	8	8
Visiting friend/relative	9	9
Amusement	0	0

3. Where are you going
   immediately after you
   leave Wienerschnitzel? Is it:

Zoo	1	1
Church	2	2
Park or athletic field	3	3
Theatre	4	4
Hospital	5	5
On inter-city trip	6	6
Other	7	7

(continued)

EXHIBIT 6.3 (continued)

4. Would you show me on this map approxi-   8-9
   mately the area where you said you are now
   coming from? (Show map—place dot on map)
   On Map _____ (Write in city)
   Off Map _____ (Write in city)

                                                                            10-13
5. Who are you with? Are you: 14

   Alone   1
   With your husband/wife   2
   With your family and children   3
   With your friends   4
   With your coworkers   5
   (on lunch, coffee break)

6. How many are with you? (If with family)   15-16
   (By observation or asking)
   Children _____
   Adults _____
   Total _____

7. How much do you think your total check will   17
   be while eating at Wienerschnitzel today?
   Under $.50   1
   $.50–$.99   2
   1.00–1.49   3
   1.50–1.99   4
   2.00–2.99   5
   3.00–3.99   6
   4.00 or over   7

8. In which age group do you belong?   18
   Under 18   1
   18–24   2
   25–34   3
   35–49   4
   50–64   5
   65 and over   6

9. Sex: 19
   Male   1
   Female   2

THANK YOU

Differentiating Your Store from Competitors

This is the place where we will apply the creative strategy concept to your retail store. We will deal with the questions: "Why should a customer spend money at your store and not with a competitor?" "What is your basic benefit?" "How will you differentiate your store from your competitors?" There are no automatic answers to these questions. If you have done the work described so far, you will have a great number of facts about your market, your competitors, your store, and your customers to help you come up with the answers to those questions. But, in the end, it will be your creativity, experience, judgment, and good business sense that provide the answers.

A GOOD EXAMPLE—FOR A WHILE

In 1977, Mel and Patricia Ziegler were living in the San Francisco Bay area, trying to make a living as a freelance writer and artist. They shopped at Army/Navy stores for two reasons. One was that the Army/Navy surplus store prices fit the budget of aspiring, but not yet established, freelance artists. The second reason was that the surplus stores were one of the few places where they could buy all-cotton clothes and they were convinced that all-cotton was the most comfortable type of clothing.

The surplus store clothes weren't always in good condition, however. Patricia removed tattered collars and cuffs and replaced them with ones of her own design. Their friends liked Patricia's work so much that they pestered her to make similar clothes for them, which she eventually began to do. They sold rehabilitated surplus clothes from the living room of their Mill Valley, California home. Although it was on a small scale, the venture was successful.

Then Mel suggested that if they could get just a little business going, they would have a "floor" under their freelance careers. So they went to Spain and bought a lot of Spanish Army used paratrooper shirts. They paid for them with the $1,500 line of credit on their bank charge card because that was all the capital they could raise. When they received the shirts back in Mill Valley, they discovered that the sleeves were too short. After some seriously worried moments, Patricia suggested they simply roll the sleeves up and consider it part of the design.

The success of the Spanish paratrooper shirt venture encouraged them to open a retail store in Mill Valley. They were so short on capital that they roamed the surplus stores of the world to find surplus clothing they could alter themselves.

They called their store "Banana Republic" and decorated it with fake palm trees, plastic parrots, and a rusting Land Rover. They hung zebra skins on the wall and used packing crates for merchandise display cases. They designed the clothes that the employees would wear, wrote the script for answering the telephone, and specified every aspect of their business. They produced a small black and white catalog that they stapled together themselves and mailed to friends.

It is now eight years later and the Banana Republic Travel & Safari Clothing Company has 65 stores throughout the United States that produced about $115 million in gross sales in 1986. The catalog is now in four colors, is 66 pages long, and is produced and distributed four times a year to 14 million customers. Mel still writes copy for the catalog and Patricia still does the illustrations.

The Zieglers say they have concentrated on the "experience of shop-

EXHIBIT 6.4

ANOTHER SIGN OF BANANA REPUBLIC'S SUCCESS?

Reprinted by permission of Newspaper Enterprise Association, Inc.

ping." They believe they have managed to treat retailing as "theater," which is probably why their Beverly Hills, California store sports a fifteen-foot high rampaging elephant made out of fiberglass.

The Zieglers now define their business as being the "travel business." They are introducing travel bookstores inside of their Banana Republic stores, selling travel and guidebooks. They have started a "climate desk" service that allows people to call a toll-free number for up-to-date weather information from around the world. They have just co-authored a book, *The Banana Republic's Guide to Travel and Safari Clothing*.

Future plans call for a travel magazine and organized travel tours. Mel points out that they are as much in the travel business as American Express Company is, except American Express entered it with financial services while Banana Republic entered it with clothing.

Exhibit 6.4 illustrates Banana Republic's success and Exhibit 6.5 is typical of the way that the Banana Republic differentiates itself (and its advertising) from competitors. The theme carries through into their catalogs as well. Exhibit 6.6 is a sample page from a current catalog.

If you have never been in a Banana Republic store, make an effort to visit one. You will never mistake shopping in that store with shopping somewhere else. That is the task of the retailer—differentiate your store from all of your competitors and give your customers real reasons for shopping at your store.

EXHIBIT 6.5

BANANA REPUBLIC AD

EXHIBIT 6.6

BANANA REPUBLIC CATALOG

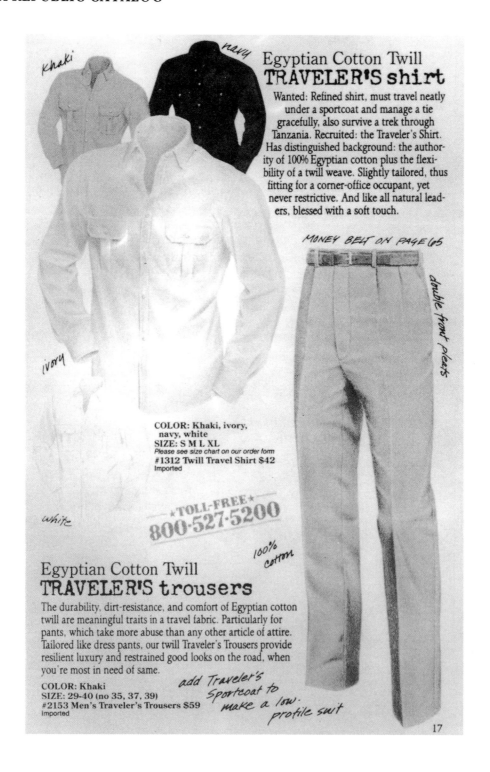

Khaki

navy

Egyptian Cotton Twill
TRAVELER'S shirt

Wanted: Refined shirt, must travel neatly under a sportcoat and manage a tie gracefully, also survive a trek through Tanzania. Recruited: the Traveler's Shirt. Has distinguished background: the authority of 100% Egyptian cotton plus the flexibility of a twill weave. Slightly tailored, thus fitting for a corner-office occupant, yet never restrictive. And like all natural leaders, blessed with a soft touch.

MONEY BELT ON PAGE 65

double front pleats

ivory

COLOR: Khaki, ivory, navy, white
SIZE: S M L XL
Please see size chart on our order form
#1312 Twill Travel Shirt $42
Imported

white

★TOLL-FREE★
800-527-5200

100% cotton

Egyptian Cotton Twill
TRAVELER'S trousers

The durability, dirt-resistance, and comfort of Egyptian cotton twill are meaningful traits in a travel fabric. Particularly for pants, which take more abuse than any other article of attire. Tailored like dress pants, our twill Traveler's Trousers provide resilient luxury and restrained good looks on the road, when you're most in need of same.

COLOR: Khaki
SIZE: 29-40 (no 35, 37, 39)
#2153 Men's Traveler's Trousers $59
Imported

add Traveler's Sportcoat to make a low profile suit

17

BANANA REPUBLIC UPDATE

This is a small aside about how fast the world changes. The Zieglers sold the Banana Republic to the Gap, Inc. in 1983. The Gap is a successful retailer of men's, women's and kid's clothing. In 1990, the company operated over 1,100 stores and recorded total sales of $1.9 billion.

The section you just read ends by recommending you visit a Banana Republic store to see an example of successful differentiation; you can no longer do that however. Here's why.

From 1983 until 1988, the Zieglers continued to run Banana Republic stores as a division of the Gap. By 1988, they had expanded to 129 stores and experienced its first "same-stores year-to-year" sales decreases and its first ever losses. Some people said the safari look went out of fashion. Some said the stores expanded too fast. Whatever the reason, the financial results lead to a dust-up between the Zieglers and the Gap management, and when the dust settled, the Zieglers were gone.

Also gone was their concept for differentiation. The Gap management gutted all of the Banana Republic stores and substituted its distinctive interiors, special merchandise, and advertising with bland, me-too replacements.

In any event, the decisions created a financial nightmare. The Gap does not report store division results separately, but their 1990 annual report indicated a $4 million charge for restructuring Banana Republic and then had this to say about Banana Republic: "In addition to generating positive comparable store sales growth, this division was once again profitable. Although its financial performance was modest compared to overall company results, these results nonetheless evidenced the correctness of our repositioning efforts." Perhaps. Time will tell.

This is an example of a company that has purposely and successfully adopted a "me-too" market position. To succeed in the market, however, it will have to differentiate itself. You can follow the developments to see what actually happens.

Your assignment now is to watch the Banana Republic store in your neighborhood compete with all of the other men's and women's clothing stores in your local shopping mall. If it succeeds, you will learn a good deal about retailing from your observations. If it fails, you may not be surprised.

A LIVE CASE STUDY

The single, most important idea in this book is that successful companies differentiate themselves from all of their competitors in a way that is meaningful to their customers and then communicate that difference to current and future customers. Glenfiddich did it with the smoothness of their scotch and communicated that message beautifully. Burger King has a clear difference in their broiled, not fried, hamburgers, but has not yet figured out how to communicate that difference in meaningful fashion. Banana Republic had the differentiation in the past, but lost it.

Here Is the Situation

The consumer electronics market is huge. Total retail sales for southern California are the largest market in the United States. According to the Los Angeles Times Marketing Research Department, southern California consumers spend over $445,680,000 on consumer electronics. If you think this is a competitive market, you are exactly correct!

At the end of the 1980s, the major retail competitors in southern California, and their competitive differentiation, were in place. The basic four dimensions of competition in electronics are location, product quality, price, and service level. Every major competitor attempted to manipulate these four elements to create a unique position. The competitive positions looked like this early in 1990:

High end of the market: These stores tend to be single- or two-location stores, and carry top equipment at top prices. The salespeople are extremely knowledgeable and helpful; these stores cater to the real "audiophile." Beverly Stereo, Supervision, and Audio Concepts are examples of such stores.

Full-line department stores: Sears and Montgomery Ward focus on "white goods" (refrigerators, washers, and dryers) and carry a frequently limited line of TVs, VCRs, camcorders, and stereo equipment. Quality is usually average and the merchandise tends to be overpriced for the market. There are lots of locations but service is nonexistent.

Independent white goods stores: These stores focus on white goods at the lowest possible prices and carry consumer electronics. Service is minimal. Phil & Jim's is an example; they operate eleven stores.

Focused merchandise lines: These retailers focus on a limited set of consumer electronics merchandise, have few locations, high-end merchandise at high prices, and lots of service. Paul (The KING of Big Screen TV) and Ken Crane (Home Entertainment Center) are examples of this segment. Leo's Stereo tried to focus on automotive stereo and portable telephones with multiple locations and some service until they went bankrupt.

Absolute lowest prices: These few stores offer brand-name merchandise at the lowest possible prices and not much more; customers are on their own. Adray's is an example.

Super Stores: These large (average 32,000+ square feet), multiple location stores have extensive inventories of middle-range merchandise, low prices, and at least an attempt at service (even though the management often seems to think it is delivering a lot more service than the customers think they are getting). Circuit City Stores, with its Richmond, Virginia headquarters and annual sales over $2 billion, is the premier example of this kind of retailer. Its 157 stores nationwide give it real bargaining power with its suppliers. The Federated Group and Pacific Stereo attempted this concept, but failed and ended up bankrupt after a series of competitive and management errors.

But Here Come New Competitors

The Good Guys is a San Francisco-based chain of 25 consumer electronics stores, that survived an invasion of their home territory by Circuit City in 1987. The Good Guys did this by moving up-market from Circuit City. They moved higher up the merchandise scale with higher prices and much higher service levels. The Good Guys followed this same strategy when they expanded into the highly competitive southern California market. As a result, they are more likely to compete with Rogersound Labs than with Circuit City. They did such a good job they put Rogersound Labs out of business.

Our real interest lies with Silo, a 217 store chain. Headquartered in Philadelphia it is a wholly owned subsidiary of the world's largest consumer electronics retailer, the London-based Dixon's Group. Silo's 1989 sales were over $1 billion, about half of Circuit City's sales.

By late 1990, Silo had 15 stores ready to open in southern California, with an additional 15 planned by 1993. Chuck Jacoby, national advertising director for Silo, and Monte Zator, management supervisor, Saatchi & Saatchi Pacific, collaborated on producing a high-profile "teaser" TV campaign to lead up to Silo's introduction into the Southern California market on Labor Day, 1990.

The first three commercials never explained what Silo was all about. Exhibit 6.7 shows a storyboard from that group and Exhibit 6.8 shows a supporting newspaper advertisement. These ads carried a toll-free number for viewers whose curiosity had been piqued. When they called the 800 number, they were told that Silo was a new consumer electronics store and directed to the store location closest to their homes. They were also promised a gift at the store. Those callers willing to leave their names and addresses were sent a Silo brochure and T-shirt with the inscription, "I feel better with a Silo nearby."

Over 30,000 calls were received in the first 30 days the advertising ran. Of those, 382 callers were seriously annoyed, and the operators gave them another toll-free number to call to complain. The 52 people who called the second 800 number spoke directly to Chuck Jacoby in Philadelphia. Jacoby said he made friends with almost all of the people who placed the personal calls to him.

The Results

Here are highlights of the advertising and sales results from the Silo introduction into southern California:

• The teaser phase generated nearly 40 percent advertising awareness (up from 0 percent initially, of course)

• By the grand opening, 65 percent of all southern California households were aware of Silo stores

• By Christmas, 1990, store awareness had reached 80 percent

• Grand opening sales exceeded projections by 40 percent

• In the four periods since the grand opening, sales have exceeded projections three times.

The Challenge for the Future

Silo successfully expanded into southern California on the sole premise that they were an alternative to Circuit City. What this book has called the "principal consumer benefit" Silo calls the "single-minded proposition," which they say is "Silo has come to Los Angeles to offer consumer electronics/appliance shoppers a new and better alternative."

This single-minded proposition was the basis for their entry into southern California and there is little question that the introduction was extremely successful. The basic benefit offered to potential customers, however, is that Silo is an alternative to Circuit City. While that position was okay for entering the market, Silo will have to find some way to differentiate themselves from Circuit City stores if they are to grow and profit.

For instance, even though both chains have approximately the same number of stores in the market, Circuit City's larger stores produce greater

EXHIBIT 6.7

SAATCHI & SAATCHI DFS
RETAIL DIVISION, SOUTHERN CALIFORNIA

TELEVISION COPY

File Name: PHAZ1TV1	**Campaign/Project:**	SILO TEASE/PHASE I (1 OF 3)	**AS PRODUCED**	
Client: SILO				Page 1 of 2
Job No.: T1-101	**Title:**	"THE DECISION"	**Code No.:**	QCFY 1001
Acct. Exec.: G/AUSTIN	**Product:**		**Length:**	:30
Rev. No.: 4			**Writer/tr/wp:**	MB/kg/kf

1. VID A WELL-DRESSED MAN (LATE FORTIES, EARLY FIFTIES) IS CORNERED BY THE PRESS AND SURROUNDED BY MICROPHONES AS HE LEAVES "THE FEDERAL BUILDING." HE IS BARRAGED WITH QUESTIONS AT THE END OF HIS STATEMENT.

   AUD *WELL-DRESSED MAN:* Ok folks, alright folks. The decision's been made, the President has approved. The Silos will be located in Southern California.

2. VID ELECTRONIC WHITE NOISE FADE.
   AUD (*SFX:*   STATIC NOISE)

3. VID CLOSE-UP OF MAN ON THE STREET.
   AUD *MAN:*   They're putting Silos in the Southland? Never thought I'd live to see the day.

4. VID ELECTRONIC WHITE NOISE FADE.
   AUD (*SFX:*   STATIC NOISE)

EXHIBIT 6.7 (continued)

SAATCHI & SAATCHI DFS
RETAIL DIVISION, SOUTHERN CALIFORNIA

TELEVISION COPY

File Name:	PHAZ1TV1	Campaign/Project:	SILO TEASE/PHASE I (1 OF 3)	AS PRODUCED	
Client:	SILO				Page 2 of 2
Job No.:	T1-101	Title:	"THE DECISION"	Code No.:	QCFY 1001
Acct. Exec.:	G/AUSTIN	Product:		Length:	:30
Rev. No.:	4			Writer/tr/wp:	MB/kg/kf

5. VID   CLOSE-UP OF WOMAN ON THE STREET.
   AUD   *WOMAN*:   Oh yeah. They're building one near my sister's place in Fullerton. You can see it from her backyard.

6. VID   ELECTRONIC WHITE NOISE FADE.
   AUD   (*SFX*:   STATIC NOISE)

7. VID   CLOSE-UP OF WOMAN ON THE STREET.
   AUD   *WOMAN*:   They say the Silos are for our own protection. Is that true?

   VID   FULL-SCREEN TITLES: *THE SILOS ARE COMING 1(800)288-SILO BROUGHT TO YOU BY THE PEOPLE WHO WANT TO PROTECT THE SOUTHLAND*
   AUD   *ANNCR*: Are the Silos really here to protect us? Call one-eight hundred—288-Silo.

EXHIBIT 6.8

15 SILO SITES PROPOSED FOR DENSELY POPULATED AREAS.

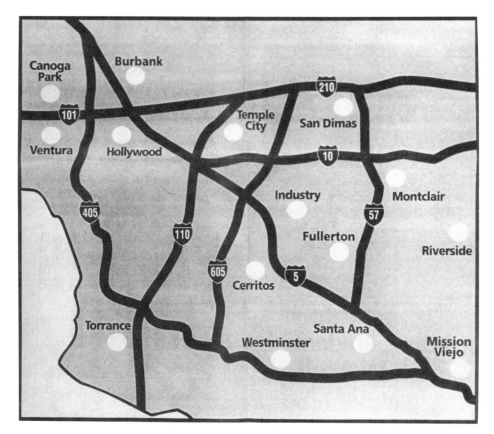

The Silos are coming to the Southland. To communities just like yours. Places like Fullerton, Canoga Park and Burbank. They say the Silos are good for the economy. They say that they'll create jobs and save us taxpayers money. And they say the Silos are here for our protection. But shouldn't we know more?

Are the Silos really here to protect us? Call 1-800-288-SILO.

BROUGHT TO YOU BY THE PEOPLE WHO WANT TO PROTECT THE SOUTHLAND.

sales and profits per store, and, as a result, a much larger budget for advertising and promotion.

Your Assignment

In the space below, write down at least three ways that Silo could differentiate its stores from Circuit City stores to continue to build on its successful introduction.

1. _____

2. _____

3. _____

Finally, watch the southern California consumer electronics market and answer these questions: Will Silo continue to grow without creating some meaningful differentiation from Circuit City? If they do create a differentiation, did they follow your advice?

Finding Affordable, Effective, Efficient Media

There are three parameters that apply to retail advertising. The first parameter is finding media whose costs you can afford over the course of a whole year, with special attention to peak selling periods.

The second parameter is finding media that work for you, media that produce sales. You will have to experiment to find the answer to this question. Start by setting up test conditions and devising methods of measuring the results produced by the tested media. Coupons are always good measurement devices. So are coded telephone numbers and coded mail addresses (one ad says write to Box A and the other says write to Box B). Some retailers have regular programs where their salespeople ask every customer, "How did you hear about us?" However you go about it, effective media can only be identified by testing and more testing.

The third parameter is finding efficient media. Efficiency is defined as getting the most sales results for your advertising investment. For retailers, that invariably means finding media that cover your trading area with the minimum amount of waste circulation outside of the trading area. That is a tough job. If you want to be clear about it, envision this scene: Every dollar that you spend on advertising outside of your trading area is a dollar bill that you hold a match to and burn until only ashes are left!

A STATE-OF-THE-ART EXAMPLE

Carl Karcher Enterprises, Inc., is an Anaheim, California-based restaurant company. Their flagship chain is comprised of approximately 400 quick service restaurants in western United States. Michelle Rose is regional marketing manager for Carl's Jr. restaurants. She uses TV and radio in all markets with enough of Carl's Jr. restaurants to support the cost. Rose uses electronic media for all of the right reasons (to demonstrate new products or promotions and to build brand awareness).

After she has accomplished her objectives in TV and radio, she still has a series of marketing programs left to do. Those new products and promotions must be turned into actual customers in the restaurants. There are slow seasons to be strengthened, low performing restaurants to be aided, and many other jobs to be done at the individual restaurant level. Ads combined with coupons have proved to be effective promotional tools in accomplishing these restaurant activities. Exhibit 6.9 is a good example of a business-building coupon ad.

Rose's objective is to deliver these coupon ads inside of each restaurant's trading area at a minimum cost. She can use direct mail to get the coupons in the hands of prospective customers. And this gives her complete control over where the coupon ads are delivered. This is called *solo direct mail* and it allows her to focus all of her resources precisely in the trading areas of the individual restaurants. But the cost per thousand (CPM) of using solo direct mail is high, which in turn, limits the number of promotions she can afford to run each year.

On the other hand, if she turns to newspapers, she will encounter two deficiencies. First, newspapers never have 100 percent coverage inside of the restaurant's trading area, and second, they have circulation outside of the trading areas, thus generating wasted dollars. Buying multiple papers in an area just makes the problem worse because there is duplication in circulation to contend with, as well as a more complicated buying situation.

Since 1986, Rose has been working with Tom Ketchum, President of the KLW Group, Inc., to develop a state-of-the-art solution to the ad coupon delivery problem. The KLW Group's computer database contains circulation data on every newspaper and shopper paper in the United States. They analyze each trading area to determine the best delivery system for each restaurant. Exhibit 6.10 is an example of the recommendations for some of Carl's Jr. restaurants in Nevada and California.

In June, 1986, Carl's Jr. management conducted a test of the new "marriage mail" concept for delivering coupons against the previous solo direct mail program. The results are shown below:

	Solo Direct Mail		Marriage Mail Insert	
	Direct mailed 7,000 per restaurant. 108 restaurants participated.		Marriage mail insert used 15,400 pieces per restaurant. 54 restaurants participated.	
Coupon Offered	Number Redeemed	Percent Redemption	Number Redeemed	Percent Redemption
Number One	79	1.1%	83	0.5%
Number Two	228	3.3	291	1.9
Number Three	413	5.9	348	2.3
Totals	720	10.3%	722	4.7%
Printing and mail cost	$1,057		$667	
Coupon redemption cost	291		291	
Total cost per restaurant	$1,348		$830	
Cost per coupon redeemed		$1.87		$1.15

The marriage mail program developed by the KLW Group reached more than twice as many households as the solo mail program, produced virtually

EXHIBIT 6.9

A TYPICAL CARL'S JR. COUPON ADVERTISEMENT

EXHIBIT 6.10

MEDIA RECOMMENDATIONS FOR CARL'S JR. NORTHERN CALIFORNIA LOCATIONS

Store #	Store Location	Publication/Zone	Zip Code(s)	Qty	Cost per/M	Cost	Total Store Qty	Total Store Cost
#761	1522 W. Charleston, Las Vegas, NV 89102	**Review Journal/TMC** (Covered by store #750)						
	LOS ANGELES							
#1	275 S. Harbor, Anaheim, CA 92805	**Pennysaver/HHD** Anaheim Central East	92805	16,229	$19.50	$316.47	16,229	$316.47
#3	6310 Platt Ave. Woodland Hills, CA 91367	**Pennysaver/HHD** Woodland Hills West	91364/67	15,715	$19.50	$306.44	15,715	$306.44
#5	10012 Westminster Garden Grove, CA 92640	**Pennysaver/HHD** Westminster Central	92683/55	13,068				
		Westminster East	92683	7,651				
		Total		20,719	$19.50	$404.02	20,719	$404.02
#6	11051 Euclid Ave. Garden Grove, CA 92640	**Pennysaver/HHD** Garden Grove North East	92640	15,032	$19.50	$293.12	15,032	$293.12
#7	4966 E. Florence Bell, CA 90201	**So. Calif. Publishing Co.** Bell/Maywood Ind. Post	90201/270	12,725				
		Bell Gardens Review	90201	7,750				
		Total So. Calif. Publishing		20,475	$22.40	$458.64	20,475	$458.64
#8	401 Los Posas Rd. Camarillo, CA 93010	**Ventura Valley Shopper** Zone 6/W. Camarillo	93010	10,000	$21.00	$210.00	10,000	$210.00
#9	7219 S. Alameda Los Angeles, CA 90001	**Independent Postal System** Custom Pattern	90001/90255	15,000	$20.00	$300.00	15,000	$300.00

the same number of redeemed coupons, and did the job at only 62 percent of the cost of solo direct mail.

A Final Thought about Retailing

If you are a retailer searching for a way to build your business by differentiating it from your competitors, you might begin by giving some thought to the results of a 1991 Louis Harris survey of adult Americans. Harris reports that 63 percent find shopping to be ''drudgery or worse.''

Is there an opportunity for you there?

CHAPTER 7

Understanding Media

Media Planning

An important part of successful advertising planning involves careful media planning. The media represent audiences made up of customers and prospective customers that you can purchase to deliver your advertising messages. The number of different audiences for you to select from is staggering. In the United States, there are approximately 530 morning newspapers, 1,125 evening newspapers, and 847 Sunday papers. There are about 4,800 magazines published. Also, there are 1,100 television stations and 4,500 cable TV systems. Add to that approximately 4,600 AM radio stations and 4,400 FM radio stations. Then there are over 8,000 markets in which you can buy outdoor advertising. Finally, include about $23 billion in direct mail and another $16 billion in miscellaneous media. You can see the problem.

To understand the second part of the media planning problem, we need some definitions:

Reach is the unduplicated proportion of a defined audience that is exposed to an advertising message. Usually this number is measured in terms of a four-week period. Media planning is usually based on the thirteen, four-week periods that occur each year. Exhibit 7.1 is an example of a typical advertising agency media planning schedule. Note the four-week modules.

In short, you can think of reach as the number of customers and prospective customers who see and/or hear your advertising each month.

Frequency is the number of times in that four-week period that your advertising is seen and/or heard by your customers and prospective customers. Frequency can be shown in two ways: a) as the average number of times a member of the target audience sees or hears the advertising (average frequency), and b) as a frequency distribution. The idea behind a frequency

EXHIBIT 7.1

A MEDIA PLANNER'S WORKSHEET

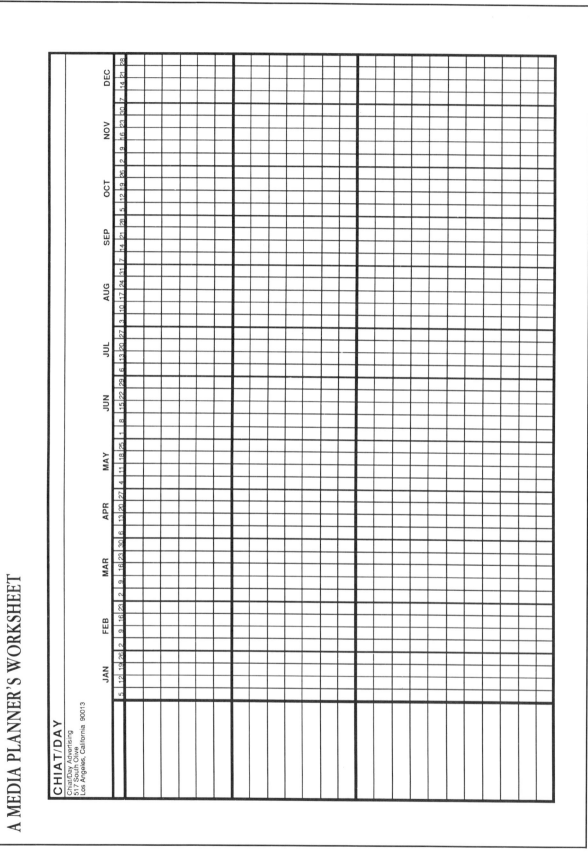

distribution is that not everybody in the target audience will see or hear the advertising the same number of times. For example:

<u>The Audience Reached in a 4-Week Period</u>

Once	10%
Twice	10
Three times	10
Four times	40
Five times	10
Six times	10
Seven +	10

Obviously, the average frequency here is four times, but the range is wide. In practical terms, you really don't have to worry about frequency distributions. The estimates they are based on are simply too crude to use for serious judgments.

Continuity refers to the number of four-week periods during the year in which you advertise. Maximum continuity would be to advertise every week all year round.

The Media Planning Problem

Each of these aspects of media has a cost attached. You can reach more and more people, but it costs more money. Or, you can reach fewer people, but reach them more often. That costs more money, too. Finally, every four-week period that you add to your media schedule takes money away from reach and/or frequency. You can visualize the media planning problem as:

$$\left. \begin{array}{ccccc} \text{Maximize} & + & \text{Maximize} & + & \text{Maximize} \\ \text{Reach} & & \text{Frequency} & & \text{Continuity} \end{array} \right\| \begin{array}{l} \text{Subject} \\ \text{to a fixed} \\ \text{budget} \end{array}$$

Unfortunately, there is only a small amount of research and hard data to guide you through this problem. Here are some thoughts that may prove helpful.

REACH

Theoretically, there is one medium that delivers an audience of customers and prospective customers at the absolutely lowest cost per customer. Then there is a second medium that delivers at the next best cost per customer, a third most cost effective, and so on until all media can be displayed in an array, representing ever-increasing costs of reaching the next marginal customer.

Your task is to reach enough of these customers and prospective customers (during the *purchase cycle* for your product or service) to have a big enough base to support your business. After that point is reached, the question becomes one of comparing the marginal revenue produced by gaining a new customer with the marginal media cost for acquiring that new customer. This requires a fair amount of estimating. On the other hand, it gives you a way to begin to analyze the question of "How much reach is right?"

FREQUENCY

What little research is available is devoted to frequency. The Association of National Advertisers, Inc., recently reviewed the woefully inadequate research database and summarized the results in *Effective Frequency: The Relationship between Frequency and Advertising Effectiveness.* The conclusions are:

1. One exposure of an advertisement to a target group consumer within a purchase cycle has little or no effect in all but a minority of circumstances.

2. Because one exposure is usually ineffective, the central goal of productive media planning should be to place emphasis on enhancing frequency rather than reach.

3. The weight of evidence strongly suggests that an exposure frequency of two within a purchase cycle is an effective level.

4. By and large, optimal exposure frequency appears to be at least three exposures within a purchase cycle.

In television advertising, it seems that the first time a commercial is seen, a decision is made based on the question, "Is this of interest to me or not?" If the answer is "yes," the viewer will pay attention to the selling points in the next commercial. A purchase decision is usually made after the second viewing; however, some people need to see the commercial once more to make a decision. Hence, two exposures are effective; three are optimal.

There is no comparable research on what happens with print advertising.

The McGraw-Hill Advertising Lab has conducted some good research on the frequency question in business-to-business advertising. The results from this area indicate that an annual frequency of four exposures, once a quarter, is optimal if the media schedule is supported with a regular sales call program. No explanation of what is going on to produce these results has been offered.

It is worth noting that all of this research was conducted on existing, established brands. That is true for both consumer and business-to-business audiences. Whether the two- or three-exposure guideline is appropriate in new product or service introductions is unknown.

CONTINUITY

The place to start thinking about continuity is with the seasonality of your business. Virtually every business has one or more peak selling seasons. Your approach to continuity should begin by identifying those periods and ensuring that adequate budgets are assigned to cover them. Also, remember that the decision-making period is part of the peak selling period, so make certain you understand how your customers go about making decisions to buy as well as when they buy.

DISTRIBUTION

The most important non-media consideration in media planning is distribution. (Remember the Porsche and New York Life examples from Chapter

4.) The best advertising in the world is of no value if the customer cannot purchase the service or product because it is unavailable.

Look at it this way: If half of the stores in a market do not stock your product, half of your advertising budget in that market is wasted (unless you can manage to advertise only in the trading areas of the stores carrying your product).

As you begin to develop your media plans on a market-by-market basis, there is another concept you should be familiar with, All Commodity Volume (ACV). If there are two stores in a market and one stocks your merchandise (Store A) but the other doesn't (Store B), you have 50 percent store distribution. If, however, Store B does 80 percent of all the business in the market and Store A only does 20 percent, you have only 20 percent ACV distribution. Because virtually every type of retailing is dominated by a few large stores, ACV distribution is much more important than store distribution.

DISTRIBUTORS

If your products are distributed by wholesalers, retailers, etc., you should consider their knowledge and preferences in your media planning. It is possible that they have observed which media really work in their markets; this can be invaluable information to you. Some may insist on local advertising that can carry dealer tags or store listings. Others may believe your products need the kind of prestige that seems to rub off on products that advertise in national media.

COMPARING MEDIA

All of the various media deliver audiences of different sizes and their charges can vary widely. The tool used most often to make media comparisons is called cost per thousand (CPM). It is calculated as follows:

$$CPM = \frac{\text{Cost per unit of advertising*}}{\text{Audience size (in thousands)}}$$

If a magazine delivers an audience of 1,000,000 and charges $10,000 for a black and white page, the calculations look like this:

$$CPM = \frac{\$10,000}{1,000,000} = \frac{\$10,000}{1,000} = \$10.00 \text{ CPM}$$

Characteristics of the Media

NEWSPAPERS

More advertising dollars are spent in newspapers than in any other media. In addition to the 1,600 daily newspapers noted earlier, there are more than

---

*Note: In print advertising, the advertising unit most commonly used is the cost of a black and white page. In broadcast, it is the cost of a 30-second commercial.

7,600 semi-weekly and weekly newspapers. The combined circulation of all these newspapers is in excess of 100 million. That is impressive, especially because there are only a little over 85 million households in the United States.

Newspapers are a local advertising medium. About 85 percent of their advertising revenues comes from retail advertising. Retail advertising is advertising placed by retail merchants and other local businesses.

In addition to retail advertising, newspapers carry national advertising. Together, these two types of advertising are called *display* advertising and carry different rates with national advertising, costing about 50 percent more than local advertising. Newspapers argue that they need the up-charge to cover the higher costs of handling national advertising (national advertising earns an advertising agency discount).

Newspapers also carry *classified* advertising. These are want ads for jobs, housing, cars, and so on.

Public notices (government reports, announcements of practices by professionals, and financial reports) also appear in newspapers. These ads are frequently called ''tombstone'' ads.

Strengths and Weaknesses

These are the major strengths of newspapers as an advertising medium.

1. Geographic selectivity. The thousands of newspapers in the United States give you the ability to pinpoint almost any combination of geographic markets. As a result, newspaper advertising can be used to support almost any pattern of distribution.

2. Broad coverage. In the course of a typical five-day week, newspapers reach a cumulative audience of 80 percent of all adults 18 years old and over. On average, 80 percent of all those readers will be exposed to the page carrying your advertising.

3. Considerable reader interest. Readers come to the newspaper looking for advertising as well as editorial content. This is particularly true for women. In addition, the news value of the newspaper lends a sense of urgency to newspaper advertising.

4. Flexibility. Newspapers will accept almost any space configuration that will fit onto a page. You can schedule your advertising any day of the week so you have the ability to be very precise in supporting specific events. Finally, closing dates for newspapers are short (24 to 48 hours before press time) so you have the capability to take advantage of fast-breaking events.

5. Low cost per thousand. Newspapers are relatively cheap compared to other media.

6. Co-operative advertising. Co-op advertising occurs when you split the cost of advertising in a market with your distributor. (Remember Porsche Cars North America's co-op program to support the introduction of the 924S?) Co-op advertising has many significant advantages. Your distributor adds his dollars to yours so that you can buy more advertising in the market than you could by yourself. Your distributor can buy the newspaper advertising at the retail rate so you both have even more dollars to spend. Finally, when your distributor decides to spend money to advertise your products, you can be sure that the distributor will have a full inventory and that the products will be well displayed.

Newspapers also have some real disadvantages as an advertising medium.

1. Wasted circulation. The other side of the broad coverage coin is that newspapers will reach a lot of people besides your own customers and prospective customers. As a result, you end up paying for all of those non-prospects.

2. High cost for national advertisers. Unless you can work a co-op deal with your local distributor, the up-charge for national advertising in newspapers is quite uncompetitive.

3. Short physical life. People read newspapers quickly and then they are discarded. Therefore, the life of your advertising is short in newspapers.

4. Poor reproduction and limited ability to use color. The newsprint that absorbs ink rapidly on today's high speed presses tends to spread that ink. As a result, newspapers are usually not suitable for detailed artwork. Color reproduction is even more limited. On the bright side, significant improvements on both of these points are being made by many newspapers. Unfortunately, if you are going to use newspapers in your media plans, you will either have to develop artwork for the poorest reproduction facilities on your newspaper schedule, or produce two versions of your advertising (one for high-quality presses and one for poor-quality presses).

MAGAZINES

There are more than 3,600 business and professional magazines published and at least 1,200 consumer and farm magazines. Consumer magazines, in particular, have been undergoing a remarkable change in the past decade. There has been a rapid shift from magazines offering broad audiences to a wide variety of special interest magazines offering very selective audiences. *American Health, Modern Maturity, American Photographer, Powder, Skateboarder, Weight Watchers, Running,* and *Cooking Light* are just a few examples of magazines targeted at selective audiences.

Most magazines are national; their readers are spread all across the United States. Some, however, are regional in their circulation and editorial viewpoint. For example, *Sunset* focuses on the Pacific coast region and *Southern Living* concentrates on the Southeastern states. One of the fastest-growing categories of magazines are the city magazines such as *Los Angeles, Philadelphia, San Diego,* and *New York.*

Magazines accept three kinds of advertising: display, display classified, and classified. Classified ads are exactly like the "want ads" in newspapers. They usually are placed at the back of the "book." Display classified uses more space and tends to be somewhat more elaborate than plain classified advertising, but is still placed with classified advertising. Mail order sales organizations are big users of display classified advertising. The rest of the advertising is display advertising.

Strengths and Weaknesses

Magazines have some specific attractions as an advertising medium. Strengths include:

1. High audience selectivity. Except for direct mail (which is expensive), magazines offer the best opportunities for carefully selecting your audiences. Most magazines will provide you with a great deal of information about the characteristics of their readers.

2. High-quality reproduction. Magazines offer the best opportunities for making your products look good. The combination of coated, high-quality papers, printing presses, and inks can reproduce fine art, make food look mouth-watering and clothing absolutely startling. In addition, the binding operations at most magazines will permit a wide variety of inserts, special sections, and even pop-up pages and fold-outs.

3. Long physical life. Magazines are a long-life medium. People save magazines. They come back to read them again and again and give the magazines to other people when they are finished with them. These "pass-along" readers can double, even triple the size of the audience that sees your advertising, and "pass-along" readers don't cost you a cent.

4. Reader interest. The fact that readers have gone out of their way to subscribe, or to buy, the magazine is evidence of a high degree of interest in the "book" and its contents. Magazine advertising tends to receive a lot of this focused attention.

5. Upscale audiences. Magazine readers tend to be more upscale in terms of education and income than non-magazine readers.

6. Prestige. It has been a long time since counter cards and sleeve tags announced, "Advertised in *LIFE*," but the idea still thrives. Advertising in certain magazines can lend prestige and legitimacy to products and services.

Here are some of the major problems you will encounter when advertising in magazines:

1. Inflexibility. Magazines require long lead times for advertising. You will have to have your materials at the printer two or three months in advance of the actual date the readers receive the magazine.

2. Thin coverage of local markets. Although magazines may offer sizable total audiences, when those numbers are broken down to individual markets, they tend to be small. Thus, it is difficult to really support local markets using magazines.

3. Lack of urgency. Given the long lead times involved with printing magazines, the propensity of readers to save the magazines, to read them again and again, and the pass-along readership, magazines tend to be a long-term medium. Not an advertising medium subjected to hurry-up pressures.

4. High cost. All of the high-quality reproduction and careful audience selection does have a price. First, production costs are high, especially four-color ads. Second, full-page costs may simply be more than smaller budgets can afford.

STANDARD RATE & DATA SERVICE

Detailed information about the mechanical requirements of the various magazines and newspapers, as well as their advertising rates and incidental charges, may be found in volumes published by:

Standard Rate & Data Service, Inc.
3004 Glenview Road
Wilmette, Illinois 60091

SRDS publishes these manuals monthly as an up-to-the-minute source of information for media buyers, and an annual subscription is moderately expensive for planning purposes. Since you do not need a current issue, you have several alternatives: (1) you may find a set at your local business library; (2) you may ask an advertsing agency to save a set for you when a new set arrives; or (3) you may write to SRDS above and ask to buy an out-dated set.

The volumes you should read are:

• Consumer Magazine and Agri-media
• Newspapers
• Business Publications

For all practical purposes, these volumes define the advertising opportunities in magazines and newspapers.

TELEVISION

After newspapers, the next largest amount of advertising dollars is spent on television. In the United States, the television industry is organized around local stations that are privately owned and operated, under a license from the Federal Communications Commission. If the station has a contract with a network, the station is called an "affiliate." A station that does not have an affiliation is called an "independent." Affiliates sell part of their broadcast time to the network at a substantial discount. In turn, the networks provide programs for the affiliates at no cost.

Because network programs usually attract larger audiences than individual station-produced programs, the affiliate can charge higher rates for commercials it broadcasts between network programs.

Independents rely heavily on reruns of programs that originally were shown on networks and relatively inexpensive programming developed specifically for the independent station market.

When we were dealing with newspapers and magazines, we were dealing with items of substance, items that exist in space. When we turn our attention to broadcast media, we deal with items of "time" and that changes things significantly. First of all, we need additional concepts. Nobody has explained these concepts better than Paul Roth did in his 1969 book, *How to Plan Media*.

1. Penetration: Start with a theoretical universe of 100 households. Ninety-eight of these households own TV sets. TV *penetration* or set ownership is $98/100 = 98$ percent.

2. Coverage area: The TV signal of a theoretical network covers 80 TV households. The coverage area, therefore, is defined as 80 out of 98 households in the universe. This equals $80/98 = 82$ percent coverage.

3. Households using television: At 9–10 p.m., 60 TV households are watching TV. Thus, Hut = 60 out of 98 households = $60/98 = 61$ percent households using television.

4. Rating: During the 9–10 p.m. period, 20 TV households are watching a particular program. The rating of this program is 20/98 = 20. A rating point, therefore, is one percent of all the households that have a TV set.

5. Share-of-audience: During this 9–10 p.m. period, 20 households are watching TV. Therefore, this particular program's share-of-audience is 20/60 = 33 percent.

The final concept is that of *gross rating points*. Gross rating points measure broadcast advertising "weight" in a market. Gross rating points (GRPs) are calculated by multiplying the rating of the program times the number of times the commercial was shown on that program in a four-week period. Thus, a TV schedule that airs a commercial once a week on a program with a rating of 20 earns 80 GRPs. (Frequency of 4 × Rating of 20 = 80.) Gross rating points are useful in comparing widely different TV advertising schedules in different markets.

Strengths and Weaknesses

Here are some positive things to consider about television advertising.

1. Television is easy to buy. Almost all network TV advertising time is sold on a "participating" basis; that means you contract to participate in sponsoring a specific program on a negotiated schedule.

2. Television can deliver huge audiences. A typical night-time program can deliver a rating of 15, and that means that about 13 million households are exposed to the advertising on that program. The 1992 Super Bowl delivered an audience of 120 million viewers. Compare that with one of the world's most read magazine's circulation of 16.6 million (*Reader's Digest*).

3. Demonstration. If your product lends itself to demonstration, TV is impossible to beat. No other medium combines sight and sound.

4. Flexibility. You can choose to advertise during any time slot on any day of the week and you can put as many commercials in a market as you can afford.

Indeed, there are some shortcomings in television advertising.

1. Television is hard to buy. If you do not want to, or can't afford to buy television time on a network basis, then you must buy it on a "spot" basis. That means you will have to negotiate with every station on an individual basis. If you use much television, that can be a demanding task.

2. Expense. Everything about television is expensive. A typical 30-second TV commercial costs around $200,000 just to produce. Then it costs an average of $125,000 to run that commercial in prime time. If you want to use a top-rated TV program, it can cost you $300,000 to run your 30-second commercial.

3. Television is not very selective. In the Clarksburg-Weston, West Virginia TV market, a soap opera like "The Young and the Restless" will deliver an audience of 10,000 women 18 years of age or older, but it also delivers 5,000 men 18 or older. You pay for those men in the audience whether you want them or not.

4. Television is in turmoil at present. After a decade of rapidly running up prices, television broadcasting has run into price resistance and time is going unsold. This is true at all levels: network, affiliate, and independent stations. At the same time that TV revenues are down, programming costs are high and climbing. While this is going on, the networks' share of the viewing audience is falling. In the 1978–79 season, 91 percent of the television viewing audience watched network programs. Now that number is down to 63 percent. Pay TV, basic cable TV, and the independent stations are all taking viewers away from network TV.

SWISSAIR Tries Television

SWISSAIR uses the services of a New York advertising agency, DoyleGrafMabley. Agency partner Charlie Fredericks is the management supervisor for SWISSAIR, and in 1985, the client and the agency were searching for ways to strengthen SWISSAIR business in the United States. Because SWISSAIR has no domestic flights within the United States and only operates out of three gateway terminals (New York, Boston, and Chicago), this was quite a challenge.

As a beginning point, both qualitative and quantitative marketing research was conducted among international air travelers. The major finding of this work was that potential passengers viewed SWISSAIR as a very efficient carrier with superior on-board service. In short, SWISSAIR was the best way to fly to Zurich or Geneva, but hardly anyone considered the airline for travel outside of Switzerland.

Based on these results, the agency was given the assignment of building on SWISSAIR's excellent reputation and increasing awareness of the destinations served by SWISSAIR outside of Switzerland. This new approach had to work well within the day-to-day demands of the airline's need to promote specific destinations, tour packages, and the like. The new work had to complement ongoing advertising and marketing activities.

DoyleGrafMabley developed nine new concepts designed to accomplish this assignment of building on existing strength and increasing awareness of additional destinations served. Concept testing indicated that the strongest concept was, "SWISSAIR—the civilized way to the world."

To build awareness broadly and quickly, the agency recommended television. SWISSAIR's management's reaction to this recommendation was negative. They simply felt that they did not have sufficient funds available to become a television advertiser in three of America's most expensive TV markets. DoyleGrafMabley believed otherwise, and set out to develop a TV plan that supported the original objectives and was affordable.

First, they developed a series of 10-second spot announcements that focused on specific SWISSAIR destinations. Exhibit 7.2 shows six of the spots from the series. Second, they developed specific TV plans for each of the three gateway markets. These media plans were sharply focused against business travellers and used spots on "60 Minutes," local market newsbreaks, and the like. SWISSAIR management liked what they saw and ran the program in 1986.

HOW DID IT WORK?

The "SWISSAIR—The Civilized Way to See the World" television campaign reached 87 percent of the target audience and produced a frequency of 11. In fact, television increased SWISSAIR's reach by 80 percent over

EXHIBIT 7.2

SWISSAIR TAKES THE CIVILIZED WAY TO DELIVER THEIR MESSAGE

How did I get to Istanbul? The civilized way. Swissair.

How did I get to Casablanca? The civilized way. Swissair.

How did I get to Moscow? The civilized way. Swissair.

How did I get to Vienna? The civilized way. Swissair.

How did I get to Hong Kong? The civilized way. Swissair.

How did I get to Nairobi? The civilized way. Swissair.

what would have resulted if only print had been used. And those reach and frequency numbers produced some real changes in the target audience.

RESULTS OF SWISSAIR TELEVISION CAMPAIGN			
Measurement	May 1985	October 1986	Percentage Points Difference
Top of the mind awareness of SWISSAIR	17%	39%	+22
Choice for multi-destination trips	6	27	+21
Advertising awareness	10	33	+23

SWISSAIR and DoyleGrafMabley made every one of TV's strong points work for them. And, best of all, SWISSAIR's business went up over 25 percent! You can make the media work for you, too. Find the exceptions that work.

RADIO

If you had to select just one word to describe radio, it would have to be ubiquitous. Radios are everywhere! An average U.S. household has five radios and that totals well over 400 million radios. There are about 9,000 commercial radio stations (4,600 AM stations and 4,400 FM stations). Radio commercial time is perishable just like TV commercial time; as a result, both are negotiable.

Strengths and Weaknesses

As an advertising medium, radio's strong points include:

1. Radio is cheap. You can produce a good 60-second radio commercial for around $5,000 or less. Sixty-second radio spots cost a few hundred dollars, not thousands as in TV. (The most common commercial length in radio is 60 seconds in contrast with TV's 30-second commercials.)

2. Radio can be very selective. You can reach farmers with weather and crop reports, you can reach blue-collar workers in drive-time as they go to and come from work, you can reach upscale audiences on classical music stations, and you can be age specific in reaching young people.

3. You have the opportunity to use local personalities. Some disc jockeys develop loyal followers and it is usually not too difficult to get these personalities involved with your advertising.

Radio also has a few weaknesses, including:

1. Radio can be hard to buy. For example, the Los Angeles metropolitan area has seven VHF-TV stations, but the market has 80 AM and FM radio stations. As a consequence, the radio audience is fragmented; it takes many stations to build reach. Also, because the price for individual commercials is low, the stations try to sell you a lot of time ("radio is a medium of frequency") without any evidence that more than three exposures are efficient.

2. Radio is only sound. Without pictures, radio commercials can be even more ephemeral than TV. It is really important to have good execution in radio commercials.

DIRECT MAIL

After newspapers and television, direct mail appears to get the biggest allocation of the advertising investment in the United States. It is also one of the fastest growing mediums. The strengths and weaknesses of direct mail are simple and clear.

Strengths and Weaknesses

Direct mail can be the most selective of all media. You can use it to deliver virtually any message to specific individuals. With direct mail, you can even deliver product samples.

As an advertising medium, direct mail is almost always expensive on a cost per thousand basis. You will have to deal with these costs:

- Mailing list. Although the cost to rent mailing lists varies widely, many lists rent in the range from $35 to $75 per thousand. Standard Rate & Data Services also publishes a direct mail list guide.

- Materials. There is a wide range of choices here.

- Stuffing, addressing, and mailing. There are firms that specialize in these functions, but you will have to pay for it.

- Delivery. Whether your material is mailed or delivered door-to-door, or in some other way, the cost for delivery can be substantial.

OUTDOOR

This is a collection of ways to deliver an advertising message to people who are outdoors. It includes poster panels (most often thought of as billboards) with pasted paper panels; painted display boards; spectacular electronic signs; display cards inside and outside of buses, trains, trolleys, and taxi cabs; and advertising signs on bus benches, inside railway and bus terminals, and generally anywhere a creative salesperson can think of to place an advertising message in front of a prospective customer.

Strengths and Weaknesses

There are two major reasons to consider investing some of your advertising dollars in outdoor advertising. One is flexibility. You can buy one outdoor message display, or you can buy thousands of them. You can buy them in a tiny part of one market, or you can buy them in hundreds of markets around the country. Another reason is generally low cost. Not only can you buy a few locations, individual ones can be expected to cost only a few hundred dollars a month.

Outdoor advertising has one huge weak point that overshadows all other limitations or concerns. It is virtually impossible to know what you are getting for your money! First, take the question of audience. You can count the number of cars that pass any given point on the Santa Ana Freeway in Los Angeles, but how can you determine if many people saw the Pepto-Bismol board? You can count the number of people using Grand Central Station in New York, but how do you know how many people saw the Kodak sign?

Consider the question of what you got for your money. The industry has adopted a standard unit of sale called a 100 gross rating points daily showing. (These are not television gross rating points.) That is what they would like you to buy. Now consider what faces you if you do buy a 100 gross rating point daily showing in 10 markets:

Market	Number of locations to obtain a 100 gross rating showing
Atlanta	120
Denver	78
Detroit	180
Las Vegas	31
Los Angeles	480
Minneapolis/St. Paul	180
New Orleans	80
Phoenix	88
Seattle	116
St. Louis	128
	1,481

How do you verify that your message was up at each of those locations for the length of time you are paying for? To some extent, this concern is true for some other media, but nowhere does it reach the proportions of outdoor advertising.

AN EXAMPLE OF SUCCESSFUL OUTDOOR ADVERTISING

The NYNEX Yellow Pages Directories built a very high level of awareness among potential Yellow Pages advertisers and users in northeastern United States during the 1980s. They used a series of clever TV commercials that played word games with the audience.

The opening of each commercial established a premise and then added clues as the commercial progressed. At the end of the commercial, the correct answer was presented and it was shown how the answer was involved in the use of the NYNEX Yellow Pages. Finally, the whole thing was tied together in each commercial under the unifying theme, "If It's Out There, It's In Here." Exhibits 7.3 and 7.4 show the photoscripts for two of the series.

EXHIBIT 7.3

NYNEX Yellow Pages

Chiat/Day

"DUMBWAITER" :30

(SFX: OPENING CHIME. RESTAURANT SOUNDS)
MAN VO: Excuse me...
WAITER: Sir!
MAN VO: What are your specials today?
WAITER: I don't know.

WOMAN VO: Do your entrees come with salad?
WAITER: I don't know.

MAN VO: Do you have escargot?
WAITER: Escargot? (PAUSE) I don't know.

WOMAN VO: May we see a menu?
WAITER: (CONFUSED) Yes! No! I don't know.

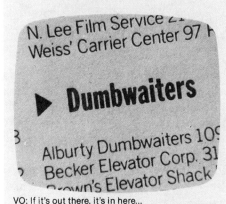

VO: If it's out there, it's in here...
(SFX: PLATES BREAKING)

VO: The NYNEX Yellow Pages.
(SFX: BOOK SLAMS SHUT)
Why would anyone need another?

EXHIBIT 7.4

NYNEX Yellow Pages

Chiat/Day

"Furniture Stripping" :30

(SFX: OPENING CHIME. AS LIGHTS GO DOWN, STRIPPER MUSIC BEGINS, CLAPPING, WHISTLING.)

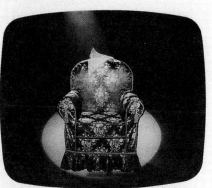

(SFX: MUSIC AND CROWD NOISE CONTINUE.)

(SFX: MUSIC AND CROWD NOISE CONTINUE; SOUND OF SPRINGS POPPING OFF.)

(SFX: MUSIC AND CROWD NOISE CONTINUE.)

VO: If it's out there, it's in here...(SFX: CAT CALL WHISTLE)

VO: The NYNEX Yellow Pages. (SFX: BOOK SLAMS SHUT) Why would anyone need another?

The Business Problem

As you know, the United States was in a recession in 1990 that was unevenly distributed across the country. Particularly hard hit were the northeastern states, NYNEX's market. By 1991, NYNEX was facing substantially reduced revenues and a number of expenditures had to be curtailed. One of them was the popular TV advertising described above.

Each year, the NYNEX Yellow Pages has roughly four months to sell directory advertising for the following year. During that sign-up/sell-in period, it is important for advertisers (prospective and current NYNEX Yellow Pages customers) to have a high awareness of the Yellow Pages as an advertising medium and to rate the Yellow Pages highly as a source of their own business.

As 1990 ended, Bernard Bloomfield, vice president of marketing, Jackie Ganim, director of advertising, and Susan Deflora, staff manager for advertising at NYNEX Information Sources began their planning for 1991. The knew they were facing the worst situation they had been in for over a decade. They needed to re-sign record levels of current Yellow Pages advertisers and sign up more new advertisers just as small- and medium-sized businesses all over the northwestern United States were going out of business. In addition, they had to get the job done with less money to spend than they had had in years.

What Happened

The management group at NYNEX turned to their advertising account group at Chiat/Day/Mojo for ideas about how to accomplish these contract signing goals. Mary Maroun, management supervisor, and Lorraine Arado, account supervisor, worked with the other members of the NYNEX group at the agency to devise an advertising plan to produce big results under difficult conditions with a minimal budget. Their basic recommendation centered on outdoor advertising. Outdoor is flexible and could support exactly those markets, and at times when NYNEX needed to deliver its advertising message. Outdoor also allowed them to work with a limited budget.

The creative content extended the popular word games that previous television advertising had made widely known. The agency created six different treatments, each consisting of two outdoor boards. The first board in the series would show a bizarre visual with no explanation (see Exhibit 7.5). This was much like the way the TV commercials opened. After two weeks, these boards were replaced with ones that identified the visual and showed it as a heading in the NYNEX Yellow Pages. Exhibit 7.6 replaced the initial showing for ''Bull Dozing.'' In another treatment, an initial board showed a large hare with blue fur. The replacement board displayed the same image with ''Hair Tinting'' as the tag line. The ''If It's Out There, It's In Here'' theme tied the outdoor advertising to the earlier TV advertising.

The Results

The advertising campaign attracted a lot of attention from other media. TV stations and newspapers throughout the Northeast covered the campaign as news. As always, however, the numbers tell the real story. Here are the crucial measures among prospective and current NYNEX Yellow Pages advertisers:

EXHIBIT 7.5

EXHIBIT 7.6

▶ **Bulldozing**

If it's out there, it's in here.

Measurement	April 1991	Sept. 1991	% Change
Aware of NYNEX advertising	62%	70%	+ 13
Aware of outdoor NYNEX advertising	32	50	+ 56
Attitudes			
Yellow Pages good for attracting potential customers	41	48	+ 17
Good value for money	28	38	+ 35
Great for generating business	22	28	+ 27
Among Prospective Advertisers			
Definitely or probably will purchase space in the Yellow Pages	46	52	+ 13
Among Current Advertisers			
Definitely will renew	55	60	+ 9

This is another example of what is true for so much of advertising. For every generalization, there is an exception. If you want to get the most bang from your advertising bucks, your job is to completely understand the generalizations and search for the exceptions because that is where the payouts are found.

YELLOW PAGES AND DIRECTORIES

A bit of history first. Before 1984, AT&T published all of the ''Yellow Pages.'' In 1984, however, the U.S. Supreme Court separated the regional operating telephone companies, AT&T, and the Yellow Pages. Today, there are over 200 publishers of over 6,500 Yellow Page Directories. (Because AT&T never bothered to copyright the term, any publisher can produce and market ''yellow pages.'')

Strengths and Weaknesses

As an advertising medium, the Yellow Pages play one of the most important parts in the purchasing decision: they tell a prospective customer where to purchase products and services. Research has demonstrated that 90 percent of all adults in the United States say they have consulted the Yellow Pages at least once in the past year and 59 percent say they consulted the Yellow Pages *last week*. Clearly, this is a widely used source of information.

Using the Yellow Pages as an advertising medium presents a few disadvantages, especially for retailers and manufacturers.

If you are a retailer, there are two difficulties in using directories as an advertising medium. One is finding the directories that match your store's trading area. As you discovered in the last chapter, an advertising dollar spent outside of your trading area is a wasted dollar. The other problem is that your funds are tied up for at least a year after you sign a Yellow Pages contract; thus, you lose a great deal of flexibility.

If you are a manufacturer trying to support your dealers with local Yellow Pages advertising, you also have two problems. One is the complexity of sorting through all of the available directories, market by market, to find the ones that really match your distribution. To give you some idea of this complexity, Exhibit 7.7 is a list of the Yellow Page directories you would need to cover the Columbus, Ohio Metropolitan Statistical Area and Exhibit 7.8 is a coverage map showing the directories available to cover the same area. If you are going to use Yellow Pages directories, you should obtain major support and assistance from their publishers. The other problem is the same as for retailers. After you sign those directory contracts, significant amounts of your advertising dollars are out of your control and tied up for long periods of time.

A Few Hints

PRINT ADVERTISING

As a rule of thumb, you can expect five times as many people to read your headline than will read your body copy. Therefore, it is important that your headline selects prospective customers and promises them a benefit. Page through any magazine or newspaper you choose and see just how few headlines do these jobs.

Also, after years of evidence that reverse type (white letters on a black background) is hard to read and reduces readership, there are still art directors that will ask you to approve reverse type ads. Do not do it.

TELEVISION ADVERTISING

The thing that you are paying the big price for in television is the pictures. You can buy just the words on radio for a lot less money. Therefore, you must make certain that the pictures work for you.

One of the first things you will be asked to approve will be a storyboard. A storyboard is a series of sketches, with copy below each picture, that is used to design the commercial. Cover up the copy on the storyboard and see if your message still comes through. If it doesn't, do not approve the storyboard.

The first five seconds of a commercial are like the headline of a print ad. That is when the prospective customers must be selected and promised a benefit. If you don't do it then, you will lose them for good. Remember the section on frequency—when a viewer sees a new commercial the first question is, "For me or not for me?"

EXHIBIT 7.7

COLUMBUS, OH MSA
YELLOW PAGES DIRECTORIES

Directory Number	Directory Name	Publisher	Distribution (000's)	Percent MSA Penetration	Percent Directory Within MSA
056145	Baltimore	GTD	9	1.5	100.0
056240	Columbus Southeast	AMP	126	8.9	100.0
056582	Circleville	GTD	17	2.7	88.5
056668	Columbus (Y)	AMP	699	78.5	100.0
056820	Delaware–Plain City	GTD	n/a	3.5	82.2
056879	Columbus Northwest	AMP	179	11.8	100.0
057099	Columbus Northeast	AMP	81	7.7	100.0
057341	Columbus Southwest	AMP	78	3.8	100.0
057535	Lancaster	AMP	57	4.4	100.0
057654	London	AMP	12	1.9	100.0
057789	Union Countywide	DA	16	1.5	92.5
057976	Mt Sterling	DA	2	0.5	100.0
058044	Newark	GTD	80	5.7	94.5
058248	Pataskala	DA	21	3.6	100.0

PROTOTYPE

EXHIBIT 7.8

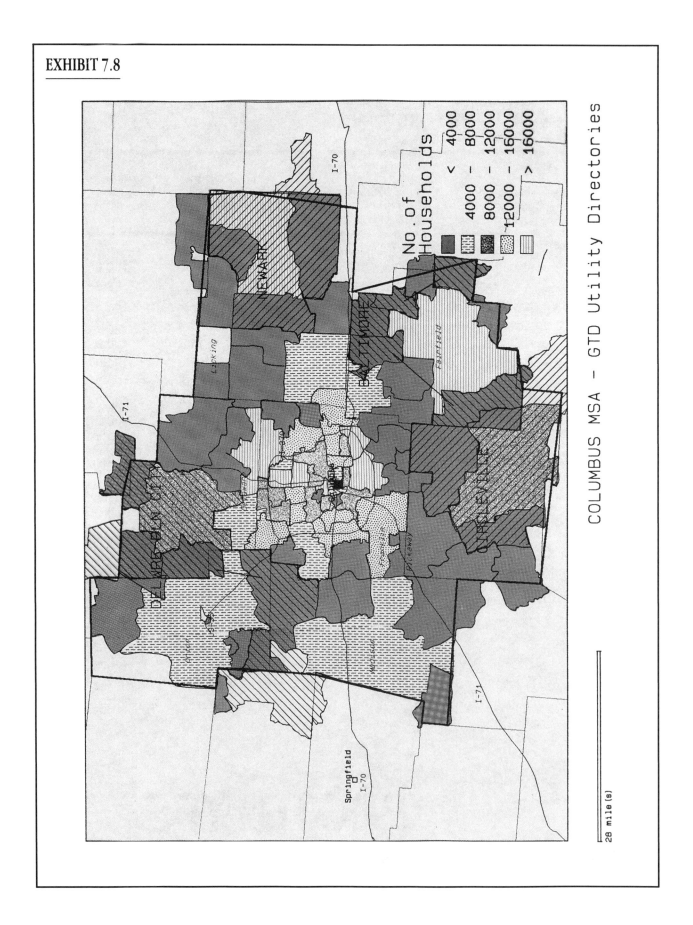

COLUMBUS MSA – GTD Utility Directories

EXHIBIT 7.8 (continued)

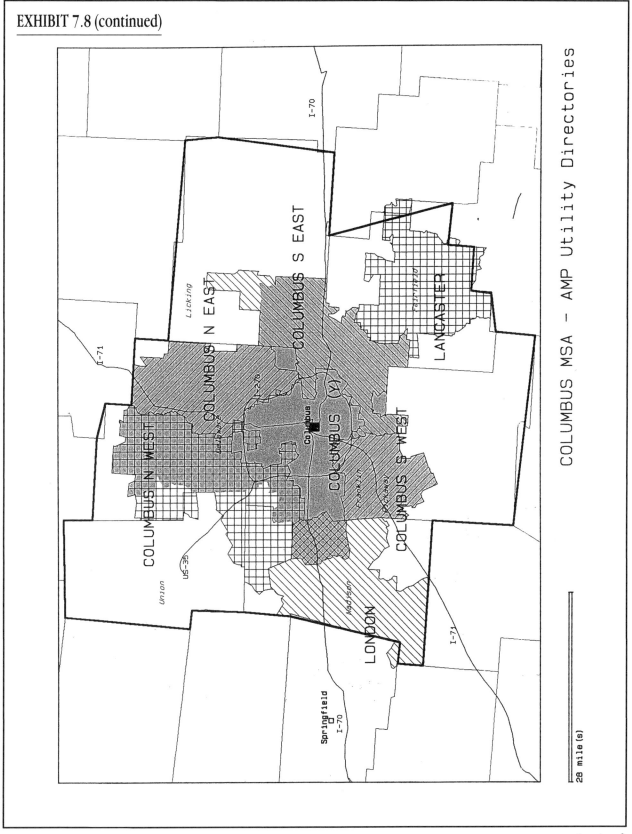

COLUMBUS MSA – AMP Utility Directories

(continued)

EXHIBIT 7.8 (continued)

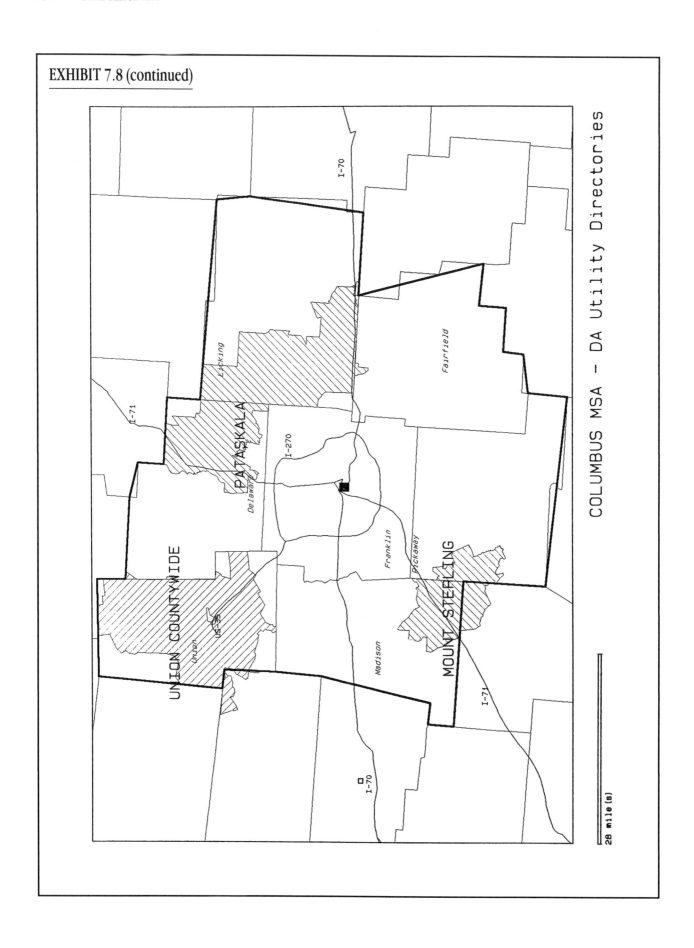

COLUMBUS MSA – DA Utility Directories

28 mile (s)

EXHIBIT 7.8 (continued)

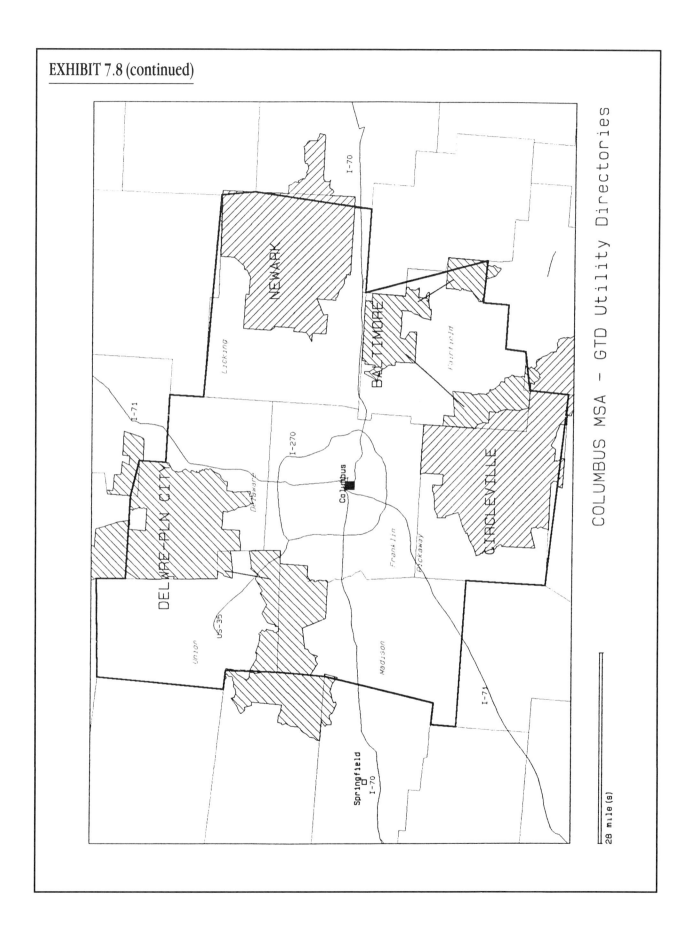

COLUMBUS MSA – GTD Utility Directories

AN EXAMPLE OF A MEDIA PLAN

Exhibit 7.9 is Yamaha's 1987 motorcycle media plan. You will notice that they invest most of their budget in the heavy buying months, each product tends to have a different type of customer, and the media choices reflect these market segments.

EXHIBIT 7.9

YAMAHA'S 1987 MEDIA PLAN

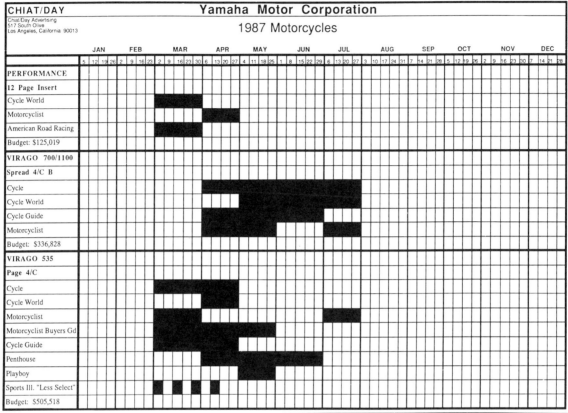

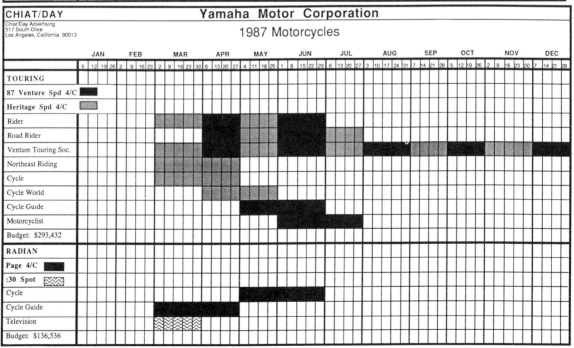

(continued)

EXHIBIT 7.9 (continued)

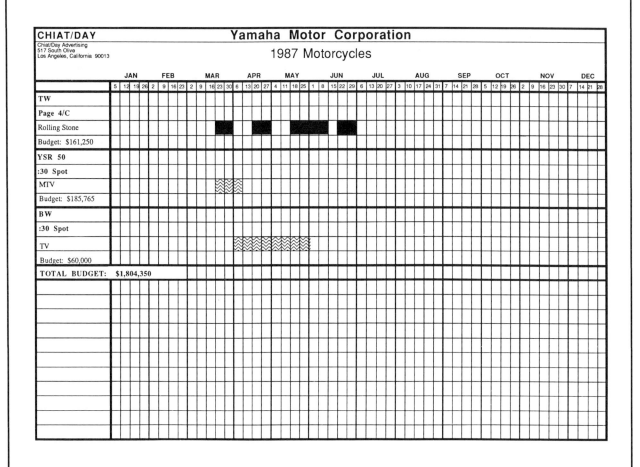

How Advertising Dollars Are Spent

Exhibit 7.10 shows a breakdown of how advertising dollars were divided among the major media in 1990.

EXHIBIT 7.10

TOTAL U.S. ADVERTISING EXPENDITURES (1990)

Rank	Medium	Volume (in millions)
1	Newspapers	$38,281
2	Television	28,405
3	Direct mail	23,370
4	Yellow Pages	8,926
5	Radio	8,726
6	Magazines	6,803
7	Outdoor	1,084
	All other	15,955

Source: McCann-Erickson

CHAPTER 8

The New Media

In this chapter we will discuss the "new media" and focus on opportunities to further reduce the "waste" circulation that you pay for that produces no results because your message is delivered to the wrong people. The driving force behind the new media is the reduction and elimination of waste circulation. That means your message is delivered to ever smaller groups of people until finally you are delivering it to "only one person" at a time.

Although things are in a state of flux among the major media, at least there are some widely known rules of thumb for making decisions there. The fundamental problem with most of the new media is that these rules for decision making don't exist. Therefore, you will have to develop your own rules. You will do that by thinking hard about what you are trying to accomplish, and then running test after test to find out what works and what doesn't.

Yes, that will be a lot harder than just signing a contract set in front of you, but you must remember that the money you are trying to save is your own money! When you develop experimental programs using the new media, you will also be learning an enormous amount about what makes your business go.

Cable TV

Broadcast television signals travel in straight lines, and in the early days of broadcasting, that presented some serious problems. Many people who lived in cities full of tall buildings could not receive a signal, nor could people who lived in hilly or mountainous areas. Anyone who lived much more than 50 or 60 miles from the transmitter couldn't receive a signal because the curvature of the earth sent the signal out into space after it had traveled that far.

To deal with this problem, companies were started that ran hard wires directly into homes so that the TV signal could be delivered by wire rather than by over-the-air transmission. To make hard wiring affordable, the cable companies had to concentrate on relatively small geographic areas. As a result, a patchwork of small areas wired by a single company sprang up all over the United States. The initial areas were those with the worst reception problems.

To continue to grow, the cable companies expanded into areas with fewer reception problems. To sign up new subscribers, the cable companies began offering more than just repeat broadcasts of network and local station programs. At first, full-length feature movies were added, then came a variety of advertiser sponsored programming, locally produced cable programming, and diversified pay-per-view programming. Later, premium services such as Home Box Office and the Disney Channel were added along with national broadcasts of single local stations, called "superstations." Ted Turner's WTBS in Atlanta was the first superstation.

The primary result of this growth pattern is that there are now over 1,000 cable TV service companies providing service to a huge collection of small geographic areas. Exhibit 8.1 shows a map of southern California where many different companies supply cable TV service in just one market. This pattern is repeated across the United States.

Today, about 55 percent of all U.S. households are wired for cable and most forecasts call for that number to reach 65 percent by the mid-1990s. Industry forecasts for the year 2000 range from 70 to 100 percent penetration.

Comcast Cablevision in Fullerton, California, is a typical cable company, serving many specific areas in southern California. Exhibit 8.2 shows the geographic areas they serve in Orange County and highlights a quality that is both a strength and a weakness of cable TV. Comcast can only deliver your advertising message within those geographic areas, and only to homes inside of those geographic areas that are Comcast subscribers. For a retail store trying to advertise only in its trading area, this geographic specificity can be a large advantage. To a national advertiser, however, trying to reach a large part of the United States at one time is a nightmare to buy.

Closely related to this problem is the question of what you actually get when you buy into a cable system. Demographics are non-existent because the audience for each system is so small that it cannot be measured economically. Add to this the fact that some cable systems can deliver as many as 50 channels for subscribers to watch (200 channels may soon be possible), and you can understand that the question of who is watching your cable TV commercial is virtually unanswerable for now.

But the unquestionable advantage of cable TV is its low cost, both for production and broadcast time. Exhibit 8.3 shows Comcast's rate card for various geographic locations. It is possible to buy a 30-second commercial to reach homes in one of the most affluent areas in the United States for as little as $25—a price worth investigating.

SO WHY BOTHER WITH CABLE TV?

Ann Bailey, senior account executive at Comcast Cablevision, has a very good answer for that question. She points out that the audience for network TV is rapidly shrinking and no end is in sight. As the audience for network TV gets smaller, the money advertisers pay the networks will shrink. With less money available, the networks will most likely reduce the quality of their programming, and audiences will continue to shrink even further. That, Bailey says, is why national advertisers should be learning how to use cable TV right now.

EXHIBIT 8.1

CABLE ADVERTISING FOR SOUTHERN CALIFORNIA

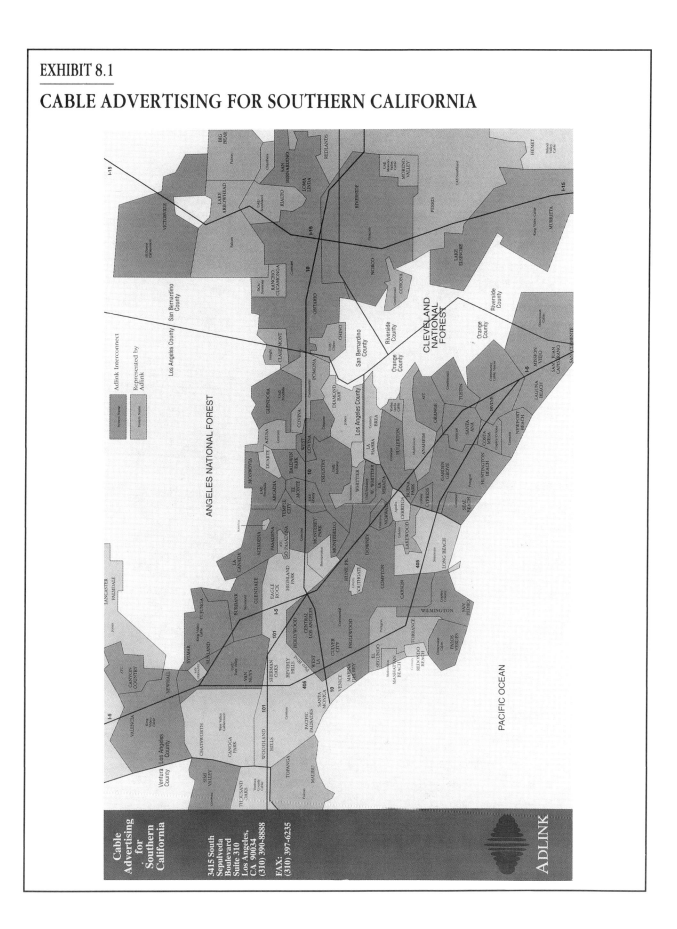

EXHIBIT 8.2

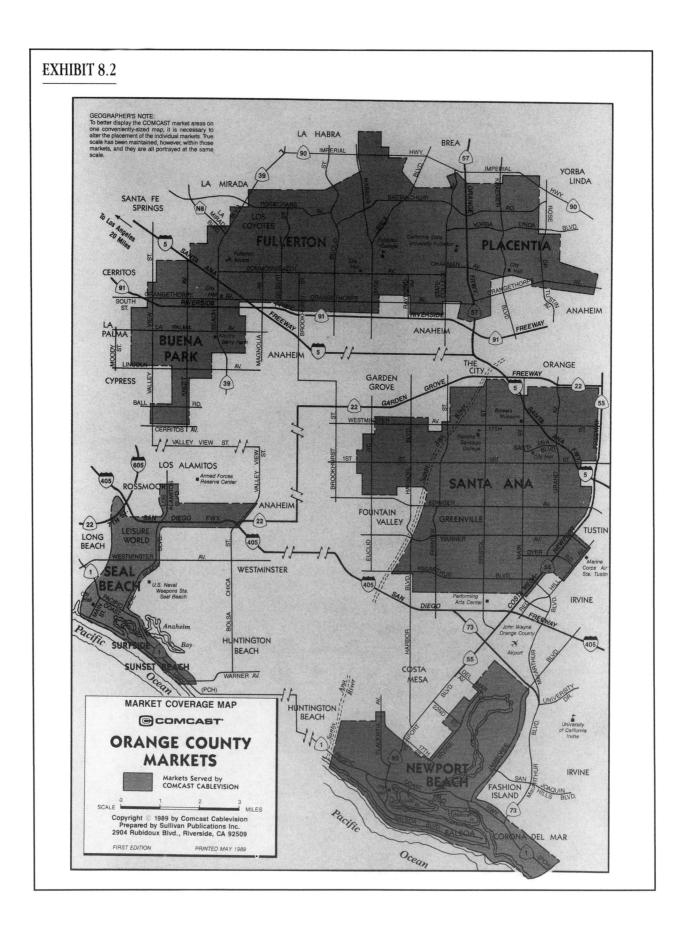

EXHIBIT 8.3

LOCATIONS & 30-SECOND RATES

	GRID I : FIXED POSITION	GRID II : PRIME ROTATION	GRID III: 6AM - 12 MID
ORANGE COUNTY	GRID I	GRID II	GRID III
CNN, ESPN, TNT, USA, PRTK	$65.00	$50.00	$35.00
MTV, A&E*, DISC*, FAM*, NICK*, LIFE*, CNBC	$55.00	$40.00	$25.00
SAN BERNARDINO	GRID I	GRID II	GRID III
CNN, ESPN, TNT, USA, PRTK	$35.00	$25.00	$15.00
MTV, A&E, DISC, FAM, LIFE, CNBC	$30.00	$20.00	$12.00
ONTARIO	GRID I	GRID II	GRID III
CNN, ESPN, TNT, USA, PRTK	$30.00	$20.00	$12.00
MTV, A&E, DISC, FAM, LIFE, CNBC	$25.00	$15.00	$10.00
SIMI VALLEY	GRID I	GRID II	GRID III
CNN, ESPN, TNT, USA, PRTK	$35.00	$25.00	$15.00
MTV, DISC, FAM, LIFE, CNBC	$30.00	$20.00	$10.00
SANTA MARIA/LOMPOC COMBO	GRID I	GRID II	GRID III
CNN, ESPN, TNT, USA	$25.00	$22.00	$18.00
MTV, DISC, FAM, LIFE, CNBC	$22.00	$20.00	$16.00

PLEASE SEE REVERSE FOR LOCATIONS AND DISCOUNT OPPORTUNITIES.
*ORANGE COUNTY NETWORKS AVAILABLE 3/92

SPECIAL NOTATIONS

1. ALL FIXED TIMES ARE SUBJECT TO AVAILABILITY.
2. RATES LISTED ARE NOT APPLICABLE TO PREMIUM SPORTING EVENTS OR OTHER SPECIAL EVENTS
   AS DETERMINED BY COMCAST.

ORANGE COUNTY
1501 W. COMMONWEALTH AVE.
FULLERTON, CA 92633
714/525-2058   FAX 714/879-3232

SAN BERNARDINO COUNTY/ONTARIO
24769 REDLANDS BLVD., SUITE D
SAN BERNARDINO, CA 92408
714/824-0520   FAX 714/796-7198

SIMI VALLEY
485 EASY STREET
SIMI VALLEY, CA 93065
805/526-0654   FAX 805/526-0832

LOMPOC/SANTA MARIA
646 NORTH "H" STREET
LOMPOC, CA 93436
805/736-3446   FAX 805/922-6794

(continued)

EXHIBIT 8.3 (continued)

13 WEEK COMMITMENT:	5% DISCOUNT	2 AREAS:	5% DISCOUNT
26 WEEK COMMITMENT:	10% DISCOUNT	3 AREAS:	10% DISCOUNT
52 WEEK COMMITMENT:	17% DISCOUNT	4 OR MORE AREAS:	15% DISCOUNT

ALL FIRST-TIME ACCOUNTS WITH NO COMCAST CREDIT HISTORY MUST PAY CASH IN ADVANCE.

ALL AGENCY AND RETAIL ACCOUNTS WITH NO COMCAST CREDIT HISTORY WILL HAVE A CREDIT CHECK WITH OTHER MEDIA TO VERIFY CREDIT.

A 15% COMMISSION WILL BE ALLOWED TO RECOGNIZED ADVERTISING AGENCIES.
NO COMMISSIONS WILL BE ALLOWED ON ACCOUNTS OVER 90 DAYS PAST DUE.

INVOICES ARE DUE AND PAYABLE WITHIN 30 DAYS, NET. A SERVICE FEE OF 1.5% PER MONTH IS CHARGED ON OVERDUE ACCOUNTS. COMCAST RESERVES THE RIGHT TO CANCEL ANY OR ALL ADVERTISERS' SCHEDULES IF THEY ARE PAST DUE 90 DAYS OR MORE.

CANCELLATIONS OF COMMERCIALS OR SCHEDULES BY ADVERTISERS MUST BE MADE TWO WEEKS PRIOR TO THAT COMMERCIAL AND/OR SCHEDULED BEGINNING. CANCELLATION OF SCHEDULES IN WHOLE OR PART BY THE ADVERTISERS WILL RESULT IN AN ADJUSTMENT OF THE RATES (SHORT RATE) BASED ON PAST AND SUBSEQUENT INSERTIONS TO REFLECT ACTUAL SCHEDULE USED AT THE EARNEST RATE.

UNLESS OTHERWISE ADVISED, ALL TAPES WILL BE KEPT BY COMCAST FOR 30 DAYS AFTER AN ADVERTISER'S SCHEDULE IS COMPLETED AND THEN REMOVED FROM INVENTORY BY WHATEVER MEANS COMCAST DEEMS APPROPRIATE.

ORANGE COUNTY, SAN BERNARDINO, ONTARIO:
    TAPE MUST BE IN BY 5PM TUESDAY TO AIR ON THURSDAY
    TAPE MUST BE IN BY 5PM FRIDAY TO AIR ON TUESDAY
SIMI VALLEY, SANTA MARIA, LOMPOC:
    TAPE MUST BE IN BY 11AM WEDNESDAY TO AIR ON MONDAY

TAPES RECEIVED AFTER THE DEADLINE WILL BE DUBBED ON THE NEXT SCHEDULED DUBBING DAY (NO EXCEPTIONS).
PLEASE SEND ALL TAPES WITH TRAFFIC INSTRUCTIONS TO:
COMCAST ADVERTISING SALES

The table below lists the top 10 cable network advertisers for 1990–1991 and suggests that some national advertisers may be listening to Ann Bailey.

Advertiser	Expenditures (in millions)
Procter & Gamble	$62.7
Time-Warner	35.4
General Motors	31.0
General Mills	30.4
Anheuser-Busch	29.2
Philip Morris	25.5
KKR	22.7
Sears	20.0
AT&T	19.2
Eastman Kodak	17.2

Bailey points out that there is also a very compelling reason for retailers to learn to use cable TV effectively. Newspapers have typically been the primary advertising support medium for retailers, but newspaper readership has been changing almost as dramatically as TV viewing.

Newspapers are caught in a double bind. Daily newspaper readership has been falling dramatically. About 70 percent of U.S. households now subscribe to a daily newspaper; this is down sharply from 100 percent from 20 years ago. Historically, newspaper readership has increased steadily with the age of the readers. This no longer seems to be true, and this failure of younger people to pick up a newspaper reading habit as they get older will simply increase the rate of decline of newspaper readership.

ONE RETAILER'S EXPERIENCE WITH CABLE TV

J. A. "Tony B" Buttacavoli learned the retail automobile business by managing an automobile dealership for Cal Worthington, a large southern California automobile dealer and something of a local TV advertising legend. In 1989, Tony B decided it was time for him to own a dealership.

When most people decide to open a new retail business, they search for locations with high demand for their product or service and limited competition. Tony B had a different idea. He began searching for an area that had superior cable TV advertising capabilities. He found what he was looking for in Fullerton, California in an area served by Comcast Cablevision, among others. Next, he located a Dodge dealership within his chosen area and began negotiations to purchase the business.

By January, 1991, Tony B had complete control of Fullerton Dodge. One of the first things he did was terminate all newspaper advertising. He replaced it with cable TV advertising (on Comcast and other cable TV companies) on a budget of $15,000 per month.

Once a week, Comcast sends a TV camera crew to Fullerton Dodge to tape commercials, which feature Tony B, the spokesman for his business. About one hour before the camera crew is scheduled to arrive, Tony B finds a quiet corner and writes down what he wants to say to prospective customers. Since there is no script for these sessions and the commercials are taped, there is no storyboard or photoscript to show you.

Since a 30-second commercial uses about six or seven seconds for an opening and the same amount of time for a close, Tony B has about sixteen seconds to get his points across. This is enough time for 30–40 words. Although he was nervous at first, practice has made Tony B much more comfortable with his on-camera role.

Fullerton Dodge sells a lot of trucks and vans, mostly to men. To reach the maximum number of men, Tony B uses sports and news programs for his commercials.

Fullerton Dodge has been using Tony B's unorthodox advertising ideas for a year now. When asked how it is working, this is what he has to say:

In January, 1991, the first full month I was running things, we sold 31 new cars and trucks and 8 used cars and trucks. We lost $43,000.

In February, 1991, the first full month of cable TV advertising, we sold 51 new units and 10 used units. We made $1,800.

In January, 1992, after a full year of cable TV advertising, we sold 88 new units and 39 used units. We made over $100,000!

His advice to other retailers considering cable TV is to be consistent and patient. Retailers are accustomed to running a sale ad in the newspaper on Friday and seeing the results in the store on Saturday. Cable TV does not work quite that fast. Tony B says, "Give your first attempt at least one month to show results."

Tony B has never lost sight of the fact that the primary rule in cable TV is experiment, experiment, experiment. He is now planning a year-long test of another cable system, KBL TV Cable Advertising, to reach a section of Orange County that Comcast and the other eight cable TV companies he now uses do not cover. Exhibit 8.4 is his plan to sell Dodge Van Conversions on the new cable system. It is worth studying.

INTERCONNECTS

Cable advertising companies recognize the complexities of buying cable TV advertising. To make it easier, some companies have banded together to create "interconnected" systems within a market. The advertiser and the advertising agency only have to deal with one interconnect to cover a market. The 20 largest interconnects in the United States, as of 1992, are shown in Exhibit 8.4 on page 188.

When Silo was introduced to the southern California market, they used Adlink as a supplementary part of their media schedule. Chuck Jacoby, national advertising director for Silo, says there is no question in his mind that the Adlink media buy brought customers into the Silo stores, but he is unable to quantify profits versus costs. This is an ongoing problem with interconnects.

Interconnect	Market Area	Number of Subscribers
New York Interconnect	New York metro area	3,487,000
Adlink	Los Angeles metro area	1,700,000
Philadelphia Cable Advertising	Philadelphia, South New Jersey, Delaware	1,200,000
Boston Interconnect	Boston	1,200,000
Greater Chicago Cable	Chicago	1,200,000
Interconnect Bay Cable Advertising	San Francisco, Oakland, San Jose	1,150,000

Connecticut Cable Corp.	Connecticut	940,000
Detroit Cable	Detroit	825,000
Interconnect Tampa Bay	Tampa, St. Petersburg	773,000
Interconnect Time-Warner City Cable Advertising	Manhattan, Brooklyn, Queens	750,000
North Carolina	North Carolina	745,300
Interconnect Cable Ad Group of South Florida	Fort Lauderdale, Palm Beach	700,900
Connecticut Cable	Hartford, New Haven	681,000
Interconnect Cable Networks	Los Angeles	675,000
Metrobase Cable	Philadelphia	673,000
Advertising Northwest Cable	Seattle	609,000
Advertising Cable AdNet-Pittsburgh	Pittsburgh	576,100
Sunrise Cable TV	Indiana	514,000
Interconnect Cable Advertising of Metro Atlanta	Atlanta	500,000
MEGA Advertising	Suburban Washington, DC	490,000

Point-of-Purchase

Another way to reduce the waste in advertising is to deliver the message closer to the time the customer actually makes the purchase. This works for you in two ways: 1) it increases the chances that your message is delivered to the "right" person, and 2) it increases the chances that your message—because of its timeliness—will be more persuasive than your competition's.

Here are two examples of how to deliver your message close to the point of purchase.

SUPERMARKETS

Companies that distribute products through supermarkets have long understood the importance of delivering a message as close to the point of purchase as possible. Over the years, they have attempted to accomplish this task by placing informational literature and coupons next to their products in the store. Exhibit 8.5 shows how the ice cream company from Chapter 1 went about that job. These are called "Take Ones" for obvious reasons.

One company that provides advertisers with an opportunity to talk to their customers near the point of purchase is Supermarket Communication Systems. They install and maintain "information" boards in more than 7,000 supermarkets around the United States. Exhibit 8.6 is an example of a Supermarket Communication System board. As you can see, public service messages and local personal ads are displayed to draw shoppers' attention to the boards.

The Adolph Coors Company sells merchandise clearly marked with its Coors brand label by allowing interested prospects to select an order form from an information board. Spiegel, one of the premier direct mail organizations, uses the system to get its expensive catalogs into the hands of interested prospects by assembling an offer combining a catalog, a merchandise certificate, and a designer tote bag. Spiegel makes it easy to order by either mailing in the order form or calling a toll-free number.

Suzanne M. Douglas, Vice President, Marketing, at Supermarket

EXHIBIT 8.4

KBL-TV Advertising Proposal
for
Fullerton Dodge

"VAN CONVERSION MADNESS"

Market Coverage: Paragon Cable/KBL-TV

Total Subscribers:	91,000
Cities Served:	Huntington Beach, Huntington Harbour, Westminster, Fountain Valley, Stanton, Garden Grove, Los Alamitos, Westminster, Midway City, Rossmoor, and Cypress.

Flight: March 9, 1992–March 7, 1993 (52 calendar weeks)
36 Weeks total on-air (3 weeks per month)

Networks: ESPN - CNN - USA

Schedule:

Network	Day	Daypart	Frequency	Cost
ESPN	TUE, WED, FRI, SUN	12 pm–12 mid	4 spots/day	$35/ea
ESPN	SAT	6 am–12 mid	4 spots/day	$30/ea
CNN	MON, THURS	4 pm–12 mid	4 spots/day	$40/ea
USA	MON–FRI	12 pm–12 mid	2 spots/day	**BONUS**
USA	SAT-SUN	6 am–12 mid	4 spots/day	**BONUS**

Total Number of Spots per Week:	46
Total Number of Spots per Month:	138
Total Number of Spots over Flight:	1656
Monthly Investment:	$3000
Average Cost Per Spot:	**$21.74**

Conditions:

1. Contract is non-cancelable.
2. Bonus spots are pre-emptible but will be made good within an equitable daypart during flight.

"The Advertising Power of Paragon"

EXHIBIT 8.5

In Store Display

"Take One" pamphlets

EXHIBIT 8.6

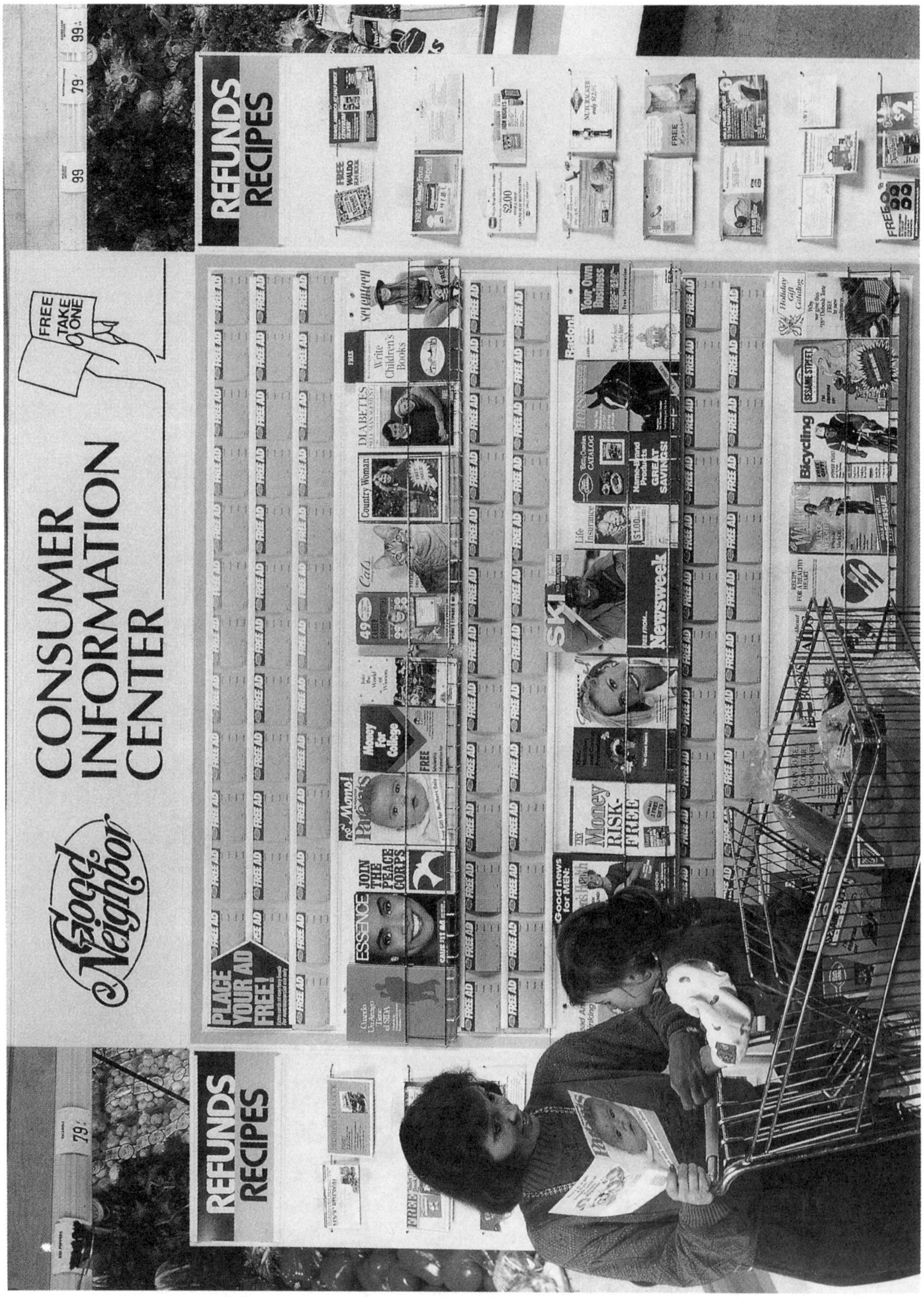
Good Neighbor
CONSUMER INFORMATION CENTER
FREE TAKE ONE
REFUNDS RECIPES
REFUNDS RECIPES
PLACE YOUR AD FREE!

Communication Systems says, "Too many media buyers and sellers still rely on the CPM (cost per thousand) when making media decisions. CPM may have been useful in the past, but today, it is simply one more source of wasted advertising dollars."

CPM ignores the most basic of all marketing facts. The only people you want to deliver your advertising message to are your customers, prospective and current. Everyone else you pay to receive your message represents wasted dollars, pure and simple! We believe that marketing people who are truly interested in maximizing their advertising investments should explore Delivered Customer Messages (DCM). DCM media comparisons often produce extremely different cost structures.

Here is an example. One of the fastest growing methods of delivering a customer message—usually a coupon—during the 1980s has been free-standing inserts (FSI), those sheets of advertising material inserted in your Sunday newspaper. An FSI in a Sunday newspaper typically costs $7–$8 CPM to deliver a coupon into the hands of customers. Redemption rates seldom exceed 2–2.5 percent, however. That means the advertiser is really spending something like $7.50 to reach 22 real customers, for a DCM of $0.34 per customer. Direct mail costs are even higher, which is one of the factors driving the growth in FSIs.

A much better value is available from Supermarket Communication Systems. They provide space for an advertiser's literature in one of their Good Neighbor Consumer Information Centers for about $3.50 per month. It is typical for a general interest subject like nutrition to have 50 interested, motivated customers select the advertiser's sales message from a Consumer Information Center in a typical month. This means that an advertiser who uses it to reach customers can do the job for about 7 cents each, a DCM of $0.07.

Douglas points out that Supermarket Communication Systems makes the primary characteristic of the new media maximum effectiveness at minimum cost—available to every advertiser who sells products in supermarkets. For more information, give them a call at (203) 852-0888.

THE ULTIMATE POINT-OF-PURCHASE MESSAGE

Until recently, laminated windshields (windscreens) were not required on automobiles or trucks in the United Kingdom. When a stone, or other object, strikes an unlaminated piece of glass it simply shatters. When the windshield shatters, the motorist is pretty much out of business right on the spot. This led to a large business of roadside replacements performed by individual owners of repair trucks.

The sequence would go something like this. You are driving along an English road and a stone from a passing truck shatters your windscreen. You pull over immediately and pick out as much of the broken glass as you can. Then you drive slowly and carefully to the nearest telephone. There you find the number of some repair service, call them and tell them your location, and then wait for someone to arrive and replace your windscreen.

Belron International BV is the parent organization of Autoglass, and is the world's largest player in the Automotive Replacement Glass (ARG) market. One of the ways they have achieved this preeminent position is through clever use of point-of-purchase materials.

Here is the business problem. Every motorist on the road in the United Kingdom is a potential customer but, on average, a windscreen is broken

EXHIBIT 8.7

BROKEN WINDSCREEN?

If you have a comprehensive Policy, you simply produce your 'Certificate of Insurance' and only have to pay the Policy Excess if applicable.

DIAL DIRECT FREE **0800 36·36·36**

AUTOGLASS

INDEPENDENT
INSURANCE COMPANY LIMITED

BROKEN WINDSCREEN, BODYGLASS

A Replacement and Repair Service is available through Autoglass and Glass Medic

AUTOGLASS

GLASS MEDIC

You only need to produce your current Certificate of Insurance and pay any Excess and V.A.T. applicable. Other policyholders will be allowed a 30% DISCOUNT ON STANDARD STOCK ITEMS, provided payment is received at the time of replacement.

DIAL DIRECT FREE
0800 36·36·36

ACCIDENT?
Accident Recovery and Repair Service
In the event of an accident where you require towing and you have Comprehensive Insurance
DIAL DIRECT FREE
0800 234 234
ALWAYS CARRY YOUR CERTIFICATE OF INSURANCE

CORINTHIAN
MOTOR POLICIES AT LLOYD'S

M521 8/91

BROKEN WINDSCREEN?
30% DISCOUNT
Autoglass will reinstate your windscreen allowing a 30% discount to standard stock items.
You must pay on the spot by cash, cheque (with bankers card) or credit card.
If your vehicle is comprehensively insured with us we will refund the cost subject to the policy conditions, provided that the new windscreen is of a similar type to the one broken.
Simply send your Autoglass receipt to your broker or to us, quoting your certificate number.
Dial direct FREE
0800 36·36·36
AUTOGLASS
ALWAYS CARRY YOUR CERTIFICATE OF INSURANCE

A.L.S. Motor Policies at Lloyd's

AUTOGLASS
TROPHY

WINDSCREENS
SIDE & REAR WINDOWS
DIAL 0800 36·36·36 24 HOUR SERVICE
AUDIO REPLACEMENT
RINGMARK SECURITY ETCHING
GLASS MEDIC WINDSCREEN REPAIR

M.926 8/91

only once every seven years. Twenty-four hour service must be provided seven days a week. And you basically never have a repeat customer because the chances for breaking a windscreen in the same location are *very* small. So how do you get your message and telephone number to a potential customer exactly when they need it? Here is how Autoglass does it.

Every year, British motorists must obtain a certificate of safety and emissions by having the automobile inspected and paying a road tax of about £100 (about $170). This certificate comes in the form of a paper disc and must be displayed prominently on the windscreen. Autoglass developed a simple, easy-to-use disc holder. Exhibit 8.7 shows examples of these simple, but obviously effective, point-of-purchase devices. They put Autoglass's telephone number right at the point of purchase!

But simply developing the disc holder was hardly enough to make inroads into the ARG, dominated by gypsy truck drivers. Autoglass had to develop a sophisticated computer system to direct their repair trucks to locations throughout Great Britain once the toll-free calls were received. They also had to distribute the holders. To do this, they developed consistent pricing policies, direct billing procedures, and standardized service programs to make it easy for insurance companies and motorists to do business with Autoglass. The insurance companies then distributed the personalized disc holders to their policyholders.

The introduction of laminated windscreens in the late 1980s has begun moving the ARG business off the side of the road and into Autoglass shops. The system works just as well with scheduled appointments in shops. It also works well with the increasing number of windows broken by vandals and thieves in major cities.

Belron International BV is now using its marketing and management skills to grow its ARG business in Germany, Italy, Portugal, The Netherlands, Belgium, France, Australia, South Africa, and the United States. Who knows—they may fix your next broken windshield.

Database Marketing

Probably the best way to approach this whole subject area is to think back to the earlier times of direct mail advertising. Profits came from doing two things successfully at the same time. One was to present your product or service to the prospective customer. That was accomplished with the headline, body copy, and illustrations in the letter, brochure, or insert (the "package") that was mailed to the prospect. Different configurations of the package could produce different levels of sales.

The other part of the equation involved the direct mail list that was used for mailing the package. Just as different packages could produce different sales results, so could different mail lists. The idea was to select lists that contained the best prospects for your product or service. That was usually hard to do, however, so direct mail testing of lists became almost mandatory.

The next improvement in direct mail list selection involved "qualifying" the list. That meant using some additional criteria to judge the appropriateness of the prospects on the list. In the early days of direct mail, the most important piece of qualifying information that could be had about a prospect is that they had previously purchased something by direct mail.

That information demonstrated that this person was willing to trust sending money to some unknown merchant at some distant location. The use of charge cards in direct marketing has removed virtually all of the risk in buying by mail.

Now we are ready to explore current database marketing. The present-day capabilities of computers to process huge amounts of information quickly and cheaply now allow for much more sophisticated qualifying of prospects. Income, age, family composition, and other straightforward demographic characteristics were the first additions. Lifestyle characteristics are the latest addition to qualifying characteristics. Exhibit 8.8 shows Equifax's approach to gathering lifestyle data through direct mail solicitation. Exhibit 8.9 is a typical product registration form that Kenwood uses to gather data about customers who have purchased any of the company's consumer electronics products.

These sophisticated qualified lists are now called "databases." The information comes from a number of sources. Some compile names and addresses directly out of the telephone book, some run lengthy consumer surveys that are distributed by mail, or in Sunday supplements to newspapers.

When consumers respond by completing and returning the survey, they are added to the list. Some companies make inferences about individual households because of the characteristics of their neighborhoods. A lot of data can come from customer records. Credit reporting agencies, for example, have extensive files of data on individual households. And, as you can imagine, some questions concerning invasion of privacy are raised here, and many have yet to be settled. Of those issues that have been resolved, all have been settled on the side of individuals' right to privacy—a good sign.

American Express (AMEX) is a long-time builder and user of databases. As you can imagine, AMEX has a great deal of information about its credit card customers and the way they spend their money. Much of AMEX's use of its database is to support its travel agency business. It is likely that a cardholder with a record of purchases in the Caribbean will receive mail from AMEX promoting Caribbean vacations. Their next step is using the database capabilities to sell other companies on participating in these promotions. Airlines and hotels are obvious prospective partners. American Express is so committed to database marketing that in 1990 they bought a company, Epsilon, that specializes in managing computer databases.

Now other companies with files on purchasing behavior are building databases to sell to other companies. Citicorp is a major player through their Citicorp POS Information Services. To expand information in their databases, Citicorp makes deals with supermarkets to gain access to their scanner data.

MATCHBOX COLLECTIBLES

Procter & Gamble, MCI Communications, AT&T, Walt Disney, Kimberly-Clark, Pepsi-Cola, Hallmark, Coca-Cola, and Philip Morris are all known to be serious database users. Although database building and maintenance are expensive, they are not limited to big companies. Here is an example of how a small, direct mail specialist in Australia built a very successful business on a database program.

Matchbox International manufactures, imports, wholesales, and licenses its products in the United States, the United Kingdom, Europe, Hong Kong, Japan, New Zealand, and Australia. Although they deal in a

EXHIBIT 8.8

Get more for your money and less for your trashcan!

I ACCEPT

Get 3 Months' Charter Membership Absolutely FREE!

BUYER'S MARKET CUSTOMER PREFERENCE PROFILE

[PLACE STICKER HERE] **YES,** enroll me as a Free Charter Member of new BUYER'S MARKET. Send my first $50 worth of BUYER'S MARKET Discount Certificates and start my subscription to new *BUYER'S BULLETIN.* During my three-month Free Charter Membership, send me an introductory copy of the members-only newsletter, include me in the extended warranty and buyer's protection coverage* and send me $50 more Discount Certificates for a total of $100. Then and only then, send me a bill for one year's Charter Membership for only $15. If I am not interested, I will write "CANCEL" across the bill, return it and owe nothing. If I decide to join, I could save hundreds of dollars a year. And if BUYER'S MARKET does not work for me, I can always cancel for an immediate and unquestioned pro-rated refund.

SEND NO MONEY NOW!

YOUR ASSURANCE OF CONFIDENTIALITY

The information you provide by completing this Checklist will be kept confidential.

Your answers will be used by Buyer's Market solely to help you receive more money-saving offers from participating merchants for products and services you want—and less for those you don't want.

Buyer's Market is a nationwide consumer group sponsored by Equifax Consumer Direct.

PREFERENCE CHECKLIST

Check "thumbs up" and receive more mail that interests you. Check "thumbs down" and Buyer's Market will advise participating merchants that you prefer no mail in that category. To enjoy all the money-saving, time-saving benefits of Membership, complete and mail this Checklist today!

YOUR PERSONAL INTERESTS For each item, please check the "Thumbs Up" column if you're interested in special offers and information. Check "Thumbs Down" if you prefer not to receive mail in this category.

CLOTHING/ACCESSORIES
Women's
Men's
Children's
Shoes/Boots
Lingerie
Cosmetics
Jewelry

FINANCIAL
Investments
Insurance
Financial Planning

HEALTH
Medical Products & Services
Vitamins/Health Foods
Diet/Nutrition

HI-TECH
Personal Computers
Stereo Equipment
Electronics

HOME
Antiques
Collectibles
Cookware & Kitchen Accessories
Furniture
Greeting Cards/Stationery
Home Appliances
Home Furnishings
Housewares
Tools/Home Workshop
Toys

LEISURE & HOBBIES
Books
Mysteries
Non-Fiction
Novels
Science Fiction
Decorative Crafts
Gardening
Gourmet/Food Specialties
Magazines
Computers
Entertainment/Personalities
Fashion
Home
Men's
News/Public Affairs
Sports
Technology
Travel
Women's
Needlecrafts
Photography
Records, Tapes, CDs
Sports
Participating
Watching
Travel
U.S.A.
Foreign
Videos
Children's
Entertainment
Self-Help

YOUR USE OF COUPONS For each of the following product categories, please tell us whether or not you would like to receive discount coupons.

Baby Products
Baking/Cooking
Beer/Wine/Liquor
Beverages
Breads/Bakery
Candy/Snacks/Chips
Cereal
Cookies/Crackers
Dairy

Fast Food
Frozen/Refrigerated
Hardware
Health/Beauty Aids
Household Products
Paper/Plastic/Aluminum
Pet Foods/Prepared Foods
Processed/Canned Foods
Smokers' Products

NEW PRODUCT PREFERENCES When you think about buying products and services, are any of the following traits Important or Unimportant to you?

High technology
Environmentally Responsible
Gourmet
Low fat/low calories

Mail this completed form in postpaid envelope to: **Buyer's Market** 801 Pennsylvania Avenue, N.W. Suite 350 Washington, D.C. 20004

YOUR PURCHASING PLANS Thinking about your plans for the next 12 months, check the appropriate box if you may consider a purchase in the following categories. Check the "Thumbs Down" column if you are unlikely to make a purchase.

May consider purchase within...	3 months	6 months	9 months	12 months
AUTOMOTIVE				
Family Car	□	□	□	□
Performance Car	□	□	□	□
Luxury Car	□	□	□	□
Truck or Van	□	□	□	□
TRAVEL				
Foreign Trip	□	□	□	□
Trip in U.S.A.	□	□	□	□
REAL ESTATE				
Residence	□	□	□	□
Vacation Home	□	□	□	□
Rental Property	□	□	□	□
Investment	□	□	□	□
FINANCIAL SERVICES				
Insurance				
Life	□	□	□	□
Medical	□	□	□	□
Auto	□	□	□	□
Homeowner's	□	□	□	□
Property & Casualty	□	□	□	□
Investments				
Open Money Market Account	□	□	□	□
Invest in CDs	□	□	□	□
Invest in an IRA	□	□	□	□
Invest in Stock, Bonds, Mutual Funds	□	□	□	□
Credit				
Apply for Mortgage or Home Equity Line	□	□	□	□
Apply for Auto Loan	□	□	□	□

ABOUT YOU... Understanding more about you will help BUYER'S MARKET better direct product and service information of interest to you. This section is optional and all information is treated confidentially.

YOUR AGE
□ Under 21   □ 45–54
□ 21–24   □ 55–64
□ 25–34   □ 65 or
□ 35–44   older

INCOME
□ Under $10,000
□ $10–$24,000
□ $25–$49,000
□ $50–$99,000
□ $100,000 or more

MARITAL STATUS
□ Single   □ Divorced
□ Married   □ Widowed

HOME OWNERSHIP
□ Own home
□ Rent

LENGTH OF RESIDENCE
□ Less than 1 year
□ 1 to 5 years
□ 6 to 10 years
□ Over 10 years

SIZE OF HOUSEHOLD
□ One
□ Two
□ Three
□ Four or more

CHILDREN BY AGE (Enter Number)
____ Under 2 years
____ 2 to 5 years old
____ 6 to 10 years old
____ 11 to 15 years old
____ 16 to 18 years old

PERSONAL COMPUTER
Do you have a computer at home?   □ Yes □ No
Does it have a modem?
   □ Yes □ No
Do you use a computer at work?   □ Yes □ No
Does it have a modem?
   □ Yes □ No

*Some conditions and restrictions apply.

CL4A

Thank You.

EXHIBIT 8.8 (continued)

NO POSTAGE
NECESSARY
IF MAILED
IN THE
UNITED STATES

BUSINESS REPLY MAIL
FIRST CLASS MAIL   PERMIT NO. 18316   WASHINGTON DC

POSTAGE WILL BE PAID BY ADDRESSEE

BUYER'S MARKET

PO BOX 96845
WASHINGTON DC 20077-7161

EXHIBIT 8.9

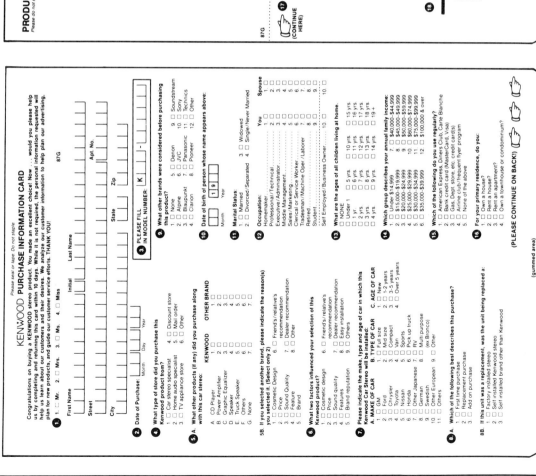

number of toys and games, the little matchbox cars that you are probably familiar with have been one of the mainstays of their business for over 40 years. Matchbox cars are sold through a variety of retailers and have their sales peak at Christmas. The company supports its retailers with a wide array of television and print advertising during the peak selling period.

In Australia, Matchbox Toys also markets a line of special model cars and trucks. The "Models of Yesteryear" are pre-WWII models and "The Dinky Collection" covers 1945 and later. They retail for $15 to $19, but some special models can sell for up to $79.95. These models are extremely well-crafted and packaged. As you can imagine, these are *not* toys for little children.

At first, Matchbox Toys Australia tried to sell this line through its usual distribution channels, but met with little success. In 1989, Matchbox International asked Alan Maclean, Rankin Direct Pty. Ltd., Australia, to develop a marketing program suitable for the products in Australia.

MacLean began by studying all of the records that Matchbox Toys Australia maintained about its Australian business. Three conclusions emerged: 1) the customers appeared to be men aged 20 to 50; 2) the customers did *not* shop in department stores nor did they shop in specialist toy stores (they did, however, appear to patronize specialist hobby stores); and 3) there was entrenched competition at both ends of the price range, from plastic models (five for $19.95) to the Franklin Mint's model collection ($125 each).

MacLean's advice was to throw out the existing program and start all over. Matchbox's Australian management agreed and started by withdrawing the collectible line from all of the existing outlets. They then appointed 15 hobby shops in Australia's main cities as exclusive Matchbox Collectibles Centres with the stipulation that these stores trade in *second hand models.* If the investment potential of these models were to be promoted, there had to have been an accessible marketplace.

Next, they ran a split-run newspaper test to determine which position was the strongest, "Collecting is a fun hobby," or "The investment potential of collecting." (Exhibits 8.10 and 8.11 show these two ads.) Approximately two-thirds of the responses supported the position of building up a collection and having fun doing it. As a result, the basic customer benefit became, "An affordable, ongoing hobby," and a new company, Matchbox Collectibles Pty. Ltd., was organized to focus this new direction.

To develop a database, they began with a list of 7,000 names of people who subscribed to the Matchbox International Collectors Association. Many of these people were already buying the collectibles in stores, so little additional sales growth was expected here. The importance of this list was that it provided a base for starting database development. The split-run test and a series of small space ads that were run in newspapers throughout Australia developed additional inquiries. By Christmas 1989, the database consisted of 30,000 names (6,000 previous customers and 24,000 prospects from leads).

For the first time, a pre-Christmas catalog was developed that presented the entire range of models. The models that were no longer available were highlighted with the message, "Look what you have missed out on by not buying when you had the first chance. Buy now before what is left sells out!! Or you could have to pay higher prices on the collectibles market."

The Christmas campaign results delighted Matchbox Toys Australia. The response from the mailing was a whopping 12.7 percent. That produced gross sales of $215,465 from 3,699 orders.

EXHIBIT 8.10

EXHIBIT 8.11

In 1990, Rankin Direct mailed a questionnaire to extend their knowledge about the database. They asked for information on topics such as:

* How long have you been collecting Matchbox cars?

* How many do you have now?

* Do you collect other things in addition to model cars?

* Are you satisfied with our service level?

* Demographic information

* Newspaper and magazine readership

All of the results were entered into the database.

Maclean understands the importance of experiment, experiment, experiment when it comes to using the new media. He says, "Research results were cross-referenced against measured results from previous advertising. The database correlation proves yet again the unsurpassed power of measurable direct marketing linked to a customer database. The products people claim they want to buy or collect are seldom what they actually part with money for. The magazines and newspapers they claim they read are not the publications that generate maximum replies at the lowest cost. Motoring magazines 'bomb' nearly every time when we run an advert, but prospects will telephone in if they read about us in the editorial. Women's general interest magazines pull best, but the coupons are filled out by men! You figure it out."

A small aside about this successful program: The North American Division of Matchbox International tried to use the Australian program in the U.S., but they made several major mistakes. For one, they failed to recognize the full value of a customer in a database over the whole life of the customer. For another, they concentrated only on direct sales and ignored inquiries that could have built their database. They also failed to remove the products from existing distribution, or to create Collectible Centres to develop a secondary market for second-hand models.

And finally, by the time the agency was finished, it was impossible to distinguish the advertising for Matchbox Collectibles from the Franklin Mint advertising. They felt that the original Australian advertising was not creative enough. Apparently, the "Not Invented Here" (NIH) syndrome did in the U.S. version. The whole program folded in less than a year.

Does that sound familiar to you? If not, return to Chapter 1 and re-read the words, "Don't ever let your agency talk you into something against your better judgment!"

Frequency Marketing

A good rule of thumb in marketing is that 20 percent of your customers will account for 80 percent of your sales. It is based on the work of turn-of-the-century Italian economist, Vilfredo Pareto, and has come to be called the Pareto effect. If you haven't already done so, this might be a good time to stop and check your own business to see just how closely the Pareto effect applies.

In every business, there are a limited number of customers who provide the majority of the sales. These relatively few customers are valuable to your business because they provide you with a disproportionate amount of your profit. Therefore, you should take good care of them and communicate with them regularly. Retaining one of these frequent, or heavy, users is usually much more profitable than obtaining a half dozen average new customers.

The way to do that is to add a characteristic to your database: frequency of use. Otherwise, you may have a database comprised only of heavy users. The airlines were among the earliest businesses to recognize their best customers. The frequent flyer programs have been smashing successes. If you are like most, an important decision about your last business trip was in which frequent flyer program you wanted to log miles.

Many other businesses have also set up programs to deliver special value to their best customers. Here are some examples.

GATEWAY FEDERAL

This savings & loan bank operates five locations in Cincinnati. They started their "Statesman's Club" back in 1972. Basic membership is maintained by keeping a minimum of $10,000 on deposit, and allows entry into the "Club Room" where 26 different services are available. These include free checking, money orders, traveler's checks, guest lectures, card games, social gatherings, complimentary refreshments, and private offices that can be reserved.

Club members average $25,000 in deposits versus about $7,000 for the average Gateway depositor. When you remember that gaining deposits at a low cost is half of the equation for profits in that business, their Club Members are a very impressive group.

VON'S GROCERY COMPANY

Von's is a leading southern California food marketer that operates several hundred supermarket stores. Its management has studied the market in southern California carefully. They have decided that the best way to differentiate their stores in this competitive market is to design a new specialty store that caters to upscale customers, but still serves all of their needs. To accomplish this task, they decided to build all new stores, using this concept, under the name, "Pavilions." Pavilions are large stores that contain dozens of specialty stores under one roof. A typical Pavilions store carries 45,000 items. The stores are decorated in a contemporary fashion and stress nutrition and value in their products.

Von's has taken the typical supermarket check-cashing prior authorization applications as a point of departure and created PAVILIONS VALUE PLUS CLUB to tie their best customers more closely to the stores. To become a member, you must complete an application form that is also the information required to pre-authorize personal checks (see Exhibit 8.12). There is no charge to the customer for joining the Club. By using your Value Plus Club Card at the check-out stand, Club members are entitled to additional discounts on a wide variety of items.

Although it is not specifically part of the Value Plus Club, Pavilions also distributes a catalog so customers can telephone or fax in their orders for later pick-up or delivery (for a fee). In addition to the regular grocery items, customers can order completely prepared dinners for one.

EXHIBIT 8.12

QUESTIONS AND ANSWERS YOU MAY HAVE ABOUT

How do I get my instant Club savings?
Select any of the items on the monthly product list. Then, when you go to check out, simply swipe your ValuePlus Club/VonsChek card through the VonsChek terminal. It will automatically deduct your ValuePlus Club savings from your total purchases. On your register tape, you will see a summary of the total ValuePlus Club savings.

What if I swipe my card after they have rung up my order?
While it is best to swipe your card before the order is rung up, the computer will still give you your discounts if your Club identification card is swiped after the checker has started ringing up your groceries. But you must swipe your card before you have paid for your purchases.

If your Club identification is swiped in the middle or at the end of the checkout process, your register tape will not list the Pavilions ValuePlus Club savings separately for each item. Instead, it will summarize the total ValuePlus Club savings for your order.

Should I swipe my Pavilions ValuePlus Club card even though I don't think I have any ValuePlus Club items in my shopping cart?
Yes! If you use your card every time you shop, you will not miss out on any savings. You might not have noticed the ValuePlus Club sign when you picked up the product or the sign may have fallen off the shelf. Using the card every time insures that you will get the instant savings.

How many ValuePlus Club items can I purchase?
Each time you shop, you can get instant savings on multiple purchases of each product on the list, unless a specific limit is stated.

Where can I find the ValuePlus Club monthly shopping lists?
The ValuePlus Club monthly shopping lists are available in the store. In addition, Pavilions ValuePlus Club items are clearly marked on the shelves and throughout the store.

(continued)

EXHIBIT 8.12 (continued)

Are Pavilions ValuePlus Club savings doubled?

NO! The Pavilions ValuePlus Club savings is the actual amount which will be deducted at checkout. But, unlike paper coupons, most ValuePlus Club savings can be used more than once!

What about double paper coupons?

Pavilions ValuePlus Club members can still use paper coupons. If a paper coupon is presented for an item which is a Pavilions ValuePlus Club item on the monthly shopping list, Club members will get the BEST DEAL... either the doubled paper coupon savings *or* the *regular* coupon value plus the Pavilions ValuePlus Club savings.

Item	ValuePlus Savings	Paper Coupon	The Best Deal	You Save
Sara Lee Pound Cake	30¢	25¢	ValuePlus Savings Plus Paper Coupon	55¢
Skippy Peanut Butter	25¢	25¢	ValuePlus Savings Plus Paper Coupon	50¢
Coca-Cola	25¢	30¢	Double Paper Coupon	60¢

Since my Club identification is on my VonsChek card, do I have to pay by check when I use the ValuePlus Club?

No! Even though your Club identification is on your VonsChek card, the ValuePlus Club is not connected with your method of payment for your purchase. You may pay via cash, check, or electronic check as you normally choose to do. **The ValuePlus Club is equally convenient for members paying with cash.** When you pay with cash, remember to swipe your card and push the **blue** ValuePlus Club Benefits key on the VonsChek terminal.

What if I move?

If you move, just fill out a change of address form at your local Pavilions store. It will let us know where to send you any special mailings informing you about new ValuePlus Club offers. Often these mailers will include personalized Bonus Certificates for dollar savings to help you discover the many departments and services Pavilions has to offer.

WALDENBOOKS

The second largest chain of bookstores in the United States, the company began its "Waldenbooks Preferred Reader" program in 1990. Nearly four million customers have signed up, each paying a $5.00 membership fee. In return for their fee, members get 10 percent discounts on books, 5 percent rebates on other purchases, automatic check approval, toll-free ordering and a variety of other services. By 1991, thirty-five percent of the chain's revenue came from Preferred Readers.

All of the new media are just waiting to help you get more results from your advertising budget. But the rules for how to use the new media are few and far between. So the best advice seems to be:

- Think carefully about what you want to do

- Plan experiments carefully

- When you get the results, think it through all over again

CHAPTER 9

Advertising Budgeting and Measuring Results

The purpose of advertising is to increase sales. Presumably, those increased sales will return increased revenues greater than the advertising costs associated with increasing the sales volume. Therefore, a short review of the nature and behavior of costs is a good beginning to the difficult subject of establishing budgets.

Basic Cost Concepts

All businesses incur costs. What those costs are, however, varies widely among different businesses. Some costs come from the production of goods or services that the business sells. Raw materials, semi-finished goods, subassemblies, and labor are production costs. Some costs are incurred by the selling and marketing of the firm's goods and services. Warehousing, transportation, sales commissions, and advertising are marketing costs. Other costs involve the processes that enable the firm to produce its goods or services. Heat, rent, electricity, insurance, and taxes are process costs. The point is, that varying levels of business activity affect costs, both individually and collectively, and the purpose of advertising is to increase those levels. Depending on their short-term behavior, costs can be sorted into two classifications: variable and fixed.

VARIABLE COSTS

Some costs vary in direct proportion to the level of business activity. For instance, when production doubles, raw material costs also double, and when production drops in half, raw material costs also fall to half. Variable costs display this kind of proportionate increasing and decreasing behavior as overall business activity varies.

In real life, however, there are few variable costs. For example, the raw materials you use may have a minimum order quantity that is larger than your initial production requirements. Therefore, your raw materials costs at lower levels of production would not vary proportionately. At high levels of production, you may have to add second shift workers that will not be as productive as your first shift workers because they are less experienced and/or skilled. In this situation, labor costs frequently rise faster than production.

Accountants use the idea of *relevant range* to deal with this insensitivity of cost behavior at very low and very high levels of production. By definition, the relevant range is the range of output over which costs are proportionate, or directly variable.

FIXED COSTS

Fixed costs remain the same regardless of the level of business activity. Suppose you lease your plant and equipment for an annual payment of $100,000. Each year, you pay the landlord $100,000 whether you produce 2,500 units or 25,000 units, or no units at all for that matter. Your lease costs are not responsive to volume output level—they are fixed.

The important point is that fixed costs behave differently than variable costs. Per unit variable costs do not change as output levels change, but per unit fixed costs do change. Look at the example below to see this effect. The variable costs are for materials and labor, and total $4.00 per unit.

	Production Level	
	2,500 Units	25,000 units
Per unit variable costs (material and labor)	$ 4.00	$ 4.00
Per unit fixed costs (plant and equipment lease)	40.00	4.00
Per unit total costs	$44.00	$ 8.00

Some managers have been known to observe the effects in the example above in their own costs and, based on that observation, come to the conclusion that they are reducing their costs. Wrong. In the example above, materials and labor still cost $4.00 per unit and the landlord must still be paid $100,000 annually. All that has happened is that per unit costs have fallen because of higher output levels.

This is a trap that exists with advertising costs as well. You can drive CPM down without affecting total advertising costs at all.

The Break-Even Point

The interrelationship of a business's three major components—revenues, variable costs, and fixed costs—determines the break-even point. *The break-even point* is the volume level that produces just enough revenue to cover the total fixed costs and the total variable costs incurred at that level of output. There are no profits or losses at the break-even point.

The formula for calculating break-even is as follows:

$$\text{Break-even} = \frac{\text{Fixed costs}}{\text{Selling price minus variable costs}}$$

If we had a selling price of $36.00 in the example above, the calculations would look like this:

$$\text{Break-even} = \frac{\$100,000}{\$36.00 - \$4.00} = 3{,}125 \text{ units}$$

This is a useful formula for evaluating individual advertising projects.

Contribution

After the break-even volume point has been reached, each additional unit of activity produces revenues greater than the variable costs required to produce that additional unit. This difference between revenues and variable costs per unit of activity is called the "contribution to fixed costs and profits," or more commonly, it is simply *contribution*. After break-even, profits increase at a rate equal to the contribution multiplied by the number of additional units.

To put it in a slightly different way, when production or sales reaches the break-even point, the fixed costs are covered and only the variable costs remain. That is why contribution is such a powerful strategy concept and should be used in developing your plans and strategy. The question becomes, "What increases in contribution can we expect from this strategy versus that strategy?"

Advertising Budgeting

There are four widely used methods to develop advertising budgets. Each has advantages and disadvantages, and none of them is best. That presents a real problem because setting advertising budgets is a difficult job. The best managed companies use several different methods in an iterative process. That is, they develop a budget with one method and examine the results in detail. Then they use the assumptions in the first method to develop a second budget using a second method, and so on.

THE AFFORDABLE METHOD

Begin by forecasting your total revenues for the upcoming year. Then subtract all expenses except for profit and advertising and set a profit objective for the year and subtract that amount. Whatever is left is spent on advertising.

The major advantage is the ease of use; however, the advertising budget bears no relationship to the marketing programs that it is supposed to support. Thus, this method of budgeting is most likely to be found in companies that don't bother to develop marketing and advertising plans.

THE PERCENTAGE OF SALES METHOD

Decide on a fixed percentage of sales, or a fixed amount per unit sold, and multiply that number by forecasted sales either in dollars or units. If you have multiple products or services, you can use this method to set budgets for the individual lines.

The percentage can be last year's actual adjusted for anticipated changes in the marketplace, or it can be the industry average, or it could be a competitor's percentage spending level. The great flexibility of this method has contributed to its wide use. It is used by the smallest retailers and the largest automobile manufacturers.

This method acknowledges that some level of advertising support will always be required. It also makes the advertising budget responsive to the success, or failure, in the marketplace. However, it still does not reflect the marketing job to be done. In the case of multiple product lines, it does not reflect differing contributions among the differing products.

THE SHARE OF ADVERTISING METHOD

The third method has grown out of research that has shown a close relationship exists between a company's share of the market and its share of the total advertising dollars spent by all of the competitors in the market. To develop an advertising budget using the share of advertising method, set a marketing objective in terms of market share and then estimate the total industry's advertising expenditures. Set the advertising budget by matching your market share goal percentage against the total expected advertising expenditure. Exhibit 9.1 shows this relationship in four Western beer markets for the years 1977 through 1981. In San Francisco, the relationship is almost perfect. The effect is present in all of the markets.

The share of advertising method certainly focuses on the need to support marketing objectives with sufficient advertising dollars. It does, however, tend to focus on advertising to the exclusion of all other marketing activities.

THE TASK METHOD

The task method supports marketing objectives and is rigorously analytical. When you budget using the task method, you must specify in considerable detail what is to be accomplished, the necessary steps, and the amount of money required to accomplish each step. That total is the budget. Here is an example:

1. Our marketing objective for FY__ is a 25 percent market share. Given our forecast of total industry sales of 2,000,000 cases, our sales goal is 500,000 cases.

2. With a 24-unit pack case, this means we will have to sell 12 million individual packages.

3. At an average purchase rate of one package per month, we will have to sell one million households.

4. However, we expect that only 50 percent of all households that make a trial purchase will make repeat purchases at the rate of one package per month. Therefore, we will have to have 1,550,000 households make a trial

EXHIBIT 9.1

THE RELATIONSHIP BETWEEN MARKET SHARE AND ADVERTISING INVESTMENT: FOUR WESTERN MARKETS FOR BEER

OBCo.'S ADVERTISING SUPPORT HAS NOT BEEN EFFECTIVE IN CAPTURING MARKET SHARE.

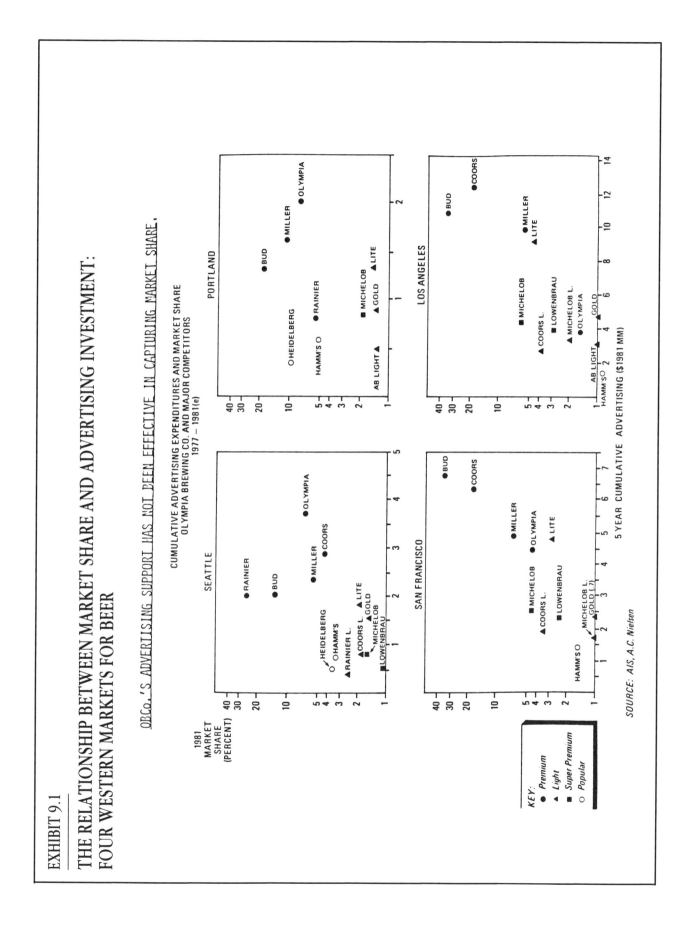

CUMULATIVE ADVERTISING EXPENDITURES AND MARKET SHARE
OLYMPIA BREWING CO. AND MAJOR COMPETITORS
1977 – 1981(e)

1981 MARKET SHARE (PERCENT)

5 YEAR CUMULATIVE ADVERTISING ($1981 MM)

KEY:
● Premium
▲ Light
■ Super Premium
○ Popular

SOURCE: AIS, A.C. Nielsen

purchase (950,000 households making 12 purchases equals 11,400,000 units and 600,000 households that make only one purchase to sell a total of 12 million packages).

5. We expect to experience a 40 percent trial rate. Therefore, to achieve trial purchases among 1,550,000 households, we will have to create awareness among 3,875,000 households.

6. We anticipate it will take three exposures to our advertising to stimulate a trial purchase.

7. Therefore, our advertising program must reach 3,875,000 households with a frequency of three. This means our advertising program must be able to generate a total of 11,625,000 gross advertising impressions.

8. The budget required to accomplish this task is $XXXXX.

Because the task method specifies each part of the marketing job separately, it permits identifying specific costs associated with each job so that alternatives can be compared for cost effectiveness and contribution. On the other hand, the assumptions underlying each step may be more tenuous than expected—the necessary precision may not be available.

Payout Plans

Essentially, the budgeting methods discussed so far envision an annual expenditure; however, advertising strategies are frequently multi-year programs. A payout plan involves making an advertising investment in the immediate future and examining the resulting contribution over a longer period of time.

A payout plan specifies three things for management consideration: (1) amount of money to be invested in the project; (2) length of time until the investment is recovered; and (3) profitability after the investment is recovered. A three-year payout plan might look like this:

Payout Plan	Year 1	Year 2	Year 3
	Cases and Dollars (in thousands)		
Total market in cases	1,000	1,200	1,440
Our estimated market share (percent)	15	20	25
Our sales in cases	150	240	360
Funds available* ($8.00 per case)	$615	$984	$1,476
Investment expenditure	1,200	800	800
Economic profit (or loss)	(585)	184	676
Cumulative economic profit (or loss)	($585)	($401)	$275
Cost per Case	$8.00	$3.33	$1.24

*Equals the per case dollars remaining after all of the fixed and variable costs, except advertising and profit, have been covered.

Characteristics of this particular payout plan are:

1. Rapidly growing market
2. Product permits us to penetrate the market rapidly
3. Opportunity to build a substantial business quickly
4. Negative cash flow is anticipated in the first year
5. Project turns profitable in Year 2
6. Total investment is recovered early in Year 3

Budgets: A Potential Source of Conflict

Budgets, and the ability to stick to them, have great potential to become serious irritants between advertisers and advertising agencies. If you want to get the best work out of your advertising agency, you must not let this happen. The next "Life's Little Lesson" describes an encounter between the legendary Ernest Gallo and his agency over a budget item. This is a scene you should avoid. (Remember that Monty is carrying his agency's letter of resignation in his briefcase all through this episode.)

A Cautionary Tale about Budgeting

Dr. Edward Ojdana is now principal in the management consulting organization, The Windsor Park Group, Los Angeles, California, but he remembers the lessons he learned during his years as director of corporate planning for the Olympia Brewing Company, Tumwater, Washington. During the 1970s, Olympia's management did all of their advertising budgeting using a single method, percentage of sales. They executed the budgets on a fixed amount per barrel of beer sold.

In following this single-minded, narrow focus budgeting procedure they missed the fact that their share of advertising was falling dramatically in a market that is driven by advertising expenditures. Exhibit 9.2 shows Olympia's advertising expenditures in their major markets in absolute dollars (left-hand graph) and it indicates that absolute dollar expenditures showed very little growth from 1973 through 1981. The graph on the top right shows what Olympia's management missed, the drastic fall in their share of advertising in their best markets. The graphs at the bottom of the page show what was happening to a major competitor, Anheuser-Busch, Inc., during the same time period in the same markets.

Beer is one of those markets where shares of market and advertising are closely related. Exhibit 9.3 shows what happened to Olympia's shares of market and advertising in four of the company's most important markets. Because market share declines lag behind advertising share of declines by eight to twelve months, all that management ever saw was a picture of endlessly declining sales throughout the 1970s.

So, what was the management of Olympia Brewing Company doing with the money that they failed to invest to support their brands? Well, the answer is that they were using it to expand geographically. Considered by

LIFE'S LITTLE LESSONS

Gallo Time, Again

Over the years I have often said that when I write my book, Ernest Gallo will get two chapters, and he's the only one who will.

One chapter would surely include the following little drama, but it should really be told by someone besides me. My preference as narrator would be Ben Norman, former TV producer at DDB/L.A., but he is not readily available. The fact is, Ben was not only a witness, but it was he who actually described the event to me. While it all happened, I was, at best, only semi-aware of what went on. Furthermore, although I may have been victim-turned-hero, I was acting purely on dumb and dangerous instincts.

The occasion was a big day-long meeting in Modesto. The morning was filled with creative presentations by AE, Ed McNeilly and me. Just before noon we broke for a showing of a re-shot Gallo commercial at the local theatre. Re-shot commercials and morning use of the theatre for projecting 35 mm film were standard practice at Gallo. So were high-pitched Gallo diatribes about who should pay for re-shoots, and this one was a true classic. Accusations, defensive statements, more accusations, etc.

Lunch later in a private corner of a Modesto restaurant, was pleasant enough and reasonably quiet until about time to return to headquarters.

At that point, Ernest arose, turned to me and unleashed a world-class tirade on how the agency had negotiated studio charges on the re-shoot with less than total dedication and forcefulness. Having finished loudly, he turned toward the only exit and started out around the table toward it—and toward me.

It was a familiar tactic in which Ernest pounded home his points and then stormed out, absolutely precluding any effective response.

This time, from some dark unfamiliar region of my gut, an uncontrollable and compulsive explosion occurred.

Ben Norman claimed later that what came out of my mouth was, ''Goddammit, Ernest, you sit down, and I'll tell you again exactly what we did.''

I take Ben's word for it. All I remember is that Ernest did sit down, and I did tell him again. And the charges were paid as billed without further discussion.

Lesson? You bet, and I learned it well.

Be sure you're right and don't try it twice.

Monty McKinney
Chairman, DDB/West
July 31, 1986

EXHIBIT 9.2

ADVERTISING EXPENDITURES VS. ADVERTISING SHARE (OLYMPIA BREWING AND ANHEUSER-BUSCH— MAJOR WESTERN MARKETS)

OLYMPIA'S DECLINE IN THE WEST IS IN PART DUE TO A REDUCTION IN ADVERTISING SUPPORT, 1975-1980, WHILE OTHER BREWERS DRAMATICALLY INCREASED SPENDING.

OLYMPIA BREWING CO. AND TOTAL MARKET ADVERTISING EXPENDITURES
PRIMARY WESTERN ADI's
1973 – 1981(e)

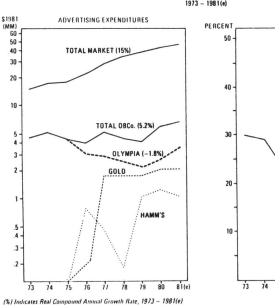

(%) Indicates Real Compound Annual Growth Rate, 1973 – 1981(e)
SOURCE: AIS

ANHEUSER BUSCH AND TOTAL MARKET ADVERTISING EXPENDITURES
PRIMARY WESTERN ADI's
1973 – 1981(e)

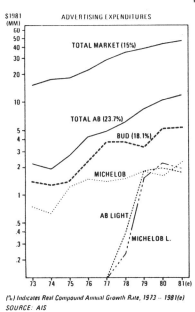
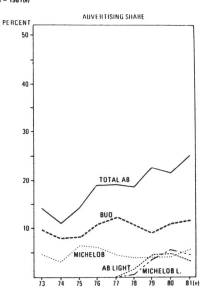

(%) Indicates Real Compound Annual Growth Rate, 1973 – 1981(e)
SOURCE: AIS

EXHIBIT 9.3
OLYMPIA'S MARKET SHARE AND ADVERTISING SHARE (FOUR MAJOR MARKETS—THE 1970s)

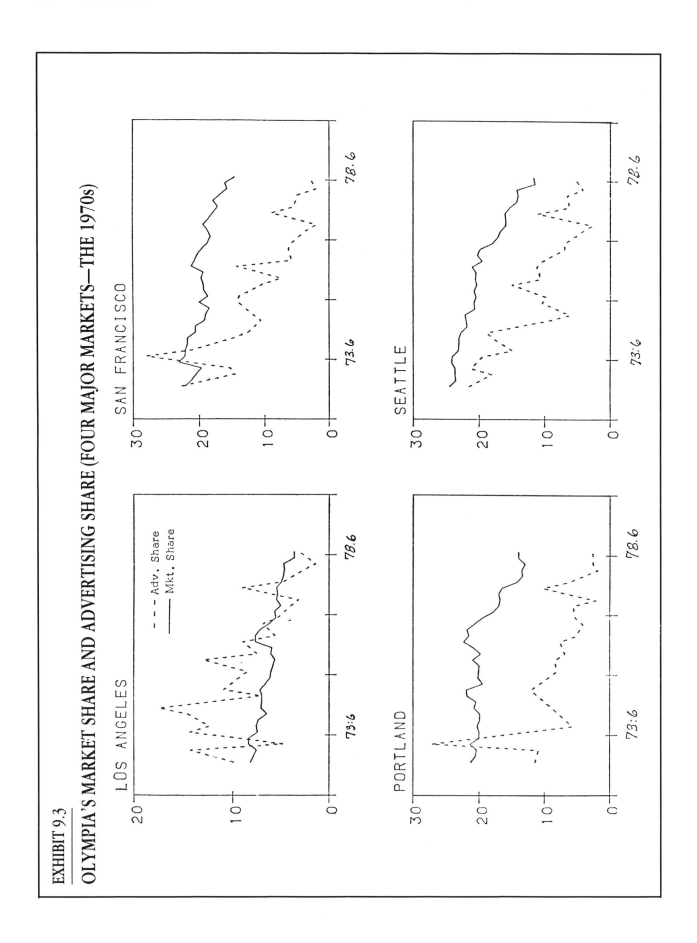

itself, that was not a bad decision for management to make. Per capita beer consumption (excluding imported beers) was flat, population in Olympia's major markets was flat, and the fall-out of the intense competition between the industry's leaders (Anheuser-Busch and Miller Brewing) on small regional brewers marketing in limited areas was devastating. What better reaction than to expand into other geographic markets in order to better weather the storm since the beer business is fought market by market.

As Olympia used the contribution margins generated in their established markets to investment spent in expansion markets, they eroded their market shares in virtually every state they operated in. Even worse, they eroded their expensively acquired market position in the established markets just the way they did in the expansion markets. Exhibit 9.4 shows more than two decades of Olympia's market shares on a state by state basis. It will be worth your while to study it at great length and detail—it is a picture of a company going out of business.

As you may know, Pabst Brewing Company saved Olympia from bankruptcy by acquiring them in 1981.

Ed Ojdana's best advice is to measure your markets and your competitors in many different ways because each one will tell you something you should know. Then, he says, "Develop your budgets in several different ways. It pays!"

Measuring Results

This final topic is meant to cover the entire field of advertising research. This is an emotion-packed subject that sometimes seems to border on craziness. The difficulty lies in the fact that so much money is at stake and so little is known about how advertising actually works. In this environment, you will find managers pressing hard to gain assurances that their decisions about advertising expenditures are good ones, willing to spend additional funds to prove the goodness of those decisions with a little research.

Into that environment rush serious researchers and an occasional flake, all attempting to respond to the advertising manager's needs to make better decisions. Unfortunately, the truth of the matter is that we know little that supports advertising pretesting of any kind, and that for most products, measuring sales results is an exceedingly difficult task, not to mention expensive.

As a consequence, the best place to begin is to examine what you should attempt to research. It is clearly desirable and within the capabilities of the research field to identify your customers and their media habits. That work basically is descriptive and researchers have long shown they can produce good work in descriptive studies.

The closely related questions of what needs your products satisfy for your customers and how you and your competitors are rated in the minds of the customers gets somewhat more vague. The problem is nobody knows exactly what those things are, so it is hard to know how to measure them. Yet, those are important questions, and you should try to answer them, taking the results with a grain of salt.

Hence, what position you should attempt to hold in the market and how you should differentiate yourself from your competitors is not a researchable question, it is a skilled management decision. Then the question

EXHIBIT 9.4

Olympia funds its geographic expansion out of the funds generated in estimated markets. Observe carefully what happens to Olympia's share in the expansion markets as well as in the established markets.

OLYMPIA BRAND MARKET SHARES 1966-1978

Established Markets	1966	1967	1968	1969	1970	1971	1972	1973	1974	1975	1976*	1977	(Est.) 1978
Alaska	26.9	24.5	22.6	24.2	24.1	22.7	21.2	24.6	26.0	25.2	23.5	18.3	16.8
Arizona	2.5	2.6	2.7	3.2	3.1	2.6	2.8	3.3	3.5	3.2	3.9	2.9	2.6
California	15.1	16.1	16.8	17.5	15.7	12.7	12.1	11.2	10.2	9.2	9.4	7.5	6.2
Hawaii	7.2	6.5	5.8	6.2	7.3	11.6	16.4	30.0	37.7	30.5	27.4	19.8	16.7
Idaho	29.6	27.8	25.6	25.4	24.3	20.3	19.4	16.7	15.2	13.9	14.7	12.5	10.4
Montana	15.7	16.2	17.2	19.4	21.5	22.5	24.9	27.8	30.1	31.7	31.3	28.7	27.0
Nevada	9.9	10.7	12.1	12.9	11.6	11.8	10.4	10.5	10.1	9.2	8.8	7.9	7.2
Oregon	25.5	24.1	23.5	24.1	23.2	22.9	23.7	24.6	24.9	24.3	23.4	19.2	16.8
Utah	20.3	20.8	22.1	23.7	21.3	16.7	15.6	14.6	13.2	11.2	11.2	7.9	6.2
Washington	30.5	29.3	28.0	28.1	25.8	22.8	23.6	24.0	23.1	21.9	20.7	17.9	15.7
Wyoming	3.5	3.7	4.5	4.8	4.5	4.4	6.0	5.2	6.3	6.8	6.8	6.5	6.2
Expansion Markets													
North Dakota						5.5	5.0	5.7	7.0	7.5	6.1	4.1	3.6
South Dakota							12.8	11.5	8.9	7.3	5.9	4.1	3.2
Colorado							5.2	6.5	6.6	6.1	6.3	5.8	4.2
Nebraska								8.6	7.8	6.6	6.2	4.0	2.2
Minnesota									9.1	5.4	3.7	2.4	1.5
Iowa									9.0	7.9	6.9	4.3	2.8
Illinois										.9	1.6	1.6	3.2
New Mexico											6.4	4.5	3.4
Missouri											4.7	5.9	4.5
Kansas											5.8	2.8	1.8
Wisconsin											4.5	2.8	1.4
Florida													.4
Indiana													3.8
Kentucky													.4
Michigan													1.7

*Anheuser-Busch strike.

becomes, "Fine, we've studied the customers and competition carefully and staked out a position for ourselves on a conceptual basis. Can we research that? Can we find out if it is important to customers?" And the answer is most likely NO! The problem is that customers can't tell you with any great degree of accuracy what they will actually do.

What you can reasonably test is whether you are *communicating* the ideas you wish to communicate—an important distinction.

A Story about Confused Concepts

The ABC Entertainment Complex is a clutch of restaurants and theaters located in a large office building, shopping center, hotel complex located in West Los Angeles. The ABC Entertainment Complex hired an advertising agency to attract customers to its many offerings. Before they would run the advertising, however, the Complex management wanted to know if it was "good" advertising so they hired a research firm to find the answer. The results were confusing and the client and the agency got into a large row over whether the advertising was any good.

Everyone failed to ask the right question, which was "What does the advertising communicate?" The answer to that question was extraordinarily clear. The advertising said, "ABC Entertainment Complex is just as exciting as Las Vegas" to everyone in the research study. The problem was that some people love Las Vegas and others hate it with an equal passion. When all of their reactions were mixed together, confusion soup was created.

What Can Happen When Concepts Get Unconfused

As you learned in Chapter 5, SmithKline Beecham Consumer Brands has been successful in Japan with their various versions of CONTAC. Management, however, has long been concerned about being a "one pony act," and they have made major efforts to develop and market additional products to reduce their reliance on CONTAC and, in particular, lessen the cash flow problems that accompany a product line like CONTAC that has highly seasonal sales.

One of the first new products was a hemorrhoidal preparation, in suppository form, initially, with an ointment to soon follow. After clinical trials demonstrated the efficacy of the product, the marketing department and advertising agency went to work to decide how best to position and introduce it.

The new product relieved four primary symptoms: pain, bleeding, swelling, and itching. It contained a higher level of the major ingredients that relieved these symptoms than any competitive product.

The product name, G4, grew out of concept testing of a number of possible names. The pronunciation of "G" in Japanese is "dzi," the Japanese word for hemorrhoids. "4" indicates the four symptoms the product relieves.

Retail pricing, wholesale pricing, and pharmacists' margins were all carefully researched and studied because (as you know from Chapter 5) almost half of the OTC products sold in Japan are sold on the pharmacist's recommendation. The final suggested retail prices, Y1,200 ($6.00) for the suppositories and Y900 ($4.50) for the ointment, placed G4 at the upper end of the price range for these products. These price levels gave pharmacists a good margin and, hence, a strong incentive to recommend G4 to their customers. Consumer research strongly suggested that the personal nature of the customer/product involvement would support a higher price for a product that really delivered results.

An introductory test market program was developed with heavy emphasis on TV because this product category was only lightly advertised. TV was supported with print, coupons, sampling, and a comprehensive trade promotion package. Test marketing began in the smaller market of Fukuoka. Based on early results, the test market was expanded to include Tokyo by 1980 and a national rollout began in late 1980.

By 1983, G4 had achieved wide distribution and a significant market share, however, an unforeseen problem developed. The target market, males aged 30 to 50 years, had several attacks of symptoms, lasting three to seven days, several times a year, and as noted previously, there was little seasonal variation here. Sufferers have three choices for dealing with these attacks: they can do nothing and suffer through them, they can use home remedies, or they can use commercial preparations. The problem was that reaching this relatively "thin" market when the symptoms occurred required advertising all year long with a heavy schedule. This heavy advertising investment meant that SmithKline Beecham had a new product success on their hands in terms of sales, but a dud in profitability.

THE CONFUSED CONCEPT

As CEO, Richard J. Findlay, tells the story, the marketing group created the problem for themselves. The advertising was all about "product as hero" and concentrated on the product, not the benefits. Exhibit 9.5 is the storyboard from one of the original introductory TV commercials. As you can see, the commercial is all about the product and the package.

The marketing group forgot that consumers do not buy products, they buy benefits. When they were reminded of this, a creative strategy statement was developed for G4 that focused directly on the single benefit that most potential customers said was the most important, pain relief. A single 15-second commercial was produced. That commercial is called "The Prayer" and the photoscript is shown in Exhibit 9.6.

Did it work? Like gangbusters! By 1988, market share was almost double the 1983 share, awareness of G4 reached 78 percent, and, most importantly, those results were achieved at a spending level of less than one-third the 1983 GRP level. Exhibit 9.7 shows the results. A well-crafted creative strategy may be the most important financial tool available to smart advertisers.

If you have any lingering doubts about the importance of having a well-crafted creative strategy that supports each of your products and services, you would do well to carefully study the photoscript shown in Exhibit 9.6. Although American television may not be ready to air "The Prayer," there is no doubt that it conveys a clear message and that it turned a big problem into a big winner, making a lot of money for the company.

EXHIBIT 9.5

VIDEO

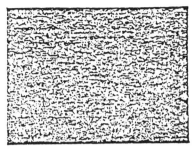

AUDIO

It thunders in the dark.

G4 package appears
lighted by the lightening

(Narration)
G4!
G4's "G" means
hemmorroids.

Japanese characters for the
four symptoms: pain,
bleeding, swelling, and
itching; appear and they
are torn into pieces.

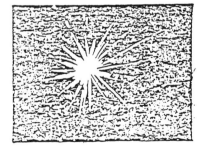

(G4's) "4" means four
symptoms.

EXHIBIT 9.5 (continued)

VIDEO

AUDIO

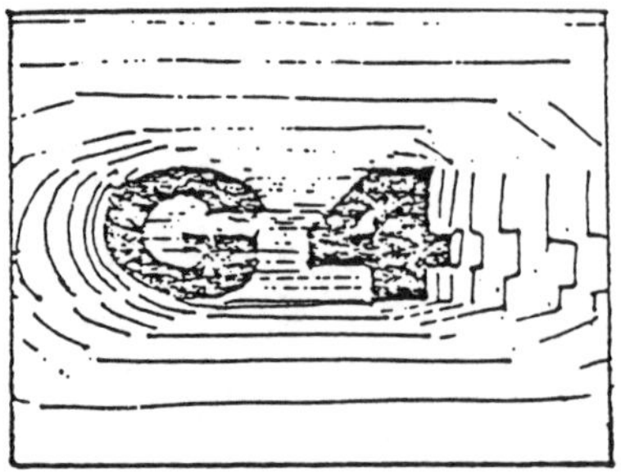

ジーフォー

G4

Shot of the package

G4 relieves four
hemorrhoidal symptoms,
pain, bleeding, swelling
and itching—it is named
''G4''.

Shot of a suppository

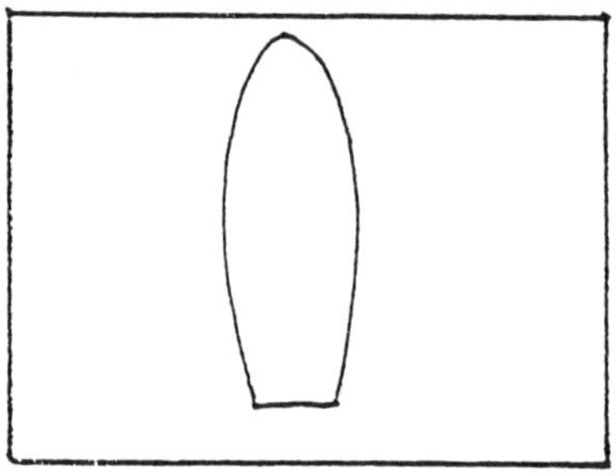

Visual device shows the
suppository melting.

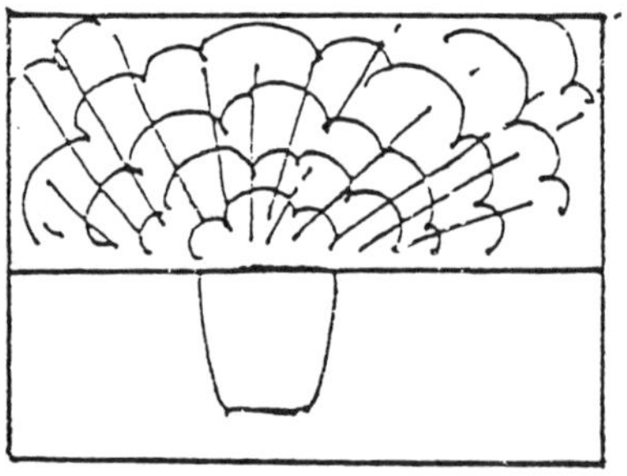

The bright and fresh
morning comes with birds
singing.

G4
Now on sale.

(continued)

EXHIBIT 9.5 (continued)

VIDEO	AUDIO
Product shot of suppository and ointment.	

G4
G4
新発売

What Your Creative Strategy Does for You Now

As you will recall from Chapter 5, one of the uses for a creative strategy is as a "benchmark for evaluating advertising." You and your advertising agency have agreed on what you are trying to say to your customers and you have written it down in your creative strategy document. It is not impossible for responsible, experienced professionals to have disagreements about advertising and one of those areas of disagreement can be "What does the advertising communicate?" Remember to stick to that one question.

The rest of the research that purports to measure the effectiveness of advertising before it is run is wishful thinking. Nobody knows what to measure.

Always remember there are many folks out there who are anxious to sell you a system for measuring the effectiveness of advertising before it runs. And remember that they are good salespeople. Keep on asking for proof that their system correlates closely with later sales results. That will send most of them away.

How Do You Know If Your Advertising Works?

The answer is simple—you run the advertising and see what happens. That is easy to say, but hard to do. What it means is that you must plan to evaluate your advertising results as carefully as you planned the advertising in the first place.

If there are big dollars at stake, the smart thing may be to use a test market and limit your financial exposure. There are usually two arguments against this course of action. One is that it will disclose your plans to your competitors. This is probably the most overrated worry in all of business. The truth is that if those other guys were smart, they would already be doing what you are doing. At best, they have already looked at it and concluded that "it'll never work." What do they know?

The second argument is more serious. The use of test markets will slow you down. In fact, that is exactly the point of using the test market(s). It is not difficult, however, to calculate the cost of being wrong and the cost of being late. If the cost of being wrong is larger than the cost of being late, you test. If being late costs more, you skip the test.

EXHIBIT 9.6

THE PRAYER

Please, God, help me!
I'm afraid of pain.

I'm afraid of pain.

I'm afraid of pain.

Pain, bleeding, swelling,
and itching.

To soothe the four symptoms
of hemorrhoids.

White G4.

EXHIBIT 9.7

G4 VALUE SHARE AND TV GRP SHARE OF VOICE

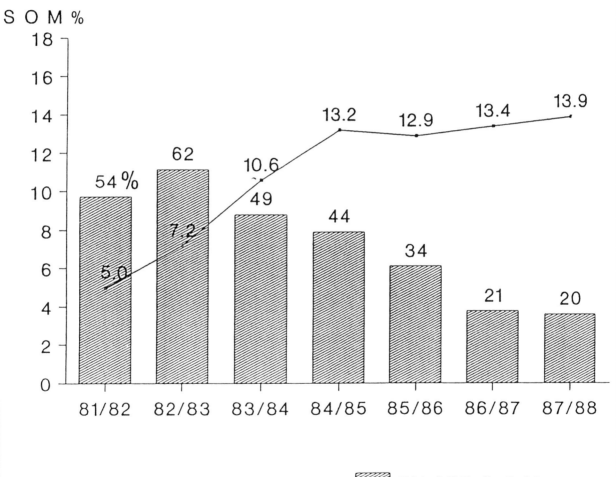

When you do test actual sales results by running the advertising, there are three things to concentrate on measuring and understanding:

1. What did the advertising actually communicate when it ran live in the real world?

2. What were the response rates by media? Which media produced the most sales results? The second most?

3. Among those prospective customers who saw and/or heard the advertising, but didn't buy, why didn't they buy?

Those are three tough questions, but they can all be answered with great profit to you if you gather the information before the advertising runs.

Another of Life's Little Lessons

Monty McKinney has some pertinent observations on advertising testing.

One Final Tale

If you have followed all of the ideas in this book and have done all of the recommended work, you now have a pretty classy advertising strategy, one that will likely make a lot of money for you. But if you think you have a guaranteed success on your hands, you are badly mistaken. Sorry to say, the best conceived strategies and the most carefully wrought plans can still go astray for reasons you never could anticipate.

Richard L. Fogg is the chief operating officer of Land O' Lakes, Inc., a Minneapolis, Minnesota-based farmer-owned cooperative. You may have a box or tub of their real butter, with its Indian maid trade character, in your refrigerator right now. Fogg is the kind of manager who meticulously studies his successes and his failures to learn everything possible about how to manage better in the future. He agreed to share one of Land O' Lakes' less successful new product experiences with you to demonstrate that great strategy, great planning, and great executions won't win every time.

LAND O' LAKES POUR-A-QUICHE

MISSION: Land O' Lakes is a member-owned farmers' cooperative, producing primarily dairy products. The mission is to find new creative uses for member-produced raw materials.

PRODUCT: Pour-A-Quiche was a frozen quiche filling made from milk, cheese, and cream; all products from Land O'Lakes members. It was offered in three flavor varieties (3 Cheese; Bacon and Onion; Spinach and Onion) and sold as a frozen entree through retail grocery stores. Packed in 26-ounce pure pack cartons—like milk cartons—the product was thawed, shaken, poured into a pie shell, and baked. It was a high-quality product, stored in the freezer section of a refrigerator.

MARKET: Competition was believed to be frozen complete dinners, frozen entrees, and frozen other main dish foods, about a $4 billion market

LIFE'S LITTLE LESSONS

Pre-Testing Ads

The search for a reliable method of pre-testing advertising effectiveness is as old, I suspect, as the business, itself. Although I never actually heard that history's first client (the guy who advertised for the runaway slave) conducted a test, it would not surprise me to learn that he had done so.

Regardless, plenty of advertisers *and agencies* since have sought the infallible touchstone which would guarantee the success and profit of campaigns in advance.

My earliest and somewhat vague recollection of a pre-testing program was one offered in the 30s by a pair of brothers named Townsend. They had (and don't trust me for the accuracy of all details) a set of 26 criteria which they would apply to a client's proposed campaign. The criteria included length of headline, size of illustration, length of copy, size and position of logotype, etc. Having applied the criteria, one of the Townsends would then consult with client and/or agency and advise on modifications necessary to assure success.

The Townsend program was briefly very popular even with large and successful advertisers.

Later, each in its turn, came other systems. Among my favorites for the oblivion which most of them deserved were these:

The Eye Camera—Developed originally and, I think, touted heavily by McCann-Erickson, the eye camera photographed the movement and even the dilation of an ad reader's eyes on the theory that this could measure interest reaction and purchase intent.

Psychogalvanometer—This device consisted of assorted sensors attached to as-sorted parts of the anatomy of the person being tested. The sensors produced measurements of the victim's pulse, respiration, perspiration, emotional tension, etc. In combination, according to the theory, these readings produced projectable predictions of the ability of advertising to gain attention, to maintain interest, to influence attitudes, and to make sales. The big weakness, in actuality, proved to be a total lack of correlation between sales and predictions—a fairly significant weakness.

The critical weakness of the devices discussed above is the fact that they cannot reasonably claim to measure or predict persuasiveness, and that's what advertising is all about. They are a little like trying to evaluate persuasiveness by a decibel meter. Louder is not necessarily better.

Other pre-testing methods, some still available, some once favored and now abandoned, suffer the same or similar weaknesses: Schwerin, Starch, ASI, Burke, Nielsen, and many more.

Conscientious advertisers and agencies keep trying to find a reliable system of pre-testing. Less conscientious advertisers and agencies turn to these kinds of research techniques primarily as tools for selling campaigns.

All advertisers and agencies, in my not so humble opinion, must still wait for a system which is as reliable but is less expensive than full-scale test marketing.

November 14, 1986

through retail grocery stores. It was recognized that quiche was a new and undeveloped market/segment.

TESTING: After extensive concept testing, R & D, product testing, and volume testing, the brand was test marketed for six months in three small markets supported by a full package of consumer and trade research. Brand awareness, trial, and purchase levels were on-target; store audit reports indicated acceptable volume movement, although below projections.

ROLLOUT: Quiche was subsequently offered for sale in 80 percent of the United States as part of a one-year rollout. The rollout was accelerated due to increased competitive activity in the quiche category, and a desire to ''pre-empt'' the frozen quiche market. Excellent retail grocery store distribution was achieved, and the brand was supported by a very competitive consumer advertising and couponing program. Pour-A-Quiche was widely recognized as a high quality, original, and creative product. It generated substantial interest in the grocery trade.

RESULTS: After 18 months in market, Pour-A-Quiche was removed from the marketplace due to declining sales volumes and a lack of profitability. The formula and concept (not the brand name) were sold to a small manufacturer who continues to produce the product on a very limited volume basis. Trial rates and brand awareness levels failed to match original test levels; low repeat and long purchase cycle led to slow sales which caused product discontinuance by the grocery trade. Follow-up research indicated that the long thaw time (12 hours in refrigerator) and lack of microwavability were major consumer negatives, although users of Pour-A-Quiche were satisfied with product performance and quality. Additionally, quiche was not seen as a regular menu item; rather, as a more specialized dish served at unique meal occasions.

LESSONS LEARNED:

1. Initial consumer testing failed to clearly identify long thawing and lack of microwavability as negatives.

2. The initial market testing failed to fully identify the long purchase cycle problem.

3. Points one and two above were compounded by the rush to expand Pour-A-Quiche into 80 percent of total U.S. as fast as possible, which then identified regional quiche consumption and seasonality patterns.

4. Quiche also proved to be more of a ''fad'' product than anticipated, but this can't be quantified.

In net, Pour-A-Quiche was a high-quality product that appealed only to a very limited market and couldn't develop the necessary volume to maintain grocery store distribution. The comprehensive development and testing program was accelerated due to perceived competitive conditions, but this program failed to clearly identify several major negatives—in part due to the newness and undeveloped aspects of this market segment.

EXHIBIT 9.8

Usually, advertisers are delighted to get free publicity for their products or services. That is especially true for new products. But not this time!

Reprinted by permission: Tribune Media Services

What an Advertising Plan Might Look Like

Market Review

1. **Market Growth**
   A brief review of the total industry sales for the past five years.

2. **Regional Variations in Market Development**
   A brief summary of the market development indices.

3. **Your Sales**
   A comparison of your actual sales for the last fiscal year with your last year's forecasted sales, on a monthly or quarterly basis.

4. **Market Shares**
   The market shares of your three or four major competitors compared with your own market share, nationally and regionally.

5. **Distribution**
   A brief summary of your distribution levels for the past three years, nationally, regionally, and by type of distributor, if appropriate.

6. **Advertising and Promotion Spending Levels**
   A summary of the dollars spent on advertising and on promotion for the past two years by you and your major competitors. Include an estimate of dollars spent per unit sold.

7. **Product Tests**
   Include the results of any tests done on your products or on competitors' products during the past year. Mention any significant field reports. Also include R & D activity, if any.

8. **Marketing Research and Advertising Research**
Summarize the findings of any marketing or advertising research that was conducted during the year.

9. **Special Events or Activities**
Review important activities during the past year by you or any of your competitors.

Summary of Market Review—Problems and Opportunities
List specific conclusions drawn from the market review that directly pertain to advertising.

Marketing Strategy

1. **Major Objectives**
Forecasted sales for planned year compared with current year, in total, by region, by size of package, or any other meaningful dimension. Include market share estimates.

2. **Marketing Strategy**
List the specific activities that are planned for the year to support the sales objectives.

Advertising Strategy

1. **Advertising Objectives**
Describe advertising objectives for the upcoming year in terms of effects on customers—increase awareness, increase repeat purchases, increase sales in a new segment, get trade-up to larger sizes, and increase frequency of use.

Also include advertising objectives for distributors, if applicable.

2. **Advertising Strategy**
List the specific activities that are planned for the year to support the advertising objectives.

3. **Creative Strategy**
Show creative strategy here.

4. **Media Strategy**
Describe briefly the rationale supporting the media choices and schedule. Show media schedule here.

5. **Sales Promotion**
List and describe planned sales promotion programs here.

6. **Special Events or Activities**

   List and describe special activities here. Participation in trade show(s) is an example. A new product test is another. A heavyweight advertising test is still another.

7. **Budget**

   Show the advertising budget for the year in terms of how it will be spent and by month in which it will be spent. Always hold back some of the budget (5 percent?) for emergencies, contingencies, over-budgets, and opportunities because one or more of those items is sure to occur.

8. **Calendar**

   Include a month by month calendar that summarizes when all the planned activities will take place.

APPENDIX B

Selecting an Advertising Agency

This section is based on what little research has been done and on a lot of observation. The topic is treated separately because it is always such a personal decision. Virtually everyone agrees that a successful advertiser/advertising agency relationship depends first and foremost on the chemistry of the people involved. An advertising agency selection is not all that different from selecting someone to marry.

There are two conditions that can lead to the search for an advertising agency. One is that you have grown big enough so that the specialized skills found in an advertising agency can now be of value to you. This will be the first advertising agency you hire. The other condition is that you already have an advertising agency, you have grown dissatisfied with something about their performance, and you have decided that the only way out is to hire a new advertising agency.

Let's deal with the second condition first. It may not be necessary to fire the current agency. If it is absolutely required that a new agency is selected, then the process is the same for the experienced advertiser as it is for the inexperienced advertiser.

First, everybody agrees that the compatibility of the people involved is the single most critical element in a well functioning advertiser/advertising agency relationship, so you should start by trying to identify the cause of your dissatisfaction. You, or somebody on your side, may actually be the cause of the problem. If that is the case, then firing this agency and hiring a new one won't change a thing.

Now suppose that you have given your operation a thorough examination and the problem truly does lie with the advertising agency. It is still not time to fire them. There are three major areas that can cause advertiser unhappiness that usually can be fixed if they can be identified and discussed by the top people on both sides.

One area is *inadequate service*. The account people call off scheduled meetings too often because they are not ready for the meeting at the last minute. The TV commercial did not run on schedule in Boise, Little Rock, and Binghamton because traffic did not get the reel to the stations on time. The big spring campaign print ad did not run in *Ladies Home Journal* because the media buyer forgot to send the insertion order. Or, the billing from the agency does not match the plans you authorized, again!

All of these things, and many more, do happen in advertising agencies. The first thing to do is document their occurrence, write down when, where, and what. Then your discussion can be about specifics instead of impressions. Second, call a couple of the agency's other clients to determine whether they are experiencing any of the same difficulties. Then you can discuss the problem as agencywide or specific to your account.

A second area is *inadequate advertising ideas.* In the beginning, the agency used to bring in many great ideas, but now they just show you a couple of ideas and they look like derivatives of what somebody else is already doing. This is a little tougher to get at because the agency will hardly admit that they are sending you second-rate ideas, even if it is true. However, tired ideas frequently are the product of tired people, that is, people who have just burnt out working on your business. You've seen all of their good ideas and now the well is dry.

It is easier to change people inside of the agency than it is to change agencies. Therefore, it may be worth the effort to see if you can't get the agency management to attempt to produce even better work by changing some assignments, or bringing new people in. However, what may look like burnout on your creative team actually may be the third source of client/ agency friction, top management inattention.

A third area is *inadequate attention by top management at the agency.* Maybe they are spending all of their time chasing new business, maybe they are burnt out on the agency business and they are spending a lot of time in Palm Springs or Palm Beach, or maybe they spend all of their time holding hands at a problem account. In any event, they are not paying attention to your business and everyone at the advertising agency gets the message that your business is not important to the agency. And guess what? Nobody is paying much attention to your business.

The top management at any reasonably well-run advertising agency should be able to document how much time they have spent on your account. It is a subject that you have every right to bring up for discussion because you, after all, are paying the bill.

All three of these areas are certainly subject to negotiation and change, and in most instances, that will produce a much better solution than searching out a new advertising agency. The reason is that searching out, reviewing, and hiring a new advertising agency, while terminating an old advertising agency, is a time demanding, expensive exercise. And the more important the advertising function is to your business, the more time and money will be required.

Also, remember that inadequate compensation may be at the heart of the three problems just discussed. That subject is also negotiable.

Nonnegotiable Problems

There are two major areas where the problem is so serious that no attempt should be made to negotiate the difference and a new agency search should be made. One nonnegotiable problem is basic disagreement over marketing strategy. The agency may feel you are asking them to produce advertising that they are convinced won't work, or they may feel your marketing strategy won't work no matter how good the advertising is that they produce. When this kind of basic disagreement arises, it is pointless to induce or intimidate the agency to go against their better judgment. Even if you succeed, you will not get their best work and you cannot accept anything less than their best work.

The other nonnegotiable problem is rapid growth, yours or theirs. In real life, big advertising budgets belong in big advertising agencies and little budgets belong in little agencies, and either one of you can upset the balance. The fundamental problem for the ice cream company in Chapter 1 was that it was a little account in an advertising agency that had grown large quite rapidly. As a consequence, nobody in the large agency had enough time to think seriously about the life-threatening problems facing such a small account.

On the other hand, your business may outgrow your agency. In the 1960s, in Los Angeles, Honda (USA) outgrew its first advertising agency, Chiat/Day Advertising, and Datsun outgrew its first agency, Parker Advertising. Both agencies had done brilliant work that had made major contributions to the success of both automakers, but when the difference in the size of their budgets and the size of their agencies became too great, Honda and Datsun both went on to select much larger advertising agencies, as they should have done.

The loss of a major client was painful to both advertising agencies. In fact, it was fatal to Parker Advertising. Chiat/Day went on to grow into a successful mid-sized agency that could now handle just about anybody's auto business, and it is proving that point right now with Nissan.

Starting an Agency Search

For whatever reason, it now becomes necessary for you to select a new advertising agency. What you have to accomplish is conceptually clear and both advertisers and advertising agencies see the job in the same terms. Dr. James W. Cagley[1] asked a sample of advertisers and advertising agencies to rank the things that are important in the advertising agency selection process.

There was virtually perfect agreement between advertisers and agencies on all 14 of Cagley's items. There was agreement on the top five most important attributes of an advertising agency in the selection process. Those attributes are:

1. Quality of people assigned to account.

2. Complete agreement between the agency and client on goals and objectives.

3. Need for agency personnel to thoroughly learn the characteristics of the advertiser's business.

4. Reputation for integrity.

5. Willingness of agency to make recommendations and to object to advertiser decisions when the agency perceives them to be wrong.

---

[1]Cagley, James W., "A Comparison of Advertising Agency Selection Factors: Advertiser and Agency Perceptions," *Journal of Advertising Research,* June/July, 1986, pp. 39–44.

Therefore, your task is to locate a group of high-quality advertising people with lots of integrity who understand your business (or who can learn it quickly) and agree with your marketing strategy, but also have enough guts to tell you when they think you are wrong.

DEVELOPING THE LONG LIST

First, develop a list of advertising agencies that might meet your criteria. To accomplish that task, you should form a committee so that you get many viewpoints now, and the reactions of people who will be working with the agency later. The first thing that the committees should do is to develop a set of minimum criteria that agencies on the long list should meet. Here are some issues the committee should consider for inclusion in the minimum criteria.

Location

If you are not located in New York, Los Angeles, or Chicago, you should consider the importance—or lack of it—of where your advertising agency is located. In these days of jet airplanes, high-quality telephone lines, overnight mail delivery, and fax machines, distance between you and your advertising agency may not be so important. If your business requires many last minute changes, however, proximity may be important.

Size

If you have a small account, forget about the prestige of having a big, international advertising agency. If you have a large business, forget about that "hot little creative boutique." In both cases, you will save yourself a lot of grief. Size is important and it is real. Here are some rough rules of thumb: A large advertising agency has media billings over $500 million in the United States, a middle-sized agency has billings over $100 million but less than $500 million, a small agency has billings between $15 and $100 million, while a really little agency bills less than $15 million.

What is important is how big your business is in relation to the other accounts that the agency handles. One thing to watch out for—large advertising agencies have offices in lots of cities and each one is a profit center. You may be able to find a branch office of a large agency where you can be a big account for that office even though you are small in the overall scheme of things. That situation may get you the services of a large agency and the attention of a small agency.

Specialization

Some advertising agencies specialize in specific types of accounts— consumer package goods, industrial products, high technology products, and direct marketing. How important is specialist skill to your business?

Account Conflicts

This is one of the most bizarre aspects of the advertising business, defining an account that conflicts with your business—a competitor. One soft drink manufacturer defines a conflict as anything liquid that is drunk by anybody.

There are no rules here. That is why you should give it some thought in advance.

BUSINESS DATA DESCRIPTION SHEET

Your committee should prepare a short summary of the business that you are seeking an advertising agency to handle. Here are some ideas of what to include:

- Company name, address, and name of key contact person
- Exact description of brands, products, and business for which you need an advertising agency
- Last year's advertising and promotion expenditures
- This year's advertising and promotion budget
- Next year's advertising and promotion budget
- Service requirements anticipated
- Any special requirements
- Intended method of agency compensation
- How new advertising agency will be selected
- Agency location requirements (if any)
- Agency size requirements
- Agency specialization requirements
- Unacceptable account conflicts

Sources for the Long List

There are two useful tools in developing the long list, *Advertising Age's* Annual U.S. Advertising Agencies Profile Issue (See Chapter 1) and the *Standard Directory of Advertising Agencies* available from National Register Publishing Company, Wilmette, Illinois. They will tell you agency size, location of offices, current accounts, and length of time in business.

Nominations for the long list can come from a number of sources. Talk to your friends and have committee members talk to their friends. Look for advertising you think is particularly effective and find out who the agency is. Talk to your distributors for ideas.

You will find the advertising agency business well organized to deal with news of prospective new accounts or existing accounts on the loose. At one company, the marketing vice president and director of marketing got together for a weekend meeting and decided it was time to look for an advertising agency for a new product they had been working on. They talked to no one else, but somehow, there were telephone calls from three advertising agencies before 10:00 a.m. Monday.

You may wish to engage a consultant to assist in the selection process. This can be an inexpensive way to gain a great deal of additional perspective.

Advertising Agency Questionnaire

Next, you should develop a questionnaire that provides you with key data you want from the long list agencies so you can get down to a short list for personal contact. What you need to know depends on your specific situation, but here are some major topics that apply to most businesses:

- Agency history, ownership, management, backgrounds of key executives
- How the agency is organized and why it is organized as it is
- Account gains and losses, and reasons
- How top management is involved with accounts
- Agency financial position, financial controls, and financial policies
- Agency approach to advertising
- Agencies' current experience in your type of business

Send the final questionnaire, along with a cover letter, to the agencies on your long list. Be sure to include a specific date for reply.

You can learn a great deal from the ways that agencies respond to your request, if you plan it correctly. Laura Scudder, Inc. is an Anaheim, California, snack foods manufacturer. It competes in virtually every market in central and southern California. Competition is intense and is at the local level. Advertising frequently is required on short notice to deal with a specific situation in a specific market. At one agency search, the questionnaires were delivered promptly at noon on Friday with the instructions that the questionnaire must be returned by noon the following Monday.

Half of the agencies never replied at all, which Laura Scudder management accepted as a good indication of the interest of those agencies in working with short deadlines.

The Short List of Advertising Agencies

After you have used the questionnaire results to reduce your long list down to no more than five agencies, you should telephone the key person at the agency and arrange an informal get-acquainted meeting. Most agencies have a fairly standardized "capabilities" new business presentation. This is often a good place to begin to get acquainted. Have the meeting at the agency's offices. Have the agency include the key people who would be working on your business at the meeting.

At this meeting, the agency will show examples of their best work. Be certain to find out what role each of your proposed account people played in developing the advertising you will be shown.

Since one of the primary purposes of the first meeting is to evaluate the people who would be assigned to work on your business and to test the "chemistry," be sure to have each agency person at the meeting describe their own background in detail and indicate what special skills they would be bringing to your business. Get them to tell you what the weaknesses of the agency are as well as pointing out the strengths. Find out what they are doing about correcting the weaknesses. If an agency ever tells you that they have no weaknesses, you can end that meeting on the spot!

The Second Informal Meeting

This meeting will be at your offices and its purpose is to provide an intensive briefing about your business, your problems, and your opportunities for the agencies that survived the first informal meeting. Your people run this meeting and it should have a well thought-out agenda. The agency people who attend should be those who will work on your business, plus any top management people who choose to attend. (This is your first clue about top management involvement in your business. If they are too busy to attend at this point, it will only get worse when they actually have the business.)

It may be useful to have someone assigned to record the questions and comments made by agency people at the meeting, tour, and so on.

The Formal Presentation

The last thing that happens in the agency selection process is the formal presentation. There are a number of choices to be made here.

Location: Your offices or theirs or a neutral meeting ground? No clear choice here. All three have advantages and disadvantages. Just think the decision through carefully.

Presentation content: You can either give each surviving agency an assignment to work on and the formal presentation is their recommendations about how they would solve the assignment, or you can let each agency decide on what to put in their own presentation. The argument for the assignment approach is that it provides a common ground for evaluating each agency. The arguments against an assignment center around the fact that the agencies' knowledge of your business is so limited at this point that their solutions can only be superficial and shallow.

Payment for presentation: If you do decide to give the agencies an assignment, also give them a flat amount to cover their expenses. You may want to keep some of the presentations of agencies that do not win your business and payment upfront avoids bad feelings (lawsuits?) in the future.

Evaluating Financial Performance

While all of these meetings are going on, one or two of your financial people should be meeting separately with financial people from the agency to review how budgets get authorized, how media contracts get done, how invoices are handled at the agency, how performance is checked, and how invoicing is handled. Although a smooth-working financial operation will not supply the right chemistry by itself, a badly working financial operation can sour an otherwise fine chemistry. What happens is that repeated problems and errors lead you to begin to distrust the agency in other areas as well.

Also, other people in your organization begin to wonder about your abilities since you cannot select a business partner who can keep his books straight. Then you start getting defensive and so it goes.

Making the Final Decision

Your committee should have an agreed-upon set of items that will be used to evaluate the final presentation, the people making it, and the agency itself. After the agency people have left, each member of the committee should have a chance to list his or her favorable and unfavorable evaluations of each agency before the discussion starts. After that, how to make the decision is up to you.

The agencies that do not win your business should be informed by telephone as soon as possible. Do not let them learn about your decision from the "street." You should offer to go over their presentation with them to explain what you found to be strong points and weak points. Remember, the world goes around and some day in the future you may want to give them another chance at your business.

The Second-Choice Agency

And finally, Monty McKinney has some thoughts to share with you on being the advertising agency that comes in second in a new business presentation.

LIFE'S LITTLE LESSONS

"It was a terribly tough decision—and *your agency was a very strong second . . ."*

That is the hated phrase heard almost every time an agency fails to win the account in a highly contested review. It's so common, in fact, that it has become one of the really threadbare cliché jokes in the business. In fact, in many competitions there will be one delighted winner and four others who ran "an incredibly close second."

Attending an industry workshop recently on the subject of new-business approaches and techniques, I was not surprised to hear three heads of top agencies reminisce about separate agency pitches and to hear each say, "Of course, although we lost, we were told that we ran a very, very close second."

I guess it is understandable (maybe even forgiveable) that advertisers hope to soften the blow when they announce his loss to an executive who with his associates had probably sweated nights, Saturdays, and Sundays for weeks putting together the agency's best presentation for a big desirable account.

One odd thing about these awful calls is that the experienced agency guy knows the full import of the call the minute he picks up the phone. Admittedly, it is a call as tough to make as to receive, and the caller's discomfort is really audible even to the most hardened ear. Almost the only unknown is the name of the winning agency, and about that the loser doesn't truly care. He just knows he and his agency lost.

So the fact is that there is no way to soften the blow for him. Only time can do that.

But once a little time has passed, most losers want to learn what they did wrong; where they came up short; how they can do better next time. So they call some key executive in the prospect's organization (necessarily a participant and voter at the presentation) and request his critique.

Now actually, it is quite rare that anyone learns much from such questioning. Often the prospect doesn't really know or doesn't want to tell the basis for the decision. So he reverts to the cliché, "It was a terribly tough decision—*and your agency was a very strong second.*" The con-versation ends aimlessly with each person wishing the other the best of luck—and saying, "Let's keep in touch. Good bye. Good bye."

It's a little like an unmating dance, but we all do it, playing our prescribed roles to the inaudible music.

A few years ago at Chiat/Day we participated in a full-scale presentation for PSA, the Pacific Southwest Airlines account. It was elaborate, comprehensive, expensive, and included some excellent speculative creative work.

We were competing against five other agencies and, although there had been the usual rumors about the choice being pre-determined, we thought we did well.

We were wrong.

The account was awarded to a small, little-known, and not very good agency.

Jay Chiat and I both knew PSA's advertising director reasonably well, so in due course we decided on phoning him—"to learn from our failure."

On a speaker phone, with me little more than an auditor, Jay opened up by saying, "Dwayne, we know it was a terribly tough decision—and we ran a very strong second—." That's as far as he got before Dwayne (who was completely familiar with the traditional patterns) interrupted to say amicably, "Like hell! Jay, you ran dead last!"

He violated the polite rules of the game, but he was right. We found out later that our speculative creative campaign had cast the PSA president as a spokesman, and that that was a role he would never agree to play. We probably would have run dead last in a review of 100 agencies.

Now I don't know about Jay, but I haven't made one of these "We-want-to-learn-from-our-mistakes" calls since.

Monty McKinney
Chairman, DDB/Needham West
October 15, 1987

INDEX

Page references to illustrations are indicated with boldface type.